100
GREATEST
TRIPS

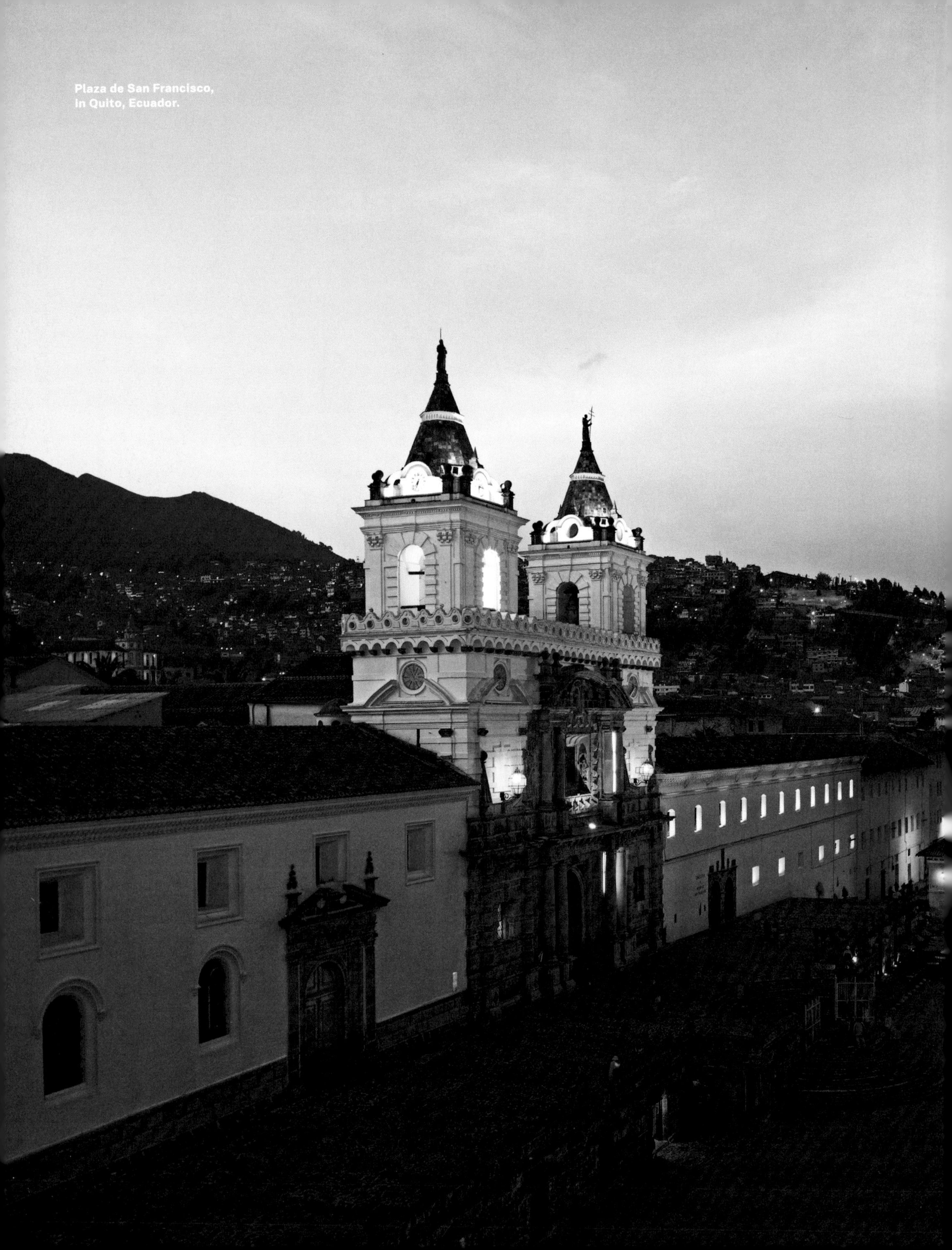

Plaza de San Francisco,
in Quito, Ecuador.

100
GREATEST
TRIPS

EIGHTH EDITION

TRAVEL+
LEISURE
BOOKS

AMERICAN EXPRESS PUBLISHING CORPORATION
NEW YORK

Travel + Leisure
100 GREATEST TRIPS
EIGHTH EDITION

Editor Clara Sedlak
Consulting Editor Laura Begley Bloom
Art Director Phoebe Flynn Rich
Photo Editor Zoey E. Klein
Consulting Photo Editor Elizabeth Boyle
Production Associates Andre Bassuet, David Richey
Assistant Editor Nate Storey
Reporters Heidi Mitchell, Lindsey Olander,
Marguerite A. Suozzi
Copy Editors David Gunderson, Mimi Hannon,
Mike Iveson, Ed Karam, Libby Sentz, Suzan Sherman
Researchers Kyle Avallone, Tomás Martín,
Paola Singer, Stephanie Sonsino

TRAVEL + LEISURE
Editor-in-Chief Nancy Novogrod
Design Director Sandra Garcia
Executive Editor/Content Strategist Jennifer Barr
Managing Editor Laura Teusink
Arts/Research Editor Mario R. Mercado
Copy Chief Kathy Roberson
Photo Director Scott Hall
Production Manager Ayad Sinawi

AMERICAN EXPRESS PUBLISHING CORPORATION
President and Chief Executive Officer Ed Kelly
Chief Marketing Officer and President,
Digital Media Mark V. Stanich
CFO, SVP, Corporate Development and Operations
Paul B. Francis
VP, General Managers Frank Bland, Keith Strohmeier
VP, Books and Products Marshall Corey
Director, Books Programs Bruce Spanier
Senior Marketing Manager, Branded Books
Eric Lucie
Associate Marketing Manager Stacy Mallis
Director of Fulfillment and Premium Value
Philip Black
Manager of Customer Experience and Product
Development Betsy Wilson
Director of Finance Thomas Noonan
Associate Business Manager Uma Mahabir
Operations Director Anthony White
VP, Operations Tracy Kelliher

Cover: A view of Bled Island, in northwestern Slovenia.
Photographed by Christian Kerber.

Back cover, from top: Biking along the main road in Tulum,
Mexico; the restaurant at Tetamanu Village, a guesthouse
on Fakarava, in French Polynesia; a pizza with prosciutto,
pea shoots, and egg at Cotogna, in San Francisco.
Photographed by Moses Berkson (top),
Jessica Sample (middle), and Alanna Hale (bottom).

Illustrations by Ben Wiseman

Copyright © 2013 American Express
Publishing Corporation

ISBN 978-1-932624-66-3

Published by American Express Publishing Corporation
1120 Avenue of the Americas
New York, New York 10036

Distributed by Charlesbridge Publishing
85 Main St., Watertown, Massachusetts 02472

Printed in the U.S.A.

Swimming in the
Mediterranean
off the coast of
Ibiza, Spain.

Walking past the
Stockbridge
General Store, in
the Berkshires.

CONTENTS

A peacock at
Lisbon's
Jardim Botânico
d'Ajuda.

HOTELS* **$** *Less than $200* **$$** *$200 to $350* **$$$** *$350 to $500* **$$$$** *$500 to $1,000* **$$$$$** *More than $1,000*
RESTAURANTS† **$** *Less than $25* **$$** *$25 to $75* **$$$** *$75 to $150* **$$$$** *More than $150*
*Starting price for a standard double; for resorts, rates indicate the starting price in high season. †Price for a three-course dinner for two, excluding drinks.

A view of downtown Los Angeles from the Griffith Observatory.

INTRODUCTION

In our hyper-digitized era, there is increasingly a degree of urgency about travel—a race to "get there now," as the world's distant recesses become less remote and our awareness of the singularity of experiences on offer grows. To unlock what is essential and distinct about each destination is one great way to stake a claim against the global blending that is an inevitable result of the proliferation of products and brands across cultures and continents.

Tapping into the authentic and unique is what we do at *Travel + Leisure*, and in this, the eighth installment of our 100 Greatest Trips series, we present enticing narratives and unforgettable photographs that capture the intrinsic qualities that define a place. Culled from the year's top stories and the thousands of locations we've featured in the magazine, as well as in T+L's five international editions, this volume offers inspiration for an enticing array of journeys—from a weekend excursion to a trip of a lifetime—and the expert advice you need to get you there.

One of the joys of travel is the opportunity it brings to transcend the everyday, to step beyond the world you know and encounter new places and adventures. In this volume, we take you to up-and-coming neighborhoods such as the seaside arts district of Barranco in Lima, Peru, and to distant islands, including Moorea in French Polynesia, where you can live out the ultimate castaway fantasy. We spotlight such timeless destinations as the Berkshires in Massachusetts, home to a growing artisanal food movement; take a tour of Rome's classic and contemporary art treasures; and retrace the footsteps of the great American food writer M.F.K. Fisher in Provence, France. We stop by the historic neighborhood of Casco Viejo, in Panama City, which is the site of a vital urban redevelopment project, and sample Amsterdam's emerging dining scene, where culinary invention meets cutting-edge design. In China, we take stock of the fast-rising architectural landscape, pushing beyond Shanghai and Beijing to Guangzhou and Hangzhou.

At T+L, we believe in the power of travel—to open hearts and minds, to inform and delight, and to counteract fear of the unknown. Whether you're headed to new places or revisiting the ones you think you know, we hope this book serves as a reminder of the joys of experiencing the world firsthand.

NANCY NOVOGROD EDITOR-IN-CHIEF

Chris Burden's
Urban Light
installation at
Los Angeles County
Museum of Art.

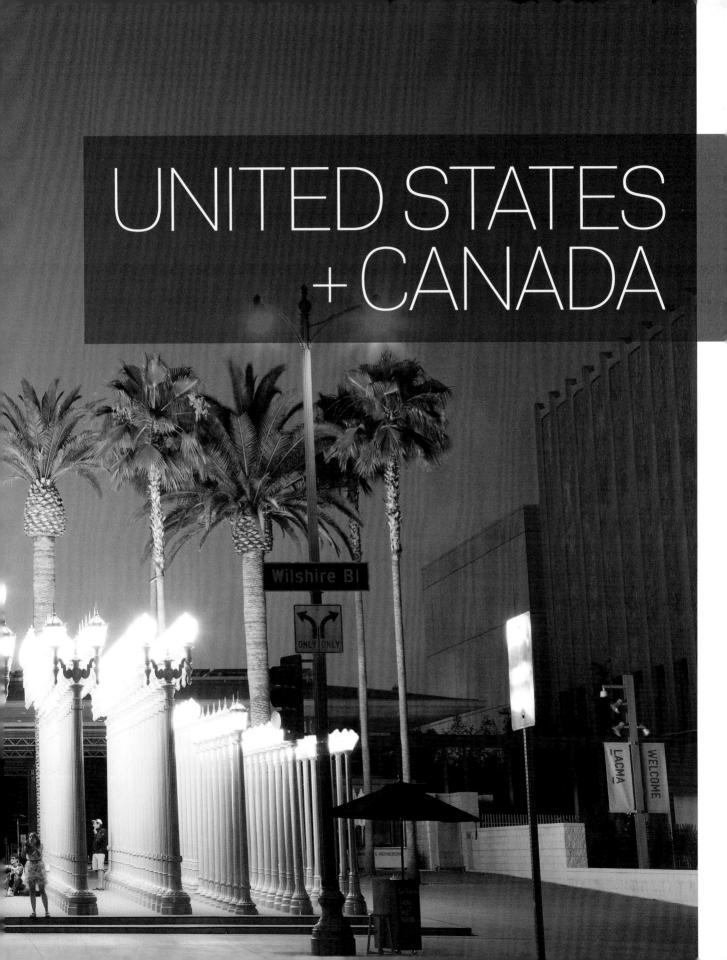

UNITED STATES
+ CANADA

THE BERKSHIRES

New farm-to-table sophistication in a Massachusetts country retreat

The restaurant at Dream Away Lodge, in Becket.

Kayaking on Stockbridge Bowl. Below: Tomatoes at the Great Barrington Farmers' Market.

THE FIRST TIME I MET Berkshires butcher Jeremy Stanton, he asked me if I wanted an interesting pig. "You know, a rootin', tootin', mushroom-hunting one." I didn't know anything about pigs, much less that they could be interesting. But my husband and I were hosting a pig roast with some friends at their Connecticut home, and an interesting pig was in order. These friends were old-school Czech, and before he knew it, Stanton was not only supplying an interesting pig but had been handed elaborate recipes—only partly in English— that I had discovered for things that could be done with pig organs, skin, and feet. I didn't eat much at that pig roast, but its mastermind made an impression. A couple of years later, when Stanton opened the Meat Market in Great Barrington, Massachusetts, I sensed that a key moment in the evolution of the Berkshires had arrived.

The Berkshires have long been a cultural destination, of course. Tanglewood, the Lenox summer home of the Boston Symphony Orchestra, provides a soundtrack ranging from Shostakovich to James Taylor. Driving past those legendary gates on a summer afternoon, it's possible to hear Yo-Yo Ma or Joshua Bell rehearsing through your open car window. The historic Jacob's Pillow Dance Festival is 30 minutes east in Becket. Some of the best regional theater in the country can be found at the Williamstown Theatre Festival—where regulars include Patricia Clarkson, Sam Rockwell, and Blythe Danner. The area also has a significant literary history: Edith Wharton considered the Mount, in Lenox, her first real home; there, she wrote *The House of Mirth* and entertained her good friend Henry James. In a later era, the Berkshires saw many of the most famous children of the 1960's; on any given night, you might hear Bob Dylan or Joan Baez making music at the Dream Away Lodge—a magical, hard-to-find bar, restaurant, and live-music joint in Becket, on the edge of October Mountain State Forest, where diners now wander the wildflower meditation labyrinth, cocktails in hand.

A selection of cheese at Rubiner's, in Great Barrington. Right: Strolling down Railroad Street in town.

The entrance at the Blantyre hotel, in Lenox. Left: Jeremy Stanton's Great Barrington butcher shop.

The Meat Market

This varied history can be found—and felt—in the community's passionate commitment to the arts, as well as in the style of the place, its homegrown, neo-bohemian atmosphere. But a different kind of worldliness has recently emerged, epitomized by a new group composed of both urban transplants and Berkshires natives, all of whom have made the conscious choice to live and promote a life of rural sophistication.

In the Berkshires—a craggy, hilly region stretching from western Massachusetts to the Connecticut border that is traversed by winding country roads and dotted with charming villages—you can find your way around by following the food. Matthew Rubiner, who opened Rubiner's Cheesemongers & Grocers in 2004 in a former bank on Main Street in Great Barrington, and followed it up with the popular Rubi's Café, was the first in the area

■ A different kind of worldliness has emerged, epitomized by both urban transplants and Berkshires natives, to promote a life of rural sophistication.

to create a gleaming, high-end retail establishment. It prompted a friend who had wandered in when the shop first opened to call me, practically hyperventilating. "I feel as if I'm in Fauchon," she said, referring to that Parisian mecca of all things culinary. And indeed, Rubiner's is a gourmet's paradise, and Rubiner himself, the poet laureate of cheese. Some 125 artisanal cheeses are displayed with descriptions such as this one, for Azeitão: "Little drum of rich, dense, occasionally flowing raw ewe's milk cheese of the 'Serra (mountain)' style of southern Portugal. Sheepy and seductive." "We are in an era of extreme connoisseurship," Rubiner says. "The lay customer has incredible depth of knowledge. And there are a lot of cool, young, dynamic people who want to be butchers and cheesemongers. This probably extends across the landscape of artisanal food, to manufacturing and producing. Not just chefs are stars now."

The Berkshires have attracted precisely these young people—ones who might have gone into business or law or advertising in decades past but who, instead, are

building lives close to the earth. Maybe it's a result of watching their own parents work too hard and not enjoy the fruits of their labors—but regardless, they have redefined success for themselves. Time with family and friends, homey pleasures: this isn't 1980's-style gluttony but something altogether different. This breed of Berkshirite is interested in learning and savoring, and in giving back. Each week at the community table at Rubi's Café, the local farmers compare notes over breakfast about what's on the docket at the slaughterhouse and the price of vegetables. "Hay is a popular subject," Rubiner says. Erhard Wendt, who owns the Williamsville Inn, is known to be an expert forager. Jeremy Stanton has staked out the best spots for morels, hosts classes in introductory and advanced sausage-making, pickling, and whole-hog breakdown, and sends recipes for cassoulet and milk-braised pork to his mailing list of 500. Mark Firth, whom Rubiner refers to as one of the "new old-school hipster butcher chefs," used to co-own highly successful restaurants in Brooklyn, including Marlow & Daughters. "I would go back and forth," he tells me, "between my farm up here and my restaurants down there, and I finally realized that I really didn't want to be raising animals here, then going back to the chaos." Firth decamped to the Berkshires with his wife and young children, and opened Bell & Anchor, a 60-seat locavore restaurant that he describes as "We raise it, we kill it, you eat it."

Following the food trail leads deep into the land and the complex web of people who take care of it. Rubiner takes me down a dirt road to Rawson Brook Farm, where about 40 milking goats each yield six quarts of milk a day at the height of the season. "This is about as low-tech an operation as there is," he says. Indeed, the goats are roaming, there isn't a soul to be seen, a refrigerator is full of the Monterey chèvre that the farm produces, and every so often someone stops in to buy some. But for a long time it was Stanton, the butcher, who delivered the fresh goat cheese all over the county each week, from the Old Mill, in South Egremont, all the way to Mezze, in Williamstown. And he still gets around, despite running his thriving new business. Why? "For the same reason that I drive to Chatham, New York, twice a week to pick up my bread," Rubiner says, referring to the camaraderie among these merchants and restaurateurs. "I wouldn't survive without it."

Three hours from Manhattan and two and a half from Boston, "Great Barrington is not a suburb of anything," says cookbook writer, food blogger—and former town selectman—Alana Chernila, who works most Saturday mornings at the farmers' market selling produce for Indian Line Farm, one of the first community-supported-agriculture farms in the country. "It will never be absorbed by a city. It never will become less of itself." Perhaps for this reason, the town and its environs easily inspire we-could-live-here fantasies among visiting urbanites. It's just big enough to feel like it wouldn't get old fast, yet retains the small-town sense of knowing and being known.

The range of accommodations the Berkshires have to offer is striking. In April 2011, Richard and Clare Proctor, a British couple, began renovations on what had once been a typical roadside motel, the Briarcliff, at Monument Mountain, and transformed it into a spare and design-centric—not to mention reasonably priced—spot. "Motels are where you go to get murdered, or go to have sex for a few hours in the afternoon," Clare says, referring to the pop-cultural preconceptions of such places, "but we were tired of B&B's. We'd stayed in lots of them and no longer felt compelled to talk with fifteen strangers at ten o'clock in the morning."

A B&B that would not fit the Proctors' scenario would be Stonover Farm—owned by Tom Werman, a former heavy-metal record producer who, along with his wife, Suky, has created a serene and airy property in Lenox, within walking distance of Tanglewood, complete with an art gallery and a one-room schoolhouse now used as a guest suite. And though modern, rural minimalism may be a hallmark of the new Berkshires, elegance and luxury abound at Wheatleigh, the country-house hotel, also in Lenox. The heart, soul, and history of the region are on full display nearby at the exquisite Blantyre. Owner Ann Fitzpatrick Brown has created an environment so cosseting that, staying there, I was overcome by a hazy, delightful sense of relaxation. There were books and magazines to satisfy every taste, from Dickens to *Hello!* In the 1902 manse's great hall, the staff posts suggestions for the day's activities: playing a game of chess in the music room. Relaxing in the sauna in the Potting Shed. Taking a walk on the Blantyre trail. Embarking on a guided tour of the extraordinary wine cellar with Luc Chevalier, the elegant maître d' and former sommelier at New York's Lutèce. The house is full of such treasures—the regal heads of a Canadian caribou named Bob and an elk called James; portraits of "the girls," Brown's late, beloved wheaten terriers, dressed in full Elizabethan garb; a portrait of a "Hoover granddaughter" leading a lamb. Brown, whose family has owned Blantyre for 32 years, is a curator of a certain magical, all-but-bygone era, and her passion is in preserving it. "One of the reasons people

GUIDE

STAY

Blantyre
16 Blantyre Rd., Lenox; 413/637-3556; blantyre.com. $$$$

Briarcliff Motel
506 Stockbridge Rd., Great Barrington; 413/528-3000; thebriarcliffmotel.com. $

Stonover Farm
169 Undermountain Rd., Lenox; 413/637-9100; stonoverfarm.com. $$$

Wheatleigh
11 Hawthorne Rd., Lenox; 413/637-0610; wheatleigh.com. $$$$

Williamsville Inn
286 Great Barrington Rd., West Stockbridge; 413/274-6118; williamsvilleinn.com. $

EAT

Bell & Anchor
178 Main St., Great Barrington; 413/528-5050. $$$

Dream Away Lodge
1342 County Rd., Becket; 413/623-8725; thedreamawaylodge.com. $$

Rubi's Café
264 Main St., Great Barrington; 413/528-0488; rubiners.com. $

DO

Indian Line Farm
57 Jug End Rd., South Egremont; 413/528-8301; indianlinefarm.com.

Jacob's Pillow Dance Festival
358 George Carter Rd., Becket; 413/243-0745; jacobspillow.org.

Kripalu Center for Yoga & Health
57 Interlaken Rd., Stockbridge; 413/448-3152; kripalu.org.

Rawson Brook Farm
185 New Marlboro Rd., Monterey; 413/528-2138.

Tanglewood
297 West St., Lenox; 617/266-1492; tanglewood.org.

Williamstown Theatre Festival
1000 Main St., Williamstown; 413/458-3200; wtfestival.org.

SHOP

Meat Market
389 Stockbridge Rd., Great Barrington; 413/528-2022; themeatmarketgb.com.

Rubiner's Cheesemongers & Grocers
264 Main St., Great Barrington; 413/528-0488; rubiners.com.

A guest room at Briarcliff Motel, in Great Barrington. Right: Picnicking on the lawn at Tanglewood.

come back is that it's always the same," she tells me. "Once, we had a problem in the Paterson Suite with the frog stopper in the bathtub. A guest came back after years and asked, 'What happened to the frog?'"

As tempting as it is to sink into the nurturing environment of Blantyre and never leave, just over in Stockbridge is the yin to Blantyre's yang: an unlikely, institutional-looking, massive brick building perched high above the Stockbridge Bowl lake, the Kripalu Center for Yoga & Health—where an entirely different kind of nurturing takes place. As is true of most things Berkshire, Kripalu is authentic, complex, quirky, storied and unlike anyplace else. It takes time to discover the beauty of guided morning kayaking on Stockbridge Bowl, or the range of programs, from the most out-there (Soul-Level Animal Communication: What Our Animals Are Really Telling Us) to the seriously cutting-edge (Stephen Cope's Institute for Extraordinary Living, which is engaged in a Department of Defense–funded study of yoga's effects on military personnel suffering from post-traumatic stress disorder). One evening, I booked an after-dinner ayurvedic treatment called *shirodhara* in the spartan Healing Arts Center. An oil was chosen specifically for my *dosha*, or bodily humor.

Anxious? Ungrounded? Restless? Fearful? Irritated by loud noise? Chilled or cold? Check, check, check. In a small, quiet room, a practitioner named Nikki draped me in towels, then began to pour a slow, steady stream of warm oil onto the center of my forehead, my "third eye." Music—meditative chants—filled the air, repeating, repeating. The sensation, at first, was almost unbearable. But then something within me began to break down, to relax. After an hour in which I lost all sense of time, having stopped wondering how I'd ever wash the oil out of my hair, and smelling, not unpleasantly, of sesame, I drifted back toward my monastic room, feeling a rare and profound sense of peace. I stopped in front of a plaque engraved with a quote from Mahatma Gandhi. It seemed to encapsulate everything there is to say about life in the Berkshires and its valiant anthem to living an authentic, grounded life: "Happiness is when what you think, what you say, and what you do are in harmony." I think the butchers, the cheesemongers, the farmers, and the artists and artisans who make up today's Berkshires would agree. ✦

Adapted from "Welcome to the New Berkshires," by Dani Shapiro.

On the grounds of the Scottish Bakehouse, in Vineyard Haven.

MARTHA'S VINEYARD

A quintessential East Coast getaway

WITH ITS STORYBOOK VILLAGES, miles of pristine sand, and fresh-caught seafood, this 20-mile-long island is the ultimate New England summer escape. Every town here has its particular appeal, from the windswept dunes of West Tisbury to Vineyard Haven, home to historic clapboard restaurants like the 52-year-old Scottish Bakehouse, where Polo-clad prepsters cluster around outdoor wooden tables for lunch. Summer crowds are drawn to the northeastern Oak Bluffs for its pastel-colored gingerbread Victorians and kitschy candy shops. From there, it's a 15-minute drive south to the former whaling port of Edgartown, where you'll find the Hob Knob, a stylish alternative to the island's slew of old-school inns. The 17 bright guest rooms are wallpapered in cheery floral prints, each grounded by an English antique or two. Spend an afternoon on a guided tour of the sound aboard the property's 27-foot Boston Whaler.

The Vineyard was a locavore haven even before the term was fashionable. Most of the ingredients at the wood-beam tavern State Road are sourced from local farms: try the beef burger topped with house-made dill pickles. If you're craving lobster rolls, it's worth the trek to the cliffside Faith's Seafood Shack, in Aquinnah, the island's westernmost town. After an early dinner, head to nearby Gay Head beach—the perfect place to take in the sunset.

GUIDE

STAY
Hob Knob
*128 Main St., Edgartown;
508/627-9510;
hobknob.com.* **$$$**

EAT
Faith's Seafood Shack
33 Aquinnah Circle, Aquinnah;

*508/645-4080;
faithsseafoodshack.com.* **$$**

Scottish Bakehouse
*977 State Rd., Vineyard Haven;
508/693-6633;
scottishbakehousemv.com.*
$$

State Road
*688 State Rd., West Tisbury;
508/693-8582;
stateroadmv.com.* **$$**

DO
Gay Head
70 Moshup Trail, Aquinnah.

NEW YORK CITY

Three neighborhoods remapping America's style capital

The Wythe Hotel at dusk, with the East River and Manhattan skyline in the background.

A guest room at Brooklyn's Wythe Hotel. Right: On Franklin Street, in TriBeCa.

Baja-style fish tacos at Super Linda. Left: Sidewalk dining at Chez Lucienne, in Harlem.

ANYONE WHO GREW UP in New York has a "remember when" story about the city's restless landscape. Remember when Hudson Street was stoplight-free? Or a bike ride across the bridge to Williamsburg meant running a gantlet of junkies? So much of the dynamic energy of New York is reflected in the ebb and flow of neighborhoods as artists, entrepreneurs, and other elements in the avant-garde of gentrification push into new territory and pioneer the transformation of run-down warehouse districts and urban wilderness into vibrant communities.

I remember in the late 1970's, when West 57th Street between Fifth and Sixth Avenues was a desolate span of construction sites, sickly health-food stores, and discount-clothing joints. It's hard to imagine that the block where my brother and I relinquished our skateboards to a pair of muggers has now become a glamorous thoroughfare of high-end boutiques and hotels. What comes into fashion in New York can just as easily go out. It seems equally hard to imagine that there was a time when the now semi-suburbanized East Sixties were drop-dead cool: the fashion designer Halston was throwing decadent parties in his Paul Rudolph town house, and Andy Warhol and Liza Minnelli were buying steaks at Albert & Sons, on Lexington Avenue. Mention the East Sixties now and most people will mutter "nowhere to eat"—a wasteland.

At the moment, three of the most dynamic neighborhoods in New York City are TriBeCa, Harlem, and Williamsburg. Although vastly different in their histories and demographics, all three have blossomed into destinations with coveted addresses and trendy denizens while maintaining an authentic sense of community. In fact, you could say they've each become brands in their own right, defined not only by physical boundaries but also by their architecture, attitude, fashion, and the ways they both embrace change—and resist it.

TRIBECA Hollywood East

"Everyone says New York is just a bunch of villages laid end to end," says writer Karl Taro Greenfeld, whose novel *Triburbia* chronicles TriBeCa's transformation from a cutting-edge no-man's-land of famous clubs like Area on Hudson Street in the 1980's and artists such as Richard Serra in the 1970's into a stomping ground for affluent celebrities including Meryl Streep and Gwyneth Paltrow.

When my husband and I moved there in the late 1990's, the neighborhood—with its cast-iron buildings and wide, cobblestoned streets—still felt like a village. It was a small community of mostly writers, artists, Hollywood types, and some prescient developers. John F. Kennedy Jr. and his wife, Carolyn Bessette, were fixtures at the Hudson Street newsstand run by Mary and Fred Parvin, two early pioneers. Fred & Mary's was a compulsory stop on every resident's daily rounds, if not to buy the newspaper, then to catch up on gossip or catch a glimpse of Julia Roberts or Eric Bogosian browsing the shelves. It was after the tragedy of 9/11 that TriBeCa began its reincarnation as an upscale district. Many of the original loft dwellers and young families fled, but even more residents stayed, determined to help the community.

Today, TriBeCa is having a second renaissance inspired by a new generation of change agents (the first being Drew Nieporent, Robert De Niro, and David Bouley, who established the place as a culinary destination in the 1980's and 90's with restaurants like Montrachet, Nobu, and Bouley). Now a younger group, including chef Andrew Carmellini of Locanda Verde and Matt Abramcyk of Smith & Mills, Tiny's & the Bar Upstairs, and Super Linda, are bringing comfort food to the 19th-century Italianate and Beaux-Arts façades of the neighborhood.

Before it was rezoned in the 1970's, TriBeCa (for Triangle Below Canal Street) had been known since the early 1800's as Washington Market, after the merchant-focused businesses that stored produce, butter, eggs, and cheese and manufactured everything from soap to glass. Passersby would smell the daily roasting coffee beans and desiccated coconuts. Once the merchants moved to Hunts Point, in the Bronx, and the artists began migrating in, the neighborhood was transformed from industrial zone to creative enclave. In the 1980's, late-night restaurants like El Teddy's and local clubs like Area catered to a cool crowd of artists. Still, some of TriBeCa's pioneers are holding on to a certain mystique. The restaurateur Matt Abramcyk moved to the neighborhood after 9/11, when it was more affordable. "I grew up in New York City, and TriBeCa was always kind of mysterious," Abramcyk says. "The buildings were different, and it had a lot of potential to be exciting." Back then, fancy restaurants weren't accessible, so he opened smaller establishments with personality. Smith & Mills, a former storage space and seafarer's inn, was the perfect

■ Harlem is still defined by a strong sense of community and history, no matter how many developers slap high-rise condos together.

backdrop for such a place. The tiny interior has a bathroom made out of a turn-of-the-century elevator with a flip-down sink from a Depression-era railway car. Tiny's is modeled after Lower East Side butcher shops with handmade white ceramic tiles and 60-year-old wallpaper. At Super Linda, a Latin grill serving ceviche and grilled meat, the banquettes are covered in vintage burlap coffee-bean sacks, and Buenos Aires phone books from the 1940's are piled on shelves behind the bar.

Although Fred & Mary's newsstand is long gone, many of the neighborhood's industrial buildings still look the same. Parking lots have given way to three-bedroom condos and fancy establishments like Robert De Niro's Greenwich Hotel. A favorite greasy spoon, Socrates, has been replaced by Tamarind Tribeca, a gigantic Michelin-starred Indian restaurant serving $35 lobster masala. Celebrities are still drawn to TriBeCa, but that under-the-radar cool has been replaced by the pack of paparazzi chasing Tom Cruise or Brad Pitt into the caravan of Escalades purring outside De Niro's hotel.

HARLEM **Uptown Renaissance**

Like TriBeCa, Harlem is still defined by a strong sense of community and history, no matter how many developers slap together high-rise condos. "Harlem has always been a neighborhood. People say hello to each other," says longtime resident Bevy Smith, the founder of Dinner with Bevy, a networking series for VIP's. And that friendly, neighborhood familiarity is what ultimately inspired chef Marcus Samuelsson to open Red Rooster Harlem—a few blocks south of the tenement where Sammy Davis Jr. grew up and not far from the YMCA where Langston Hughes lived in the 1930's.

"To me, Harlem is very Parisian, very social on the street, and with the big boulevards," Samuelsson says. "I wanted a place with a large bar where you can be social. Come in, take a book, talk to someone you've never talked to before."

A *Top Chef* Master and author, Samuelsson has found his most important role in helping to rejuvenate this historic neighborhood where million-dollar condos are adjacent to some of the city's poorest blocks. As a kid I remember taking the bus up through Harlem to school in the Bronx and passing blocks of abandoned 19th-century brownstones. You could still see the bones of once-beautiful buildings, but they had been taken over by squatters and crack dens, their windows boarded up, graffiti scrawled over doors. Certain blocks are still off-limits, but many of Harlem's brownstones have been restored to their earlier grandeur.

Harlem's latest renaissance—what was a literary and musical movement in the 1920's and 30's is now a culinary and real estate boom—respects the traditions that have made the neighborhood the center of African American culture. "If you're going to move to Marcus Garvey Park, that's lovely, but you have to know that on Saturday mornings there will be African drummers setting up there," Smith says. You also have to know that Harlem residents always say Lenox and never Malcolm X Boulevard, and Lenox is like Fifth Avenue, and Seventh Avenue is like the Champs-Élysées in a very traditional way—it's the place to stroll on Easter Sunday. On a woven flag hanging above the bookshelf at Red Rooster, Samuelsson identifies Harlem landmarks, including the Studio Museum in Harlem, helmed by his friend, the stylish director and chief curator Thelma Golden. Then there are Sylvia's soul-food restaurant and Parlor

The lunch crowd at Red Rooster Harlem.

The intersection of North Seventh Street and Bedford Avenue, in Williamsburg.

Entertainment at Marjorie Eliot's, a free Sunday evening concert series in her northern Harlem home.

Frederick Douglass Boulevard between 110th Street and 125th Street is now known as Restaurant Row, with places like Lido, Five & Diamond Harlem, and Frederick Café Bistro packed on weekend nights. A ramen place called Jin Ramen, a beer garden called Bier International, and a French bistro called Chez Lucienne all reflect Harlem's influx of multicultural residents. According to the recent census reports, now there are more Hispanics, Caucasians, and Asians in greater Harlem than there are African Americans. Yet it is still the neighborhood's history as the seat of African American intellectual culture that makes it one of New York City's prime tourist destinations.

WILLIAMSBURG The New Brooklyn

Andrew Tarlow, an artist who waited tables at Odeon, a groundbreaking brasserie in TriBeCa and model for the change-agent restaurants that would help gentrify other fringe areas of New York City in the mid 1990's, moved to Williamsburg 18 years ago for the cheap rent and abundant studio space, but he couldn't find a convenient place to get a meal. So in 2000 he opened Diner and served locally sourced food in a simple setting. "The idea was that anyone could come," Tarlow says. He followed Diner's success with Marlow & Sons, another restaurant and shop, and Marlow & Daughters, a butcher that serves organic beef and poultry. Although he is loath to agree, Tarlow is considered the unofficial mayor of Williamsburg's artisanal food movement. Tarlow is a great champion of the community, using craftsmen and resources from the area for most of his projects. The cramped shelves of Marlow & Sons are stocked with Mast Brothers chocolate bars and Really Raw Honey jars.

In 2012, Tarlow opened his fifth Brooklyn restaurant, Reynards, in the Wythe Hotel, a 1901 former barrel factory on Williamsburg's more industrial northern edge. Much like Tarlow's restaurants, the hotel has a very local vibe. Most of the interior wood in the original building was salvaged and used to create beds and ceilings. The wallpaper in each of the 70 rooms was custom-made by Flavor Paper, in Brooklyn's Cobble Hill, and the mini-bars offer fresh granola from Marlow & Sons, small-batch booze, and house-made ice cream.

Originally, Tarlow liked the site because it had a desolate feel, not unlike Broadway when he opened Diner. But in the time it's taken them to renovate, the area has filled in with music halls like Brooklyn Bowl, and another hotel, King & Grove Williamsburg, from the team behind hot spots in Miami and Montauk.

Everyone in Williamsburg seems to be making something—whether it's fixed-gear bikes or organic soaps. Michael and Rick Mast of Mast Brothers Chocolate were among the first to support this idea of local manufacturing. In 2006, they began creating chocolate from scratch. Now they have a booming business out of their North Third Street factory, where they roast, crack, and grind cocoa beans imported from Central and South America. Derek Herbster, a resident chocolate expert at Mast Brothers who has lived in the area for three years, cannot get over the changes to Williamsburg. "It's weird to me to live in the biggest city in the world and have it feel like a small town," he says.

Early one Friday evening, I had dinner at Reynards with some friends. The cavernous bar room was already hopping with Brooklyn foodies dressed in floral-print minidresses and shorts with plaid shirts. Was it possible that every diner in this restaurant was 26? Tarlow was manning the maître d's desk, smiling at drop-ins as he politely turned them away. A tattooed waiter explained that the menu changes every day and the water is carbonated in-house.

When Tarlow dropped by our table, we pressed him on his idea to open a restaurant that was a strange juxtaposition of fine dining and neighborhood joint serving food grilled or baked in a wood-burning stove—"touched by fire," as he put it. How had Tarlow known that Upper East Siders would trek all the way across the bridge for a meal? And where might he venture for his next restaurant? "The Upper East Side," he said. We all burst out laughing. "I'm not kidding. It's a wasteland." +

Adapted from "New York Now," by Kate Betts.

GUIDE

BALTIMORE

A former shipbuilding city makes a splash

FOR DECADES, BALTIMORE WAS considered D.C.'s redheaded stepchild, synonymous with the kitsch culture made famous by director John Waters. But with the arrival of the Four Seasons Hotel Baltimore, this port city is getting a much-needed dose of glamour. Overlooking the marina, the soaring glass-sheathed tower feels like it could belong in South Beach: there's a sleek marble-and-wood lobby, a rooftop infinity pool and bar dispensing cocktails and frozen grapes, and serious culinary chops thanks to renowned chef Michael Mina. The property is within easy walking distance of the city's major attractions, including the renovated Baltimore Museum of Art, which houses an impressive collection of modern works (13,000 pieces, to be exact). For a step back in time, make your way to the historic district of Fell's Point, with its 18th-century red-brick row houses, cozy taverns, and tugboats plying the bay.

It's no surprise that Baltimore is known for its seafood—after all, the city is the largest seaport in the mid-Atlantic. To sample some of the finest Chesapeake Bay blue crab in town, hop a water taxi from Inner Harbor and snag an oceanfront picnic table at local favorite Captain James Crab House—make sure to come with your claw-cracking prowess and a hearty appetite.

GUIDE

STAY
Four Seasons Hotel Baltimore
200 International Dr.; 410/576-5800; fourseasons.com. **$$$**

EAT
Captain James Crab House
2127 Boston St.; 410/327-8600; captainjameslanding.com. **$$$**

DO
Baltimore Museum of Art
10 Art Museum Dr.; 443/573-1700; artbma.org.

The rooftop pool at the Four Seasons Hotel Baltimore.

WASHINGTON, D.C.

Thanks to a coterie of young chefs who are reinventing the dining scene with farm-fresh ingredients and innovative approaches, D.C.'s foodie cred is on the rise. But that doesn't mean the old guard is resting on its laurels: mainstays like José Andrés continue to raise the bar with forward-thinking restaurants. Here, a tour of the city's top tables.

Birch & Barley and Church Key

The happy-hour brigade packs the 70-foot-long bar for Tater Tots, charcuterie, and more than 500 varieties of international brews at the second-floor gastropub Church Key. Downstairs at Birch & Barley, the vibe is decidedly more sophisticated, but beer is still the driving force: bamboo floors and exposed-brick walls provide the backdrop for glasses of cask ale paired with ricotta cavatelli. *1337 14th St. NW; 202/567-2576; churchkeydc.com.* **$$$**

Izakaya Seki

A nondescript green-brick façade and a solitary red paper lantern mark the entrance to the U Street Corridor's buzziest new addition. Sidle up to the 10-seat counter or head upstairs to the understated dining room for seafood-centric plates honed by chef Hiroshi Seki's half-century behind the cutting board. The *yuzu*-scallop carpaccio and *uni* with quail egg are crowd-pleasers. *1117 V St. NW; 202/588-5841; sekidc.com.* **$$**

Jaleo and Minibar by José Andrés

How did Spanish-born star chef José Andrés manage to reinvigorate his 20-year-old Jaleo tapas restaurant? A top-to-bottom renovation incorporating glass-topped foosball tables, funky art installations, and *croquetas* served in glass sneakers. Try the *tortilla* with *sobrasada*, onions, and Mahón cheese from the new menu. Or make your way to Andrés's reopened Minibar nearby, where one-bite molecular concoctions (a dollop of carrot gelatin and curried pig tail sandwiched between two pieces of meringue, for example) take center stage. *480 Seventh St. NW; 202/628-7949; jaleo.com;* **$$$**. *855 E St. NW; 202/393-0812; minibar byjoseandres.com.* **$$$$**

Komi and Little Serow

Johnny Monis and his wife, Anne Marler, take cues from classic Greek dishes to craft the menu at their Dupont Circle haute spot, Komi. Dinner starts with small meze and works up to creative feats such as slow-roasted baby goat. At Little Serow, the duo tackle northern Thai cuisine. There are no reservations and no groups larger than four—but once you tuck in to the pork ribs steeped in Mekong whiskey, you'll understand why devotees line up outside for hours. *1509 17th St. NW; 202/332-9200; komirestaurant.com;* **$$$**. *1511 17th St. NW; no phone; littleserow.com.* **$$$**

Pearl Dive Oyster Palace

Yes, there are standout oysters—grilled, wrapped in bacon, and accompanied by a Pimm's-based Pearl Cup—but regulars swear by the impeccably golden-fried chicken: juicy, braised essays of down-home cooking. Jeff and Barbara Black's Lowcountry recipes don't stop there, running the gamut from Creole tasso-ham gumbo to pecan pie in a ramshackle-chic space (well-worn floors; decaying walls). Don't fret the hour's wait; take a ticket, head upstairs to the speakeasy Black Jack, and chance a game on the bocce courts. *1612 14th St. NW; 202/319-1612; pearldivedc.com.* **$$$**

Rasika and Rasika West End

The city's elite, including Wolf Blitzer and the Clintons, flock to this classic Indian restaurant and its mod new sibling, Rasika West End, for authentic Indian cuisine. At the latter, Mumbai native Vikram Sunderam delivers *tawa* (griddle) and *sigri* (barbecue) staples in a whimsical space: the turquoise booths resemble traditional elephant carriages and a wild three-dimensional ceiling looks like a banyan-tree canopy. What to order? The *masala* pancakes with tomato chutney and the minty chicken kebab. *633 D St. NW; 202/637-1222; rasikarestaurant.com;* **$$$**. *1190 New Hampshire Ave.; 202/466-2500; rasikarestaurant.com.* **$$$**

Supper Club at Seasonal Pantry

Chef Daniel O'Brien has firmly planted his flag in the still-gentrifying Shaw neighborhood with a masterful cocktail tavern, A&D, and his newest venture, the multipurpose Supper Club at Seasonal Pantry. By day, patrons come to the market for jars of pickled vegetables and fruit jams. At night, the place is transformed into a convivial dinner party whose centerpiece is a 12-seat communal table. Here, the *Top Chef* alum presents dishes from an ever-changing menu that may include rabbit and foie gras accented with cherries. *1314½ Ninth St. NW; 202/713-9866; seasonalpantry.com.* **$$$**

Slices of
tomato bread
at Jaleo. Left:
The dining
room at
Birch & Barley.

Chef Johnny
Monis preparing
a dish at
Little Serow.
Right: The bar
at Pearl Dive
Oyster Palace.

Taking a break
on Charleston's
Rainbow Row.

CHARLESTON, SOUTH CAROLINA

Old meets new down South

IT'S EASY TO LOVE antebellum Charleston, with its scented gardens and live oaks, starched demeanor and polite exchanges of the day. Stroll through the circa-1804 City Market, in downtown, and you can still meet a traditional sweetgrass basket weaver; on Lower King Street, you'll find 18th-century Georgian buildings housing quaint antique shops, such as the Heirloom Book Company, filled with vintage Southern recipe collections. Farther north, a new brand of cool has taken root in Upper King. This frontier of urban renewal is occupied by a generation of tattooed hipsters who irreverently refer to the area as "Chucktown." At Worthwhile, browse the asymmetrical leather jackets by designer Rick Owens and Isabel Marant's embroidered skirts, before slipping into the speakeasy-inspired Cocktail Club for an impeccably crafted pre-dinner drink (look for the door with the "C"). Just up the road, chef Mike Lata of downtown's F.I.G. has opened the Ordinary, a seafood joint known for its clam cakes and triggerfish schnitzel. Live music is never far away here, and the nearby Charleston Music Hall is *the* spot to see homegrown Southern bands. Don't miss local favorite alt-folk duo Shovels & Rope, whose country-rock music provides the ideal soundtrack to the city.

GUIDE

EAT
The Ordinary
544 King St.; 843/414-7060;
eattheordinary.com. **$$$**

DRINK
Cocktail Club
479 King St.; 843/724-9411;
thecocktailclubcharleston.com.

SHOP
City Market
188 Meeting St.;
843/853-8000;
thecharlestoncitymarket.com.

Heirloom Book Company
54½ Broad St.;
843/469-1717;
heirloombookcompany.com.

Worthwhile
268 King St.; 843/723-4418;
shopworthwhile.com.

DO
Charleston Music Hall
37 John St.;
843/853-2252;
charlestonmusichall.com.

GASPARILLA ISLAND, FLORIDA

The Sunshine State's best-kept secret

Off the coast of
Gasparilla Island,
in southwest
Florida.

ONE-LANE ROADS WITH NO TRAFFIC LIGHTS. Mom-and-pop general stores. Suntanned fishermen casting for tarpon. Idyllic Gasparilla is the southern Gulf Coast retreat that time forgot, a barrier island of knotty banyan trees and tortoises— the antidote to the nearby hot spots of Sanibel and Captiva. Spend a few days here and the drowsy rhythm is bound to seduce you, whether you're relaxing on the powdery beaches or exploring the town, Boca Grande village.

The island's swankiest hotel is the 1913 Gasparilla Inn & Club, a throwback to Old Florida, with a guest list that has included the Vanderbilts and Du Ponts and well-heeled patrons dressed in Lilly Pulitzer playing croquet on the lawn (it's a Gilded Age fantasy come to life). Spread across the property's 180 acres are 18 sherbet-hued cottages done up in beachy wicker furniture, floral-print wallpaper, and shell-strewn hearths. While it's tempting to hang up a Do Not Disturb sign and stay put, the island has plenty of diversions to keep you entertained. Carve out time to tour the area on one of the hotel's cruiser bikes. A must-stop: Grapevine Gourmet, where chef Patty Kitchen will pack you a beach picnic of cucumber sandwiches, drunken goat cheese, and a bottle of Chardonnay.

GUIDE

STAY
Gasparilla Inn & Club
500 Palm Ave.;
941/964-4500;
the-gasparilla-inn.com. $$$

EAT
Grapevine Gourmet
321 Park Ave.;
941/964-0614. $$

NATIONAL PARKS

Windswept plains and jagged mountain ranges, spouting volcanoes and ancient glaciers: America's national parks harbor expansive dreamscapes teeming with wildlife. From the swampy Everglades of Florida to Alaska's wintry forests, here, nine places that showcase the diverse bounty of the United States.

Acadia National Park, Maine

The eastern seaboard's tallest mountains meet the Atlantic Ocean on this archipelago, where red foxes trot across rocky coastal terrain, and humpback whales swim in the surrounding waters. Fuel up on an early breakfast of blueberry pancakes and smoked salmon at the bucolic Bar Harbor Inn *(barharborinn.com; $)*, then head to Cadillac Mountain at dawn, when fog shrouds the granite ridges and the air is filled with the song of red-eyed vireo birds.

Crater Lake National Park, Oregon

Oregon may not bring to mind images of volcanoes, but the state has an explosive past. Get a front-row seat at Crater Lake Lodge *(craterlakelodges.com; $$)*, set on the end of a caldera formed by the collapse of Mount Mazama 7,700 years ago. The eruption produced 2,000-foot-high lava walls that border the nation's deepest lake. Learn about the park's geology on a guided boat tour, arranged by the hotel.

Denali National Park, Alaska

Welcome to one of the last well-preserved nature sanctuaries in the U.S., home to Alaska's version of the Big Five (moose, caribou, Dall sheep, wolves, and grizzly bears). There's only one way to see them: a spindly 92-mile road that cuts through a taiga forest to the tundra. Bed down a mile outside the park at the riverfront McKinley Chalet Resort *(denaliparkresorts.com; $$)*, also a great jumping-off point for rafting trips.

Everglades National Park, Florida

The largest subtropical wilderness in the country (some 1.5 million acres), on the southern tip of Florida, is comprised of freshwater, seawater, and terrestrial ecosystems. It's the only place in the U.S. to spot crocodiles and aligators cohabiting, and, if you're lucky, you may cross paths with an endangered manatee. The Everglades has few upscale hotels, but the 32-room Ivey House *(iveyhouse.com; $)* is a good option and can organize airboat expeditions through the marshy habitat.

Glacier National Park, Montana

Lace up your hiking boots—this land of wildflower-blanketed hills is best explored on foot. More than 700 trails cover the same passages where Blackfeet Indians tracked buffalo centuries ago. Rest your weary legs at the chalet-style Many Glacier Hotel *(glacierparkinc.com; $)*; suites are outfitted with private balconies that look out over Swiftcurrent Lake.

Great Smoky Mountains National Park, Tennessee and North Carolina

The Appalachians' Smokies are theater in its purest form. Crowds gather in June for a light show performed by thousands of synchronized fireflies. The best place to see the spectacle is from a private cabin porch at Le Conte Lodge *(lecontelodge.com; $$)*. Come September, nature does a wardrobe change to gold, purple, and red leaves, setting the forest ablaze in an organic imitation of a Tim Burton film.

Hawaii Volcanoes National Park

On the southeastern edge of this 333,000-acre park, the rugged Kilauea is called the "drive-in volcano" because paved paths allow you to see it by car. Travel 45 minutes down Chain of Craters Road to witness the interaction of lava and sea, or watch it from afar at the newly revamped Volcano House *(hawaiivolcanohouse.com; $$)*, where the Rim restaurant's otherworldly vistas come with sustainably farmed Kona lobster.

Saguaro National Park, Arizona

Darwinism is on full display at Saguaro—animals here have had to adapt to fluctuating temperatures and incessant drought. The landscape is a reptilian paradise, with tortoises, desert iguanas, and snakes. Check in to the 60,000-acre Tanque Verde *(tanqueverderanch.com; $$$$)*, a dude ranch that pairs guests with expert guides who lead excursions on horseback.

Yellowstone National Park

Known as the American Serengeti because of its sprawling landscape and rich wildlife, the 2.2 million-acre Yellowstone contains 67 different mammal species. Bison, elk, and bighorn sheep are commonly sighted, but nothing gets the crowds gawking like the gray wolves, who reappeared in 1996 after a nearly 60-year absence. Stay at the historic log-and-stone Old Faithful Inn *(yellowstonenationalparklodges.com; $$)*, with a glowing rhyolite fireplace and handcrafted clock of copper, wood, and wrought iron.

Hikers on Mount
Desert Island,
in Acadia. Left:
Yellowstone's
"boiling river."

Bald cypress
trees in
the Everglades.
Right: The
pool at Tanque
Verde Ranch,
in Saguaro
National Park.

A row of iconic balconies in New Orleans's French Quarter.

NEW ORLEANS

The Bayou gets a fresh look

THAT MIND-BENDING AFFAIR of parades, costumes, and excess may be what New Orleans is best known for, but there's much more to celebrate here than Mardi Gras. Cooking traditions have been carried on for generations, making this one of the best cities in the world to eat in. Creole cottages in pastel hues lend the place a laid-back, Caribbean-style charm. And then there's the music—it seems to emanate from every doorway along Royal, Bourbon, and Chartres Streets.

Lately, an entrepreneurial spirit has taken hold in the Big Easy, where pioneers are thinking beyond Fat Tuesday and the French Quarter. Among the flurry of debuts is chef Phillip Lopez's Square Root, a temple of molecular gastronomy in the Lower Garden District. To the east, a creative Brooklyn vibe grows in Bywater, where shotgun houses have been turned into art galleries that showcase experimental paintings and multimedia displays by local talent. Want a peek? Head to the Bywater Art Lofts to see artists at work in their open studios.

Thankfully, not everything in New Orleans is changing. Frenchmen Street mainstay the Spotted Cat Music Club is still one of the best places to catch acts such as Meschiya and the Little Big Horns. And the house band at Preservation Hall, in the French Quarter, continues to draw crowds with old-school New Orleans–style jazz—just as it has since it opened in the 1960's.

GUIDE

EAT
Square Root
*1800 Magazine St.;
no phone.* **$$$$**

DO
Bywater Art Lofts
3725 Dauphine St.; 504/945-1883; bywaterartlofts.com.

Preservation Hall
*726 St. Peter;
504/522-2841;
preservationhall.com/hall.*

Spotted Cat Music Club
*623 Frenchmen St.;
504/258-3135;
spottedcatmusicclub.com.*

DALLAS

High design emerges in the Lone Star State

THERE'S NO PLACE THAT EMBODIES Lone Star swagger quite like Dallas, a city defined by big hats and big ambition. Proud locals, who boast of having both the Neiman Marcus flagship and one of the largest state fairs in the country, are now singing the praises of the starchitects bringing international acclaim to their hometown. In the burgeoning Arts District, the sprawling AT&T Performing Arts Center houses the dramatic red-glass-clad oval Winspear Opera House, from Foster & Partners. A stone's throw away stands Joshua Prince-Ramus and Rem Koolhaas's gleaming Wyly Theatre, made from hundreds of vertically stacked aluminum tubes. Then there's Renzo Piano's glass-topped Nasher Sculpture Center, a cathedral of light with a lush garden full of live oaks and works by art titans such as Rodin and Henry Moore. But perhaps the most striking addition to the city's skyline is the $185 million Perot Museum of Nature & Science, designed by American architect Thom Mayne. The 14-story striated structure resembles a concrete cube floating in space, and has 11 permanent exhibition halls. Not to be missed: the giant Leap Frog Forest of 3½-foot-tall glowing amphibians.

GUIDE

DO
Nasher Sculpture Center
2001 Flora St.;
214/242-5100;
naschersculpturecenter.org.

Perot Museum of
Nature & Science
2201 N. Field St.;
214/428-5555;
perotmuseum.org.

Winspear Opera House
2403 Flora St.;
214/880-0202;
attpac.org.

Wyly Theatre
2400 Flora St.;
214/880-0202;
attpac.org.

Architect Thom Mayne's cubelike Perot Museum of Nature & Science, in downtown Dallas.

CHICAGO

The Windy City's dining scene continues to push boundaries—there are tasting-menu temples, gourmet-street-food havens, artisanal bakeries, and everything in between. From Lincoln Square to Wicker Park, the latest openings offer the best of the spectrum. Dig in.

Carriage House
Crowds flock to this Lowcountry-style hot spot in Wicker Park for South Carolina native Mark Steuer's inventive interpretations of soul-food staples. A rustic dining room with reclaimed-timber tables is the setting for dishes such as cast-iron-crisped Geechie Boy Mill johnnycakes topped with a dollop of peach preserves made in house. *1700 W. Division St.; 773/384-9700; carriagehousechicago.com.* **$$**

Dillman's Delicatessen
Chi-town's latest "it" chef, French Laundry alum Brendan Sodikoff, has opened his fifth restaurant on the edge of River North. Brave the lunch lines for a booth at the 200-seat new-school deli, where the kitchen turns out ribbons of paper-thin smoked prime brisket between slices of fresh-baked rye, and bagels with house-made cream cheese. *354 Hubbard St.; 312/988-0078.* **$$**

Elizabeth
Hidden between a tire outlet and a soccer store, Elizabeth is the city's unlikeliest foodie destination. Those who want in on chef Illana Regan's locally foraged degustation menu pin their hopes on scoring a prepaid ticket, which is as hard to come by as Bulls courtside seats. Once you're seated at one of the three communal tables, you're in for some serious eating epiphanies. There's the terrarium of pickled blackberry, wood sorrel, seaweed, malt soil, yogurt, and flower petals, and the slivers of rich deer heart garnished with dill aioli, celery ribbons, and salt. *4835 N. Western Ave.; 773/681-0651; elizabeth-restaurant.com.* **$$$**

Endgrain
After a garnering a following for his artisanal doughnuts at Nightwood, Enoch Simpson teamed up with his brother for this wood-lined brunch venue in Roscoe Village: the duo made the bar by hand, refinished the chairs themselves, and crafted vintage poultry feeders into light fixtures. Under the watch of a taxidermied boar's head, patrons feast on crisp pork-belly-and-egg sandwiches, then satisfy a sweet tooth with the gooseberry-elderflower-jam jelly roll and tart rhubarb trifle. *1851 W. Addison St.; 773/687-8191; endgrainrestaurant.com.* **$$**

Grace
Former Avenues chef Curtis Duffy's tasting menu at Grace is all about intricate flavors. A highlight: the lime- and coconut-scented rice topped with raw *kampachi,* fresh and candied pomelo, golden trout roe, young coconut meat, and Thai-basil purée. Duffy extends the same complexity to his desserts, taking modern art as an inspiration for dishes such as bitter chocolate with raw chestnut, disks of persimmon, and lemon mint. While the ingredients are nouveau, his approach to service is old-school—phone reservations only. *652 W. Randolph St.; 312/234-0078; grace-restaurant.com.* **$$$**

La Sirena Clandestina
The emphasis at this Brazilian restaurant is on street food—and the vibe is just as down-to-earth. Chef John Manion's bite-size empanadas are stuffed with spinach, feta, pine nuts, and chiles, then fried to a golden crunch. Cult-favorite *moqueca,* a traditional seafood stew, is briny and rich, with flaky sea bass, mussels, and sweet shrimp poured over cilantro risotto. The cocktail menu goes well past the classic pisco sour; order the Brazillionaire, made with cachaça, *branca menta, açai* liqueur, lemon, and mole bitters. *954 West Fulton Market; 312/226-5300; lasirenachicago.com.* **$$$**

Little Goat Bread
Don't bother stepping into Stephanie Izard's bakery if you're counting calories. Her tangy sourdough is laced with duck fat. The butter is infused with cinnamon and cocoa. Staff can help pair any carb-heavy morsel with a midwestern craft brew. Although the snacks may be filling, you can get a more substantial meal at Izard's adjacent diner (we recommend the kimchi goat burger). *820 W. Randolph St.; 312/888-3455; littlegoatchicago.com.* **$**

Parson's Chicken & Fish
A follow-up to the wildly successful Longman & Eagle, this no-frills shack organizes its menu into three sections: Raw, offering yellowfin tuna and oysters; Fresh, chickpea-octopus salad and shrimp toast; and Fried, where salt-cod fritters compete with classic chicken legs. While you're making the difficult choice, have a negroni slushie—and check out the rehabbed 1977 El Camino parked outside. *2952 W. Armitage St.; 773/384-3333; parsons chickenandfish.com.* **$$**

Yellowfin tuna at Parson's Chicken & Fish. Left: Behind the counter at Little Goat Bread.

Artisanal doughnuts at Endgrain. Right: A view through the window of Little Goat Bread.

SANTA FE, NEW MEXICO

New Age gurus and eclectic characters in the desert

Traditional adobe
architecture at
Santa Fe's Inn &
Spa at Loretto.
Opposite: A
chicken taco at
El Parasol.

Gleaner, a sculpture by Jeremy Thomas, at Charlotte Jackson Fine Art. Right: The Jemez Mountains, outside Santa Fe.

A moose statue on Canyon Road. Left: The Holy Spirit Espresso coffee shop.

TS SEEDS ARE ON THE OUTSIDE! The strawberry has nothing to hide! It is the perfect size. It is not too big; neither is it too small. Nature has created it so that it would fit perfectly in the mouth." If you're wondering where this juicy conversation is happening, let me assure you there is only one possible place in the universe: Santa Fe, New Mexico. I'm at a party in one of the nicer adobe homes I've seen so far (thar be mountain views), talking to the rugged and delightfully Swiss-German–accented Sondra Goodwin, photographer and cultivator of fruits and vegetables and nude wrestler extraordinaire. On her wrist there is a tattoo of a blazing, glorious strawberry approximating the Sacred Heart of Jesus ("I don't believe in the Christ, but I love the strawberry") surrounded by six stars. Why six stars? "You know how there are five-star hotels?" Yes. "This is one more."

Let me say it from the get-go: I love Sondra Goodwin. And I love Santa Fe. Much like Sondra's strawberry, this small, mountain-hugged burg in northern New Mexico has nothing to hide, its post-hippie population reveling openly and gaily in its sunny provincial decadence. The scenery, the food, the art will always play second fiddle to this delightful collection of people, most of whom are just too weird to let loose on New York or Los Angeles, where a great deal of them seem to hail from. When I myself sported a Honduran poncho with a FREE HEMP NOW pin as a senior at Oberlin College, northern New Mexico is where I dreamed I would go after graduation with my equally patchouli-scented girlfriend. Alas, it did not work out. But 16 years later, here I am, the spotless clouds embracing me, the cold desert air tingling my nose with the pine-burning scent of 10,000 expensive kiva fireplaces. Home at last.

First, the cast of characters. I'm dining at the famed Café Pasqual's, one block south of Santa Fe's epicentral plaza, with Porochista Khakpour, the excellent Iranian-born novelist; Swedish-born philosopher Jason Leddington; and a woman this whole town seems to know and adore, Nouf Al-Qasimi. Porochista calls Nouf (rhymes with "loaf") the Holly Golightly of Santa Fe. She is an accomplished angler—she first came to this part of the world for the fishing—as well as an ex–food critic, a former elk-meat cook at a prestigious local restaurant, a Yale graduate, a Chinese-medicine practitioner, and a conflict-free-diamond trader. "Of all the places where I could afford to buy a home, I thought of Santa Fe," says Nouf. "I've been here most of my adult life."

am organic!" a woman was recently overheard screaming at Santa Fe's Whole Foods. It's not a sentiment one can easily argue with around here. The search for the earthy, the authentic, the original runs strongly through the town's citizens. At first, I am confused by the overall adobe-or-death aesthetic of the place, even as my lungs are depleted by the lack of oxygen seven thousand feet above sea level. Within five days I become an earnest appraiser of *farolitos* and vigas (small paper lanterns containing a candle and wooden beams typical in adobe construction, respectively).

After 10 days nothing surprises me. There's a sensible-seeming middle-aged woman walking down the street with a parrot she has dressed up in a Santa Claus outfit. There's a guy who reputedly fixes only Mercedes-Benzes and Wurlitzers. There's a biodiesel taxi. There are battle-weary detachments of women from Dallas and Houston running up and down Canyon Road's art district, out to purchase the $70,000 life-size statues of heroic American moose that are sculpted expressly for them.

Porochista and Nouf take me to the gorgeous 1930's Moorish-style Lensic Performing Arts Center to see the Circus Luminous, a local circus show that doubles as a kind of morality play for children. The acrobatics are spectacular, but the narrative is hard to follow—a perfect village is taken over by generals who have small bodies but rule with giant telescopes. It must be a subtle critique of Santa Fe or Burma, or both. The audience loves every minute of it, but as the show progresses we all begin to suffer from clown fatigue and decide to leave.

Some of us go off to Ten Thousand Waves, a spa complex styled like a Japanese *onsen,*

The historic San Miguel Chapel, in downtown Santa Fe. Left: A local rancher and his entourage on Palace Avenue. Opposite: Dinner at Café Pasqual's.

about 20 minutes northeast of downtown. Ten Thousand Waves is pretty much the answer to all of life's problems, and when we show up, half the town seems to be in attendance. This being Santa Fe, the communal bath has been known to get randy. A sign now asks for swimsuits to be worn after 8:15 p.m. We book the Waterfall, which has a large bath, an intense wet/dry sauna, and a waterfall sputtering into the cold plunge. The crisp mountain air, if not the stars above, settles onto our steam-warmed shoulders, and all of us are very happy.

Walking through Santa Fe's central plaza the next morning, I feel the familiar languid pleasure of strolling though a sunny Italian hill town. After a shot of caffeine at Holy Spirit Espresso, on San Francisco Street, I let go of my East Coastness and check in to the rich adobe nuthouse that is Santa Fe. It will be hard to leave.

I walk down to Canyon Road to meet some friends at the Teahouse, a good place for *matcha* green tea with

ginger on the rim and a tremendous bowl of oatmeal swimming in cream and strawberries, banana, maple syrup, and sticky rice. All around us is 12-step-speak infused with Hopi wisdom and generalized arts-and-crafts blather. "I have a new anger in me today." "I would crochet hats and sell them at art sales." "The strawberry," I want to declare to all present, as I pick a specimen out of my oatmeal, "is the best fruit. It wears its heart on its sleeve. It has nothing to hide!"

Instead I decide to check out the art. Since its opening in 1995, Site Santa Fe has been gradually shifting the center of gravity of the contemporary art scene from Canyon Road to the revamped Railyard district, thanks to its superb biennial exhibitions. The space is easily the best reuse of a Coors beer warehouse ever, and has featured important artists of the day from Marina Abramović to Takashi Murakami. The Eighth International Biennial, titled "The Dissolve,"

blows me away with its take on moving-image art. Thomas Demand's 35-mm wonder *Rain* re-creates the effect of raindrops falling on a hard surface; spending 20 minutes in front of this piece is no less than an act of meditation. The Austrian Maria Lassnig's semiautobiographical blend of live action, animation, and found photography restored my faith in that Alpine nation's sense of humor. And Mary Reid Kelley's *You Make Me Iliad*, a mixture of live-action performance and stop-motion animation set in a German-occupied brothel at the end of World War I, defies any description other than *epic*.

Next to Site Santa Fe I find a cluster of the town's trailblazing galleries, including a new space for the formerly downtown fixture Charlotte Jackson Fine Art. Jackson features a delicious installation of Charles Arnoldi's *Tasty Spuds* sculptures of the beloved starch, a series of stacked tubers made of black bronze

that leaves me both hungry and more appreciative of large carbohydrates.

At the suggestion of Janet Dees, one of Site Santa Fe's brilliant curators, I pay a visit to Eight Modern, a happy place off Canyon Road where I encounter Santa Fe artist Katherine Lee's series of drawings, *Animal Violence & Topless Women Eating Jam*. True to this title, the jam-eating women are topless and the animal-on-animal violence is vivid. Eight Modern is unpretentious and fun, a modest but inspired gallery amid a sea of whirligigs on Delgado Street. Even the old-school galleries on Canyon Road can sometimes surprise. Stopping by the Matthews Gallery, I stumble upon Gino Severini's study for his famous *Pierrot the Musician*, and I also find Käthe Kollwitz's *Beggar Woman and Child*, a masterly work from the anti-Nazi artist. But what I really want for Christmas is that $70,000 moose.

And then I want me some food. The Santa Fe dining scene is hopping. There's a lot of fallback on black truffles, prized bacons, and the inspirational power of homemade chorizo, but some innovative thinking, too.

There's nothing wrong with Restaurant Martín, where *Iron Chef* loser Martin Rios ("He's still angry about that," a waiter tells me, adding, "We don't talk about it") makes good use of local ingredients, the kind of colorful plates—the organic golden-beet carpaccio couldn't be fresher—that my doctor has always supported. Restaurant Martín is swell and up-to-the-moment, but at this point what I really want to do is go on a taco crawl with Nouf.

We leave behind the manicured center of town and head down Cerrillos Road. Sunbaked, wide-open Cerrillos brings to mind the great suburban strip-mall sprawl of the American West, like something out of the hit Albuquerque-based television show *Breaking Bad*. Suddenly style has been replaced with flavor; nothing seems organic, but everything is real.

El Parasol is a counter-only joint with no tables and no nothing, but the soft shredded-chicken taco is excellent and the crisp, intense *chicharrón* in the burrito—well, let me just say that if you have one pork-rind-and-bean burrito in your lifetime, let this be the one. At Adelitas, the *lengua* taco is the best in town, house-made tortillas brimming with luscious chunks of tongue, and there's a *mole poblano* as rich as Croesus. At Alicia's Tortillería, women in drawstring pajamas queue in front of posters advertising lots of opportunities to *enviar* their dinero back to Mexico. What they're after are the piping-hot tortillas sporting what Nouf calls "a magical elasticity." The chile burritos are a standout. La Cocina de Doña Clara is a no-frills place with a dedicated clientele deep into their food, sneaking peeks of Shakira busting her moves on the TV. Doña Clara produces an outstanding *gordita de rajas con queso*, a little spicy pocket of warmth filled with chiles and cheese, and a terrific *desebrada* shredded-beef taco. The green chiles are freshly cooked every morning, and the difference shows.

Having consumed a total of 12 dishes during the taco crawl, I feel it is time for a drink. I've been staying at the Hotel St. Francis, downtown Santa Fe's oldest, its previously European interiors remodeled into a clean

Overlooking the pool at Four Seasons Resort Rancho Encantado. Below: Secreto Lounge's stocked bar.

and simple haute-monk aesthetic. The best thing about the St. Francis is its bar, the Secreto Lounge. Here I meet Bill York, owner of small-batch bitters company Bitter End, who works with computers all day for the New Mexico state government and then comes home to make his amazing essences (he has a master's degree in biology, which seems to help). He brings his bitters to the Secreto to be mixed by Santa Fe's premier mixologist, Chris Milligan. The result of their work together is something special. A classic Manhattan with Memphis-barbecue bitters, anyone? It's a complete rethink of that tired old drink. Or how about Kaffir-lime-infused vodka, green tea, fresh mint, and Moroccan (hints of cardamom and cayenne) bitters? It starts off sweet, and then it burns nicely.

Which is how I'm feeling by the end of this trip. Santa Fe is a small town, but between the bitters, the tacos and chiles, the art scene, and the fairly regular parties, it can be intense. It is time to head to the Four Seasons Resort Rancho Encantado in the village of Tesuque, a bedroom community of Santa Fe that is home to the renowned Santa Fe Opera. The hotel opened in 2008 and features one of the warmest and most attentive staffs I've ever encountered. Their pleasantness is almost enough to make up for the fact that many of the rooms look out onto the parking lot and the resort's gleaming Mercedes coupes, which, on the plus side, you can borrow (first come, first served) and speed off with into the hills. If you close your eyes and learn to ignore the parking lot, you will notice yourself lost amid lavender and the starry New Mexico sky.

The resort's restaurant, Terra, serves up a lean antelope steak with a heavy bouquet and a strong finish, and a flaky, moist trout tamale. The chef is a proponent of the "modern rustic" style, which is well matched by the cheerfully high-ceilinged dining room and its striking views of the mountain and brush surroundings. On my final day at the resort, a craniosacral massage at the spa gets my cerebrospinal fluid pumping. My masseuse, the appropriately (for New Mexico) named Anna Aura, finally gets rid of my two years' worth of sinus troubles. The massage oil, she tells me in that sweet but strong hippie-scientist voice I hear all over Santa Fe, contains spruce, lavender, and grapefruit oil—I wish to thank the gods for each and every one of them. Outside Encantado's bar, I stare at the mountainous Los Alamos lights irradiating the distance just as the sunset explodes into a spectacular Southwestern fireball, my chakras aligned, my spirit free. ✦

Adapted from "Pure Sante Fe," by Gary Shteyngart.

GUIDE

LAS VEGAS

There's more to Vegas than monolithic nightclubs, mega-casinos, and name-brand restaurants. Venture beyond the Strip and you'll find countless attractions—high and low—that beckon you to ditch the craps and cocktails.

D Las Vegas

Don't forget your quarters. At the upstairs gaming room in the D Las Vegas, you can race mechanized horses on one of the city's few remaining Sigma Derby tables, or plunk your change into retro one-armed bandits. *3150 Paradise Rd.; 702/892-7575; thed.com.*

Dream Racing Experience

Driving a street-illegal Ferrari F430 GT at ungodly speeds ranks near the top of any "only in Vegas" bucket list. Channel your inner Mario Andretti at Las Vegas Motor Speedway, whose Dream Racing Experience gives aspiring speedsters classroom training, a simulator session, and five to 30 high-speed laps (0 to 60 mph in 3½ seconds) around the track. Fancy an exotic street car instead? Take a $200,000 McLaren out for a spin. *7000 Las Vegas Blvd. N.; 702/605-3000; dreamracing.com.*

Fashion Outlets Las Vegas

Sure, the city has its fair share of high-end retail, but it's also known for having scads of discount shops; the king of them all is 39 miles south-west, in the border town of Primm. You'll find outposts of 100 stores including Burberry, Versace, Neiman Marcus, and Tod's. And this being Vegas, the complex is connected to—what else?—a resort and casino. Bored kids and husbands will appreciate the two Tom Fazio–designed golf courses and the Desperado roller coaster. *32100 Las Vegas Blvd. S.; 702/874-1400; fashionoutletslasvegas.com.*

Mob Museum

The federal courthouse, site of the 1950 Kefauver hearings on organized crime, is now a shrine to the history of mobsters (Lefty, Lucky, Bugsy, and Scarface, to name a few). Among the showstoppers: a segment of the bullet-ridden wall from the 1929 Valentine's Day Massacre in Chicago, interactive exhibits on wiretapping, and real weapons used by Mafia hit men. *300 E. Stewart Ave.; 702/229-2734; themobmuseum.org.*

Neon Museum

For years, the most iconic Vegas signs (Moulin Rouge; Desert Inn; Stardust) were relegated to the so-called Neon Boneyard, where visitors had to book tours two weeks in advance for a viewing. Now the collection of Old Vegas kitsch dating back as far as the 1930's is finally open to the public. The lobby of the renovated 1961 La Concha Motel serves as the museum's visitors' center, through which guests enter to marvel at more than 150 of the time-rubbed relics. *770 Las Vegas Blvd. N.; 702/387-6366; neonmuseum.org.*

Nevada State Museum

This $50 million museum in the Springs Preserve was built for young kids. There's a storytelling touch screen on continental drift, a stalactite cave to explore, and a 3-D movie about life in the desert by night. If you're searching for some adult diversion, head to the exhibition on Vegas's evolution into an entertainment epicenter, with a dazzling display of showgirl costumes. *Springs Preserve, 309 S. Valley View Blvd.; 702/486-5205; museums.nevadaculture.org.*

Project Dinner Table

Every month, internationally renowned chefs, including Mark LoRusso and Michel Richard, serve 150 guests at one very long table. Each meal is in a different setting—the middle of an orchard, say, or left field at a baseball stadium. Since all proceeds go to charity, it's one of the few things you can feel good about in Sin City. Caveat: seats fill up quickly, so book at least 30 days in advance. *April through November; projectdinnertable.com.*

Smith Center for the Performing Arts

The most hotly anticipated music venue in Las Vegas history is this $450 million limestone complex designed by David M. Schwarz. True to the city's spirit, austerity was thrown to the wind: expect Venetian-marble floors, zebrawood trimmings, and a 16-story campanile housing 47 bronze bells. But all this is window dressing. The real draw is the five-tier main hall, with more than 2,000 seats and state-of-the-art acoustics. *361 Symphony Park Ave.; 702/982-7805; thesmithcenter.com.*

Valley of Fire

Head an hour northeast of town and you'll reach Nevada's oldest state park, a blazing red, Mars-like landscape marked by chiseled sandstone formations and billowy dunes. Hike the mile-long Fire Canyon Road, which looks out at the multicolored rocks of Rainbow Vista. Or opt for the half-mile-long trek to see the petroglyphs, depicting Native American hunters and animals. *parks.nv.gov.*

The Stardust Resort & Casino sign at the Neon Museum. Left: Smith Center for the Performing Arts.

Sandstone formations in the Valley of Fire. Right: The scene at Project Dinner Table.

The lobby at the Ace Hotel Portland.

PORTLAND, OREGON

The West Coast's capital of cool

IN THE PAST DECADE, Portland has developed major-league hipster cachet, with coffee geeks and style junkies, tech innovators and eco-warriors unconsciously (or perhaps consciously) transforming the city into a hotbed of do-good, feel-good enterprises. That artistic, quirky tenacity has enticed the likes of writers (Chuck Palahniuk), filmmakers (Gus Van Sant), and high-profile indie bands (the Decemberists), who have all at one point called this city home.

While neighborhoods on both sides of the Willamette River are sneaking into the spotlight, the West End is now one of Portland's most popular stopovers. Its undisputed heart is the Ace Hotel Portland, where rooms have turntables and funky nightstands fashioned from secondhand books.

Nearby, Tanner Goods is the place to shop for custom-made leather belts; Canoe is full of expertly curated goods from both near (sea salt harvested in Oregon's Netarts Bay) and far (Chilean booties made of salmon skin and wool). Wander the streets and you're bound to uncover many more one-of-a-kind boutiques.

GUIDE

STAY
Ace Hotel Portland
1022 S.W. Stark St.;
503/228-2277;
acehotel.com. **$**

SHOP
Canoe
1136 S.W. Alder St.; 503/
889-8545; canoeonline.net.

Tanner Goods
1308 W. Burnside St.; 503/
222-2774; tannergoods.com.

SAN JUAN ISLANDS, WASHINGTON

Rugged adventure in the Northwest

The boat-filled Friday Harbor, off San Juan Island.

ADVENTURE IS AN UNDENIABLE DRAW of this 172-island chain 80 miles north of Seattle. Its chilly inland seas and thick forests afford some of the best hiking, biking, and sea kayaking in the world. Friday Harbor, the archipelago's only established town, is the ideal jumping-off point for exploring the area. Fortify yourself with lunch on Main Street, where organic menus are scrawled on outdoor chalkboards: locals swear by the heaping bowls of smoked-salmon chowder at Backdoor Kitchen. Once you're suitably energized, a wildlife-packed excursion awaits, courtesy of San Juan Outfitters. Sign up for the three-hour ocean safari led by a master outdoorsman, who will guide you through glassy channels and underwater kelp jungles inhabited by porpoises and seals.

Beyond Friday Harbor, the region gets more rugged. Majestic killer whales return to their mating ground each summer off horseshoe-shaped Orcas Island. For a prime viewing spot, book a waterside suite with a private balcony at the Outlook Inn. Owners Sara and Adam Farish will set you up on a sailing expedition to see nesting bald eagles, rare red-beaked puffins, and, of course, those breaching black-and-white mammals that give the place its name.

GUIDE

STAY
Outlook Inn
*171 Main St., Eastsound;
360/376-2200;
outlookinn.com.* **$**

EAT
Backdoor Kitchen
*400B A St., Friday Harbor;
360/378-9540;
backdoorkitchen.com.* **$$**

DO
San Juan Outfitters
*248 Reuben Memorial Dr.,
Friday Harbor;
866/810-1483;
sanjuanislandoutfitters.com.*

SAN FRANCISCO

From molecular wizards to comfort-food gurus, trailblazing chefs are eager to make their mark in San Francisco's ever-evolving culinary landscape. Take our tour of the most-buzzed-about new restaurants in the Mission, SoMa, and beyond.

Bar Tartine
A worldly makeover and a menu that defies classification have given Bar Tartine a burst of fresh energy. In tandem with chef Nicolaus Balla—schooled in Budapest, trained in Japan—surfer-dude owner Chad Robertson changed everything about his 2005-opened spot but the name. What to expect now? Danish smørrebrød (open-faced sandwiches), Hungarian *lángos* (fried flatbreads), and toast topped with *bottarga* (cured fish roe), dried mushroom powder, and seaweed.
561 Valencia St.; 415/487-1600; bartartine.com. **$$**

Benu
Corey Lee, former chef de cuisine at the French Laundry, has reinvigorated fine dining in San Francisco with the clean-lined Benu, in SoMa. Here, every detail is carefully considered, from the custom porcelain serving plates and impeccably choreographed service to the Eastern-inspired tasting menu: a 1,000-year-old quail egg; salt-and-pepper squid; lobster-coral *xiao long bao* (steamed buns).
22 Hawthorne St.; 415/685-4860; benusf.com. **$$$$**

Cotogna
At this convivial neighborhood restaurant, most dishes issue from the open hearth, including succulent spit-roasted meats and wood-oven pizzas. As is the case at its sister restaurant, Quince, next door, the pastas are a must, especially the buttery *raviolo di ricotta* with farm egg and the *agnolotti dal plin*.
490 Pacific Ave.; 415/775-8508; cotognasf.com. **$$$**

Mission Chinese Food
This raved-about restaurant may have a divey interior, slack service, and an hour-long wait, but the food is worth it. Chef Danny Bowien (who last year opened an outpost in New York's Lower East Side) calls his dishes "Americanized Chinese food"; think fiery kung pao pastrami and a cardamom-laced beef brisket soup. Can't brave the line? They deliver.
2234 Mission St.; 415/863-2800; missionchinesefood.com. **$$**

Park Tavern
Anna Weinberg's North Beach brasserie draws a stylish weekend crowd, who come for her robust dishes. You can't go wrong with the crisp wild-mushroom-polenta cakes and an open-faced deviled-egg sandwich with bacon and pickled jalapeños. For brunch, a hangover-helper cocktail of Fernet Branca, espresso liqueur, and cold-brew coffee is thoughtfully available by the pitcher, should you require it.
1652 Stockton St.; 415/989-7300; parktavernsf.com. **$$$**

Rich Table
You'll want to return again and again to this homey dining room owned by husband-and-wife chefs Evan and Sarah Rich. The dishes perfectly balance acidity and texture, and highlight surprise ingredients—the addictive sardine-laced potato chips are served with horseradish sauce; the chicken lasagna is sprinkled with crunchy popped sorghum.
199 Gough St.; 415/355-9085; richtablesf.com. **$$**

Saison
After its smaller, scrappier spot received two Michelin stars, the farm-to-table restaurant Saison, run by chef Joshua Skenes, moved to a grander, more grown-up space in a SoMa historic building. Choose an 18- or 20-course tasting menu—each highlights fresh local ingredients, sourced from foragers and farmers' markets.
178 Townsend St.; 415/828-7990; saisonsf.com. **$$$$**

State Bird Provisions
Waiters roam the room serving innovative small bites from carts at this casual restaurant in the Western Addition neighborhood. Luckily, the food holds up to the quirky concept: the seafood trolley in particular is worth flagging down for delicacies such as *hamachi* tuna and black-garlic aioli on a fried nori chip.
1529 Fillmore St.; 415/795-1272; statebirdsf.com. **$$**

St. Vincent
This tavern is named after the patron saint of wine- and vinegar-makers, but it's the scruffy-faced owner David Lynch who looks after the hungry here. Try the rabbit meatballs, which pair exquisitely with an earthy Catalan red.
1270 Valencia St.; 415/285-1200; stvincentsf.com. **$$$**

Tacolicious and Mosto
The Mission has always been a go-to destination for the city's best taquerias—and the brightly tiled Tacolicious is yet another celebrated arrival to the area. Regulars love the tiny tacos stuffed with succulent prickly cactus and melted *queso oaxaca*. If you need to kill time while waiting for a table, head next door to Mosto for pitchers of margaritas made with blood orange and agave.
741 Valencia St.; 415/626-1344; tacolicious.com. **$$**

Raw tuna and avocado tostadas at Tacolicious. Left: Cooking over an open flame at Saison.

A pizza with prosciutto, pea shoots, and egg at Cotogna. Right: Outdoor dining at Park Tavern.

PARK TAVERN

SANTA BARBARA, CALIFORNIA

An idyllic escape on California's central coast

An aerial view of the city skyline and Pacific Ocean beyond.

LONG A GETAWAY FOR HOLLYWOOD A-LISTERS, this untamed yet civilized landscape is dotted with Mediterranean-style mansions, sprawling orange groves, and chaparral-covered mountains that plunge into the ocean. High in the hills, you'll find the recently renovated El Encanto, an iconic retreat with Craftsman and Spanish-colonial bungalows. Start your morning at the clock tower of the Santa Barbara Courthouse, where the view stretches from the Channel Islands to the Santa Barbara Mission. It's a six-block walk from there to the Saturday farmers' market, the perfect place to watch gray-haired hippies, dreadlocked surfers, and well-heeled natives hunting for Central Coast olive oils and zingy lemon-flavored pistachios. While you could spend hours spotting dolphins on nearby Butterfly Beach, save time for the Funk Zone, an artsy industrial district opposite Stearns Wharf. Here, pick up the Urban Wine Trail (a network of 22 tasting rooms) at Municipal Winemakers, whose varietals have offbeat names such as Bright Red and Fizz. For lunch, the open-air trolley on State Street will drop you off near Scarlett Begonia; snag a table in the hidden courtyard and order the salmon carpaccio from the organic menu. Or head to the Shop Café for a dish inspired by Ugandan street food: scrambled eggs, bacon, and smoked tomato on house-made flatbread.

GUIDE

STAY

El Encanto by Orient-Express
800 Alvarado Pl.; 805/845-5800; elencanto.com. **$$$$**

EAT

Scarlett Begonia
11 W. Victoria St.; 805/770-2143; scarlettbegonia.net. **$$$**

Shop Café
730 N. Milpas St.; 805/845-1696; shopcafesb.com. **$**

DO

Municipal Winemakers
22 Anacapa St.; 805/931-6864; municipalwinemakers.com.

Santa Barbara Farmers Market
Santa Barbara St. at Cota St.; 805/962-5354; sbfarmersmarket.org.

LOS ANGELES

Thanks to trendsetting designers, indie boutiques, and a laid-back, breezy style, Los Angeles is one of the country's most exciting places to shop. Read on for our neighborhood guide to the city, from boho-chic Venice to recently hip Downtown.

BRENTWOOD

Brentwood Country Mart
A warren of food stalls and shops by fashionable clothiers, Brentwood Country Mart has come a long way since Ronald Reagan used to have his hair cut at the mini-mall's old-school barber. The highlights: designer Jenni Kayne's namesake craft store; the exceptionally well-curated Diesel, a Bookstore; and a temple to Roberta Freymann's Indian-print beach tunics, an essential for any L.A. girl's wardrobe. *225 26th St.; 310/451-9877; brentwoodcountrymart.com.*

Velvet by Graham and Spencer
In the land of premieres, the 2013 debut of this flagship captured blockbuster buzz. Bank on the usual kicked-back California look, from off-the-shoulder slouchy tees to racer-back maxi dresses. *13020 San Vicente Blvd.; 310/395-4000; velvet-tees.com.*

DOWNTOWN

Buttons & Bows
Karen Marley, daughter of the late reggae legend Bob Marley, scours Fashion District trunk shows and warehouse sales in New York and L.A. for vintage designer threads at marked-down prices. Expect cotton floral-patterned dresses and silk tops and an ever-changing range of handbags and pumps from Martin Margiela, Miu Miu, and Phillip Lim. *348 S. Spring St., suite 112; 213/622-0648; buttonsandbowsla.com.*

LA BREA

A+R
Come to this eastside home-design showroom for a selection of decorative pieces (porcelain bird statuettes; magnetic cherrywood boxes), modern lighting (New Zealand bamboo lamps; crystal LED bulbs), and contemporary furniture (matchstick side tables; Danish wire chairs). *171 S. La Brea Ave.; 800/913-0071; aplusrstore.com.*

Jack's Eyewear
Don't be fooled by this boutique's run-of-the-mill optometrist vibe—collector Jack Bernstein's rare sunnies are a favorite of Hollywood fashionistas. Perusing his shelves is like a journey through style history: Jackie O–model Diors, Nixon-age Playboys, 90's Run DMC Cazals. *120 S. La Brea Ave.; 323/933-9800.*

Kelly Cole
The stretch of La Brea Avenue between First and Second Streets is known for its surf and skate shops. At his funky store, newcomer Kelly Cole, who moonlights as a DJ, peddles classic-rock T-shirts, Vietnam-era combat boots, and hard-to-find collector's items such as retro concert posters. *175 S. La Brea Ave.; 323/692-5012; kellycoleusa.com.*

VENICE

Den.m Bar
Some of the world's most coveted jeans are produced in industrial areas outside Los Angeles. Now avowed denim junkies can custom-design their own pair at Den.m Bar (the bespoke line is so popular that shoppers are encouraged to book an appointment). Pick from a variety of Asian and European materials, choose a fit—skinny; slim-tapered; straight leg—and add personal touches such as skull buttons or a bandanna-print pocket lining. *801 Oceanfront Walk; 626/363-3444; denmbar.com.*

Huset
The streamlined Danish and Swedish furniture at this light-filled space is sourced on trips to Scandinavia by husband-and-wife owners Holly and Per Hallberg. You'll also find fanciful Louise Campbell vases, Marimekko tea towels, and Staffon Holm spin stools. *1316½ Abbot Kinney Blvd.; 424/268-4213; huset-shop.com.*

Kendall Conrad
A-listers such as Angelina Jolie and Cameron Diaz are fans of the collection of hand-cut exotic-leather bags at Kendall Conrad. Best bet: a black matte python-skin clutch—the perfect evening accessory. *1121 Abbot Kinney Blvd.; 310/399-1333; kendallconraddesign.com.*

Linus Bikes
Created by South African wave riders Adam McDermott and Chad Kushner, these French-style city cruisers are ideal for short jaunts to the beach. Bonus: you can get whimsical flourishes such as brass bells and brightly hued baskets. *1413½ Abbot Kinney Blvd.; 310/857-7777; linusbike.com.*

Strange Invisible Perfumes
Owner Alexandra Balahoutis is a perfume purist, shunning synthetic components for fragrances made of organic botanicals such as tuberose and cedar. Take home a bottle of Prima Ballerina, which layers Egyptian rose and organic lime. *1138 Abbot Kinney Blvd.; 310/314-1505; siperfumes.com.*

The entrance to Brentwood Country Mart. Left: Books at Brentwood's Diesel, a Bookstore.

A jeans fitting at Den.m Bar. Right: Tea towels and cutting boards on display in Huset.

KAUAI, HAWAII

Exploring Hawaii's lushest island

IT'S THE OLDEST OF HAWAII'S eight main islands—and arguably the most dramatic, with scenery that ranges from wind-eroded mountains and red-walled canyons to primeval rain forest and secret waterfalls. You can capture the most dazzling panoramas from the St. Regis Princeville Resort, set on a bluff overlooking a coral reef. Luxe touches mingle with natural beauty throughout the property: there's an 11,000-square-foot spa offering taro-clay wraps and native dilo-oil massages; an infinity pool that looks out at Mount Namolokama; and a Jean-Georges Vongerichten restaurant. The 251 rooms, some of Kauai's largest, are decorated in pale blue and warm wood tones. For a firsthand peek at the island's volcanic formation, book a daylong excursion with Kauai Nature Tours; geoscience professor and guide Chuck Blay will teach you about monumental geological events as well as the myths of every fruit and flower along the way. For something more adrenaline-charged, Outfitters Kauai leads sea kayaking expeditions along the rugged Na Pali coast and through misty sea caves. End the trip with live jazz and tangy mai tais at the open-air Bar Acuda in the bayside Hanalei.

GUIDE

STAY
St. Regis Princeville Resort
5520 Ka Haku Rd.; 877/787-3447; stregis.com. **$$$$**

EAT
Bar Acuda
*5-5161 Kuhio Hwy.;
808/826-7081;
restaurantbaracuda.com.* **$$$**

DO
Kauai Nature Tours
*888/233-8365;
kauainaturetours.com.*

Outfitters Kauai
*808/742-9667;
outfitterskauai.com.*

Looking across
Hanalei Bay
from the pool at
the St. Regis
Princeville Resort.

TORONTO

The Canadian city's modern makeover

A view from the roof of the Thompson hotel. Below: Lobster claws with black tiger shrimp at Frank's Kitchen.

SAFE, CLEAN, BLAND: until quite recently, these were the adjectives traditionally applied to Canada's financial and media capital. Toronto was known primarily for its livability, and for its admirably welcoming attitude toward immigrants. Yet despite a steady influx of new cultures, the city lacked verve, vitality, a sense of pride or of real identity. What Toronto was missing in character, it made up for in its rigorous pursuit of sensible liberal values. For cultural cues, the city looked to both New York and London, while keeping a disdainful eye on its more effortlessly hip older sibling, Montreal.

Lately, however, Toronto has undergone a remarkable sea change, one that's redefining the city as stylish, sophisticated, cosmopolitan—*cool*, even— yet still utterly local.

Toronto's transformation can be traced, in part, through its changing skyline. The uninspiring, 36-year-old CN Tower, the tallest freestanding structure in North America, is no longer the city's defining landmark. In the past decade, big-name architects have been reimagining downtown: there's Will Alsop's Sharp Centre for Design at the Ontario College of Art & Design, a black-and-white domino held aloft by brightly colored struts that resemble pick-up sticks. There's Daniel Libeskind's Michael Lee-Chin Crystal, an addition to the Royal Ontario Museum— all steel, glass, and hard angles that sever the stately lines of an otherwise lovely building. Most successful is Frank Gehry's expansion of the Art Gallery of Ontario, with its graceful, curvilinear glasswork melded to the exterior of the building.

Plenty of cities can lay claim to high-profile architecture. Paralleling this, however, is an insatiable boom in residential and hotel development—Toronto has more high-rises under construction than any other city on the continent. The view from the roof of my hotel, the Thompson, recalls Shanghai or Dubai; I lost count of all the cranes. Among the newer builds

Happy hour at the Drake Hotel's Sky Yard. Left: Inside the Frank Gehry–designed Art Gallery of Toronto.

are the flagship Four Seasons Hotel, featuring Daniel Boulud's first restaurant in the city, and the massive Shangri-La Hotel, which debuted with another New York restaurant import, an outpost of David Chang's Momofuku chain. Both properties arrive hard on the heels of the Ritz-Carlton and Trump hotels that opened in February 2011 and January 2012, respectively.

What makes all this especially exciting for travelers is that while downtown Toronto grows ever denser and more international, the city's creative classes have established stylish outposts all their own. Look at Queen West (one of the city's thriving art and design districts, anchored along a three-mile stretch of Queen Street); at the Distillery District (a complex of shops, restaurants, and arts organizations located on the 14-acre grounds of a former whiskey distillery, on Toronto's east side); and at Little Italy (a charming district of bars and eateries along College Street, to the north). In any of the above, you can't get too far without running into a table crafted out of a reclaimed barn door or a bountiful supply of Edison-bulb-lit restaurants emphasizing seasonal organic ingredients. Toronto feels like a frontier town—one that's in the midst of a cultural gold rush.

Queen West is the apotheosis of the city's new energy, a swath of row houses and former factories reminiscent of London's East End or parts of Brooklyn. This is where you'd want to move if you were young and in a band. "My joke was always that you couldn't find a roll of toilet paper, and now you can get an ironic Sonic Youth onesie for your baby," said singer Emily Haines, of Metric and Broken Social Scene, a longtime Queen West resident.

On weekends the neighborhood feels like a playground for street-style photographers—not surprising given the ever expanding collection of fashion boutiques. There's Sydney's, which carries men's wear from Dries Van Noten, Jil Sander, and Japanese brand the Viridi-anne. And the local label Klaxon Howl, in addition to vintage military gear, sells its own men's clothing: stiff selvage denim and chinos; flannel scarves; ultra-structured shirts. For all the global brands, there's a distinctly Torontonian flavor to Queen West.

The neighborhood's two standout hotels, the Gladstone and the Drake, both feature local art; at the former, a different Canadian artist decorated each of the 37 guest rooms, while the Drake employs a full-time curator and rotates its collection throughout the hotel every month. Both properties were 19th-century Trunk Railway lodgings that had fallen on hard times before being renovated. Jeff Stober, who bought the Drake in 2001 and reopened it three years later, sees the hotel as a cultural space for Torontonians. "As downtown becomes more dense, you can only do so much entertaining in your living spaces," he said. "What happens by default is that the city becomes your living room. From store owners to restaurateurs, everyone recognizes that this is a really good place to pitch a tent."

Or to build a brand. Stober also owns three shops across the city called Drake General Store. Their stock capitalizes on a groundswell of pride, running the gamut from genuinely desirable stuff (Hudson's Bay Company blankets) to Canadiana kitsch—maple syrup, red-cedar incense, and a decorative ceramic dish that reads I MISS THE OLD BLUE JAYS, a reference to the 1990's glory days of Toronto's baseball team.

This sense of affectionate irreverence is pervasive in the city. At Frank's Kitchen, a small, chef-owned spot in Little Italy, half the menu reads like a caricature of what you'd think Canadians might eat: rare elk loin; rarer venison tartare.

After a tour through a few shops, I headed to a boutique hotel in the Entertainment District designed by Del Terrelonge. Called the Templar Hotel, it has 27 smartly decorated suites and lofts, a spa, and a chef's-table restaurant called Monk Kitchen; deploys a Porsche Panamera as an airport shuttle; and features a lap pool with a transparent floor over the lobby's lounge area.

When I asked for dinner recommendations, I was steered to Woodlot: bakery by day, restaurant by night, in a warm, inviting, bi-level space with Native Canadian artwork on the walls and a casually stylish waitstaff. Chef-owner David Haman's style of cooking has been dubbed "urban lumberjack" by the Toronto press; though I was skeptical, his food turned out to be the finest of my trip. The bipartite menu offers both "Regular" and "Without Meat" options: whey-fed pork chop and steak; caramelized Jerusalem artichokes and roast Japanese sweet potato. Almost everything comes out of the restaurant's wood-burning oven.

There never used to be anyplace like Woodlot in Toronto. But the restaurant and its small-scale approach seem to represent the future: a well-designed, thoroughly confident experience that respects Toronto's heritage and simultaneously breaks new ground. There was no sense that the place owed its menu and genial vibe to some other restaurant, in some other city. And thanks to the wood-burning oven, I left smelling like I'd been at a campfire. How Canadian is that? ✦

Adapted from "Toronto Lights Up," by Jonathan Durbin.

GUIDE

STAY

Drake Hotel
1150 Queen St. W.; 416/531-5042; thedrakehotel.ca. **$**

Four Seasons Hotel
60 Yorkville Ave.; 416/964-0411; fourseasons.com. **$$$**

Gladstone Hotel
1214 Queen St. W.; 416/531-4635; gladstonehotel.com. **$**

Ritz-Carlton
181 Wellington St. W.; 416/585-2500; ritzcarlton.com. **$$$**

Shangri-La Hotel
188 University Ave.; 647/788-8888; shangri-la.com. **$$$**

Templar Hotel
348 Adelaide St. W.; 647/933-5546; templarhotel.com. **$$**

Thompson
550 Wellington St. W.; 416/640-7778; thompsonhotels.com. **$$**

Trump International Hotel & Tower
325 Bay St.; 416/214-2800; trumphotelcollection.com. **$$$**

EAT

Café Boulud
60 Yorkville Ave.; 416/963-6000; cafeboulud.com. **$$**

Frank's Kitchen
588 College St.; 416/516-5861. **$$$**

Monk Kitchen
348 Adelaide St. W.; 647/933-5546. **$$$$**

Woodlot
293 Palmerston Ave.; 647/342-6307; woodlottoronto.com. **$$**

DO

Art Gallery of Ontario
317 Dundas St. W.; 416/979-6648; ago.net.

Distillery District
55 Mill St.; 416/364-1177; thedistillerydistrict.com.

Royal Ontario Museum
100 Bloor St. W.; 416/586-8000; rom.on.ca.

Sharp Centre for Design
Ontario College of Art & Design, 100 McCaul St.; 416/977-6000; ocadu.ca.

SHOP

Drake General Store Queen
1144 Queen St. W.; 416/531-5042, ext. 101; drakegeneralstore.ca.

Klaxon Howl
706 Queen St. W.; 647/436-6628; klaxonhowl.com.

Sydney's
682 Queen St. W.; 416/603-3369; shopsydneys.com.

Exploring
Water Street, in
Vancouver's
Gastown area.

VANCOUVER

Where nature and urban sophistication converge

SNOWCAPPED MOUNTAINS AND expansive bays form the backdrop for the Northwest's greatest boomtown—a city of diverse neighborhoods that embraces both rugged outdoorsiness and high-minded international culture. Make your base downtown's 1927 Rosewood Hotel Georgia, with revamped Art Deco–inspired rooms and a slick, dark-wood-and-gold paneled restaurant run by star chef David Hawksworth. From there, it's a leisurely stroll to the Victorian Gastown neighborhood, where you'll get a taste of Canada's homegrown art scene. The colorful streets are lined with galleries of indigenous art, such as the three-story Hill's Native Art, which showcases ceremonial masks and totem poles, limited-edition prints, and bentwood boxes. For lunch, hop the Skytrain at the nearby Waterfront Station to suburban Richmond, home to Vancouver's Asian culinary scene: dim sum temples; noodle huts; Korean barbecue joints—you'll find them here. Cult favorite Jade Seafood is known for its tender mushroom dumplings and clay-pot chicken. You can work off the meal with a hike along the five-mile Seawall Trail at Stanley Park, where the 360-degree mountain-fringed vistas put the region's natural splendor on full display.

GUIDE

STAY
Rosewood Hotel Georgia
801 W. Georgia St.; 604/682-5566; rosewoodhotels.com. **$$**

EAT
Jade Seafood Restaurant
8511 Alexandra Rd.,
Richmond; 604/249-0082;
jaderestaurant.ca. **$$**

DO
Hill's Native Art
165 Water St.;
604/685-4249;
hills.ca.

The Zing-Zing
Villa at
Dominica's
Secret Bay
resort.

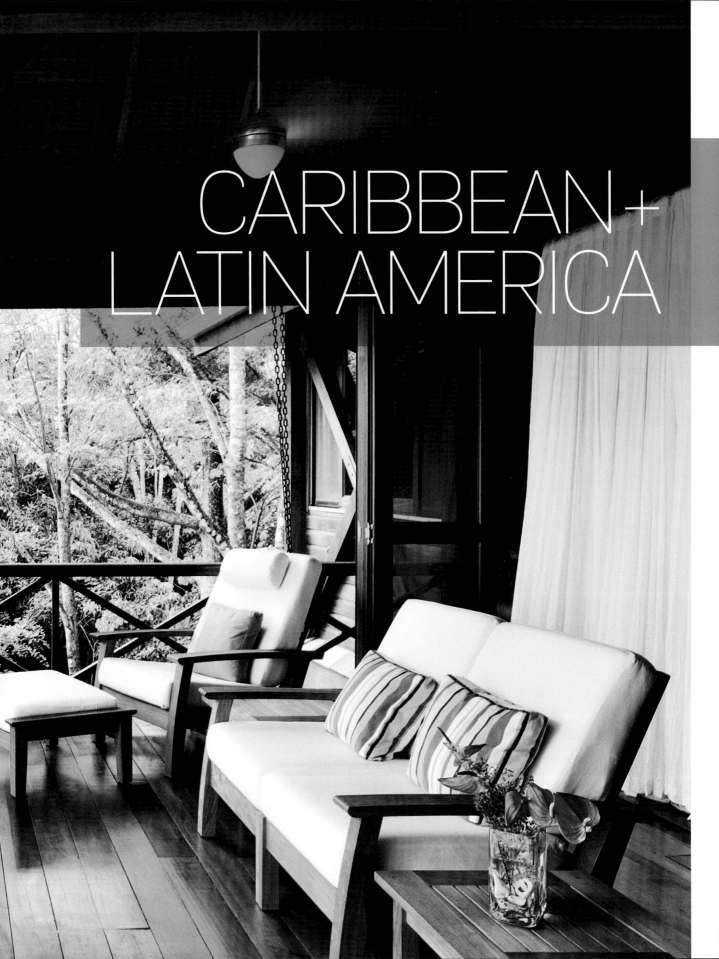

CARIBBEAN + LATIN AMERICA

Swimmers offshore from Rockhouse Hotel, in Negril. Opposite: A Rockhouse villa.

JAMAICA

Pioneering hoteliers transform the landscape

Playing on
Frenchman's
Cove beach,
in Port Antonio.
Right: A local
on his bike.

Jerk-chicken
spring rolls at
Round Hill Hotel
& Villas, in
Montego Bay.
Left: GoldenEye
Hotel & Resort
guests dancing.

T'S 11 P.M. ON THE BEACH at GoldenEye Hotel & Resort, outside of Ocho Rios, and the Jolly Boys are just hitting their stride. The old-school mento band, fronted by the 74-year-old Albert Minott, in a polyester suit and trilby, is delivering hit after hit of calypso-style classics to a large group of casually chic guests dancing in the sand. The fact that few of these guests, here to celebrate a collaboration between the resort and the New York–based Haute Hippie fashion label, were even born when the Jolly Boys first formed, in the late 1940's, doesn't stop them from jumping in and getting down. With a new album, *Great Expectation*, that features their funky mix of banjo, guitar, and marumba box, the Jolly Boys are enjoying a renaissance. They are soulful, scrappy survivors on an island that, much like the band, has been reinventing itself with an eye toward the past.

Hearing the Jolly Boys brings back my own early childhood memories of breezy, sun-filled family vacations on this island 40 years ago. The Jamaica I knew then was one still defined by the cosmopolitan sun-seekers—Errol Flynn, Ian Fleming, Elizabeth Taylor, Richard Burton, and others of their rarefied ilk—who colonized posh pockets of its coastal parishes in the mid 20th century and lent the island a palpable sense of glamour. But since achieving independence in 1962, Jamaica has had its share of growing pains. An alliance with Cuba during the Cold War took it off a short list of places for the American elite, who had been coming in droves. Headlines about poverty, unrest, and violence in the decades that followed ruled it out as an easy Caribbean destination, too, despite the popularity of Bob Marley and Jimmy Cliff. Homophobic incidents and laws didn't help. Neither did cruise-ship overload and all-inclusive overkill, phenomena that might have improved the sputtering economy, but did nothing for the reputation of the island among the sophisticated set.

But lately, a stylish crowd has been discovering Jamaica all over again, encouraged by a handful of iconoclastic resort owners. Rather than sequestering guests behind closed gates, this new breed of hotelier is tapping into what makes the island so special beyond its beaches and weather—its complex topography, rich history, and vivid culture.

"It's sometimes a fight getting guests over their negative perceptions," says the informal yet formidable Chris Blackwell, whose Island Outpost hotel brand includes GoldenEye; Strawberry Hill, in the Blue Mountains above Kingston; and the Caves, poised on cliffs in west Negril. "But the island is full of bright, talented, and funny people who love being Jamaican. They are the greatest asset of this country."

Blackwell should know. Born in London but raised in Jamaica, the Rock & Roll Hall of Fame inductee and Island Records founder produced Marley, Toots and the Maytals, and a roster of non-Jamaican musicians including Cat Stevens, Roxy Music, U2, and Tom Waits. In the early 1990's, he branched out into the hotel business, opening properties in Miami at the beginning of its revival. (His hotels played a major role in resurrecting the city's Art Deco District.) He did the same thing in Jamaica on a grander scale in the mid 1990's, as Island Outpost took the laid-back cool of reggae style and applied it to resorts. GoldenEye is a collection of 19 villas and cottages spread across 52 coastal acres. At its heart is Ian Fleming's original two-bedroom villa, where the author wrote all 14 of his James Bond books. The resort emerged from a top-to-bottom renovation and expansion that added some serious polish to the place without diminishing any of its Jamaica-influenced personality.

"The main thing for me is to attract guests who are imaginative and curious about life," Blackwell tells me over a glass of coconut water on the patio of the secluded tree-house-like cottage on GoldenEye's lagoon, where he stays when visiting the resort. "I like to create places where people can explore the area, then come back to the bar and talk."

Indeed, with a fleet of WaveRunners, boats, cars, and kayaks at the ready, guests can visit the nearby town of Oracabessa; Ocho Rios, with its blossoming local art

scene; Noël Coward's Modernist-style retreat, Firefly; and James Bond Beach, a popular weekend gathering spot for fishermen and their families. And with the road to Port Antonio paved not all that long ago, guests can also finally drive from Ocho Rios to the eastern side of Jamaica in less than two hours.

Hemmed in by the Blue Mountains on one side and the Caribbean Sea on the other, Port Antonio lured everyone from J. P. Morgan and William Randolph Hearst at the turn of the 20th century to Princess Margaret and Errol Flynn in the 1950's. Then, after decades off the radar, Geejam came along. The tiny and luxurious colony of villas with a world-class recording studio opened in 2007 and rebooted the area for hip travelers.

Jon Baker, the producer behind the Jolly Boys and Geejam's co-owner, is a visionary and champion of the island in the Blackwell mold. He fell in love with Port Antonio when visiting in the 1980's and was inspired to

build a studio there in the mid 1990's. It became so popular with musicians that Baker ended up creating a small resort to house them and other guests.

With just five accommodations and the open-air Bushbar restaurant, Geejam doesn't offer guests much in the way of on-site activities beyond a pool table and fitness room (and recording studio, of course). As an early guest there (staying in a villa with works by the infamous graffiti artist Banksy), I was encouraged to walk down to the sweet little village of Drapers and then make my way over to the beach at Frenchman's Cove Resort, a onetime jet-set destination now popular with locals who eat snapper and salt fish at the hotel's authentic shack of a restaurant.

We met welcoming people everywhere, both native Jamaicans and foreign homeowners, including Patricia Wymore Flynn, the cattle-ranching widow of Errol, and the art collector Francesca von Habsburg-Lothringen, who invited us and other Geejam guests to her raucous

Dinner at GoldenEye. Right: Round Hill's Classic villa.

New Year's Eve bash. But the best part of the visit was a trip to the Rio Grande, an hour's drive into the interior, where boatmen poled us on bamboo rafts festooned with flowers along the crystalline blue river. It was a serene experience that removed us from all thoughts of the modern world. Years ago this was the way bananas got to market, and it inspired the folk song that Harry Belafonte later made famous as "Day-O (Banana Boat Song)," as well as Errol Flynn's legendary rafting parties.

Baker, British-born, but now also a Jamaican citizen, sees this entire area, with its untouched swaths of tropical mountain beauty (lagoons, rain forests, mineral baths, and waterfalls) as an underutilized paradise. He has renovated two properties just outside Port Antonio—Trident Hotel, a series of luxurious waterfront villas that date from the 1960's, and the magnificent white Trident Castle, built nearby in the 1980's by an eccentric island architect. Baker has

also taken over the dockside restaurant at the Blue Lagoon, a 15-minute drive from Port Antonio, and plans to reopen it as a casual lunch joint that doubles as a romantic dinner spot. Next door, he's planning a spa with a freshwater bathing spring beside it. Meanwhile, he's intent on promoting the Errol Flynn Marina, in Port Antonio, as a yachting destination. It's a big to-do list. "Sometimes I feel like Fitzcarraldo," he tells me as we make our way past the Blue Lagoon's hanging moss to the dilapidated, cavelike site of his imagined spa. "But my goal is to make this area more accessible to tourists and Jamaicans alike."

What started as a tentative dip into hotels for him has blossomed into a boom for the entire area—if not the island. "There's a new positivity in Jamaica with a new government," he says of the fresh approach taken by the recently elected prime minister, Portia Simpson Miller, of the People's National Party, that includes speaking up for more education and social programs and against deep-seated homophobia. "And I've seen an upsurge in pride."

He's talking about what Novia McDonald-Whyte, a lifestyle editor at the *Jamaica Observer*, calls Brand Jamaica, something beyond beaches, reggae, and jerk chicken. "There are so many ways Jamaica pulls above its weight with its history, nature, culture, and resorts," says McDonald-Whyte, who has a penchant for wearing big white-framed eyeglasses and the best Jamaican designers. "Visitors don't just want the sun," she says. "They come here because this is home to runners such as Usain Bolt, or to raft down the most beautiful river in the Caribbean, the Rio Grande."

They can also now come to Jamaica for locally sourced meals that would have been unheard of just 10 years ago, when island food was lackluster at best. At the Jakes Hotel, a low-key resort of 27 eclectic

■ 'If you want everything smooth, you can go to St. Bart's. This island is about real life.'

cottages and two villas on the remote southwestern coast, I found chefs working with farmers and fishermen to uplift their menus. Jakes offers locavore dinners, served on-site at area farms. There's even a community-supported agriculture business, Potosi Farms, which delivers sustainable produce to hotels, restaurants, and homeowners island-wide.

Of course, some visitors still want what they always wanted from Jamaica, a quick flight to good weather in winter and an elegant experience by the sea. For this they can turn to Round Hill Hotel & Villas, a favorite of the socially prominent for 60 years, including Grace Kelly and Babe and Bill Paley, who owned grand "cottages" on the hills above the resort's beach. Today, the 110-acre resort, on its own peninsula, has 27 villas and 36 hotel rooms, recently redesigned in classic tropical style by Ralph Lauren (a property owner on Round Hill's board).

"The social history here is fascinating," says Josef Forstmayr, Round Hill's affable managing director, over a dinner of Jamaican rock shrimp and pole beans with

Owners Adam Miller and Marika Kessler at Potosi Farms. Below: Looking out at Treasure Beach from the Jakes Hotel's spa.

fresh mint (from the resort's own organic garden) at the Grill, an open-air seaside restaurant on a sprawling terrace. He rattles off a list of royals and iconic figures who have visited the resort and tells me that my own imposing cottage, No. 25, once housed John and Jackie Kennedy. What's even more exciting is the fact that Ryan Gosling, one of many younger celebrities flocking to Jamaica these days, stayed here. Rather than stick around the property, he got out on a motorcycle to explore, taking in concerts at clubs and a major street party in Kingston. "And when Paul McCartney comes," continued the puckish, Austrian-born Forstmayr, "he sails a Sunfish over to the dock and shoots the breeze with everyone. They know who he is but don't make a fuss. Jamaicans will talk to anyone."

Devoted as Forstmayr is to his world-famous clientele, who treat him as much like a friend as a manager, he's more devoted to the island itself, with all its twists and bumps. "If you want everything smooth, you can go to St. Bart's," he says. "This island is about real life."

Jason Henzell is yet another hotelier who understands that. As the owner of Jakes, in the town of Treasure Beach, he has become so integrated with the community that he might as well be mayor. His mother, Sally, designed the cluster of modest little cottages in 1991. Since then, it has developed into a popular spot for travelers in search of authenticity—thanks, in large part, to Henzell's extraordinary commitment to the Jamaican community around him. When I visited, he encouraged us to get to know the area and even joined us on a boat ride to Black River, a town of fishermen and port workers. As we zipped along the waters of Treasure Beach, a scrappy and happy little village where Henzell has many development projects under way, he sighed.

"There's so much to do around here," he said. "But it will get done through community and visitor engagement." At the time, he was getting ready to open a sports camp for 1,200 area kids funded by grants and devoted guests who support his efforts. He regularly hosts the Calabash Literary Festival, and he continues, through the local service organization he heads, to pull in funding for health care, a fish sanctuary, and agricultural projects, which include his enterprising farm-to-table dinners.

Not far from him, in Negril, the Rockhouse Hotel, a cluster of cliffside bungalows that attracts a bohemian set, has also taken community engagement to a new level. In 2008, its foundation funded a major library renovation.

In Little Bay, a small fishing village a half-hour from Negril, the foundation completed a makeover of a grammar school. (These efforts, incidentally, earned the Rockhouse a Travel + Leisure 2012 Global Vision Award.) The hotel offers guests the chance to visit the library and school every Thursday.

"Visitors want to know there's a fuller impact of their travel dollar here," Peter Rose, the foundation's president, tells me as we drive past fishing boats and coconut palms to see the school. "It makes people feel good to see the real Jamaica." Indeed, I'm impressed to find a polished two-story school that was once decrepit and inadequate.

The students look inspired. "They're passionate about education; they really want to learn," one teacher tells me.

I step into a classroom where all eyes are upon me. "Good afternoon, Mr. Morris," they say in unison. "Welcome to the Little Bay All Age School. We hope you enjoy your visit."

I do, very much. ✦

GUIDE

STAY

Geejam
Port Antonio; 876/993-7000; geejamhotel.com. **$$$**

GoldenEye Hotel & Resort
Oracabessa; 800/688-7688; goldeneye.com. **$$$$**

Jakes Hotel, Villas & Spa
Treasure Beach; 877/526-2428; jakeshotel.com. **$**

Rockhouse Hotel
Negril; 876/957-4373; rockhousehotel.com. **$**

Round Hill Hotel & Villas
Montego Bay; 800/972-2159; roundhill.com. **$$$$**

Trident Castle
Port Antonio; 888/443-3526; castleportantonio.com. **$$$$$**

Trident Hotel
Port Antonio; 888/443-3526; tridentportantonio.com. **$$$**

Adapted from "How Jamaica Got Its Groove Back," by Bob Morris.

Tropical foliage
at Puerto Rico's
Dorado Beach.
Opposite: Poolside
at the resort.

DORADO BEACH, PUERTO RICO

A former playground for Hollywood royalty reclaims its past

A Caesar salad at Mi Casa. Left: The heritage ficus tree outside Spa Botánico.

Dorado Beach's coast. Right: Golf legend Juan "Chi Chi" Rodríguez *(left)* with developer Friedel Stubbe *(right)* at the resort.

O N NEW YEAR'S 2012, eight Learjets filled with industry titans, real estate tycoons, and high-flying socialites landed at Puerto Rico's San Juan international airport. Their final destination? The famed Dorado Beach, where a $342 million renovation has transformed the palm-fringed oasis into a Ritz-Carlton Reserve. With a beachfront restaurant by chef José Andrés, a five-acre spa, and a private stretch of white sand, it is poised to become one of the most exclusive resorts in the Caribbean. Eager to see the place for myself, I hopped a flight south.

Dorado Beach's story begins in 1905, when Dr. Alfred Livingston bought 1,700 acres along the northern coast and developed a coconut and citrus plantation. His daughter, Clara, inherited the land in 1923 and lived in Su Casa, a pink colonial-style hacienda with a clay tiled roof and grand double stairway. In 1955, Laurance S. Rockefeller, the venture capitalist and son of John D. Rockefeller Jr., acquired the property and three years later opened the ne plus ultra of Caribbean resorts. Hollywood stars, who once frequented Havana, headed here—and the area became as much of a scene as St. Bart's is today. John F. Kennedy, Joan Crawford, Elizabeth Taylor, and Ava Gardner were regulars; Amelia Earhart used to fly her plane in to see Clara (the landing strip remains).

In the mid 1980's, the Puerto Rican government shifted focus away from tourism and the luxury hospitality market took a hit—and the resort eventually closed. Seeking to bring back a time when visiting the island was a bragging right, Puerto Rico has instituted new tax laws, and dozens of direct flights have been launched (JetBlue; Southwest). In recent years, the country has also put billions into infrastructure and, to lure real estate investors, offered generous tax exemptions. A handful of upscale hotels—including the St. Regis Bahia Beach Resort, in Río Grande, and the W Retreat & Spa, in Vieques—have capitalized on the incentives. But no hotel has been as anticipated as Dorado Beach. "We want to be a place where friends from the Hamptons and other summer communities gather during winter," says Caribbean Property Group CEO Mark Lipschutz, who partnered with Ritz-Carlton and developer Friedel Stubbe in 2007 to revive the property.

Amid the throngs of tourists at San Juan's international airport, a uniformed Ritz-Carlton driver materializes before I reach baggage claim and ushers me to a black Mercedes SUV. It is a far cry from my last visit to the country, when a boyfriend and I took a teetering old taxi three hours down unpaved detours to the eastern tip of the island, only to have the view of the lush hills from our hotel window collapse in a mudslide.

As we make our way down a road lined with palms and ceiba trees, I glimpse a minimalist, white-stone entry pavilion—its clean lines and pitched wooden roof blending seamlessly with the surrounding jungle. With resorts of this stature, there is no need to do anything so common as check in. My private *embajador* (ambassador) whisks me in a golf cart to my room, decorated in cream-colored fabrics and sand-tinted walls, with floor-to-ceiling windows that overlook a powdery beach.

The level of luxury at the Dorado Beach resort sets a new standard for Puerto Rico, from the delicate star designs reflecting on the sand at the outdoor Positivo Sand Bar to the spacious suites and low-lying bungalows extending out to private plunge pools and terraces. Walking along the jungle-lined wooden paths, past a series of tranquil ponds, I discover a labyrinthine infinity pool, where a plush oversize daybed beckons me to linger for hours. The hotel's legacy is present at every turn. Books about Rockefeller fill the mahogany-paneled library, and a short walk away, the restored Su Casa (which you can rent for $30,000 a night in high season) stands in all its pink-hued glory.

Over lunch in the golf club's casual bar, Dorado Beach Resort's CEO, Eric Christensen, introduces me to the property's longtime golf pro, Juan "Chi Chi" Rodríguez, who began his career working for Rockefeller and was later inducted into the World Golf Hall of Fame & Museum. Tan and lithe, with slick black hair peeping out of a Panama hat, Rodríguez reminisces about his early days. "When I first met Rockefeller, I scolded him for riding three to a golf cart," he tells me. "I was sure I'd get fired." But that didn't happen. "Instead, Rockefeller apologized and said to my boss, 'That young man is going to go places.'"

An 80-year-old ficus tree marks the entrance to the five-acre spa, which is like a mini-resort in itself with a pineapple garden, hammocks, soaking pools, steam rooms, waterfall showers, a lily pond, and two tree-house treatment platforms. The experience begins with a walk through an herbal-scented Apothecary Portal, filled with lavender, marigold, and lemongrass. Guests are offered private consultations with healing experts called "Manos Santas" (healing hands), who create bespoke concoctions using natural oils and fresh herbs. Walking through the private massage pavilions and jungle gardens reminds me of the dense, wet rain forests of Koh Samui, in Thailand. The masseuse works on my back from underneath; in the room white curtains billow in the breeze, lulling me into a deep sleep. That night, I eat dinner at José Andrés's beachfront Mi Casa restaurant, where the experimental menu plays with tastes and textures inspired by both Puerto Rico and the Iberian Peninsula. My Caesar salad "sushi roll" comes with delicate quail eggs on top, and the "*coquitos frescos,*" a small plate made of rum, lime, and coconut, is served inside a large coconut shell.

For all the changes at Dorado, what remains untouched is the terrain itself, the same undulating coastline of beach buttressed by verdant cupey trees. It's the very landscape that drew the area's first guests 55 years ago and sets the stage for Dorado's new golden era. ✦

Adapted from "Puerto Rico's Next Act," by Alexandra Wolfe.

GUIDE

STAY
Dorado Beach, a Ritz-Carlton Reserve
Dorado; 787/626-1100; ritzcarlton.com. **$$$$**

The master bedroom at Su Casa.

DOMINICA

The Caribbean's untouched island

SITUATED BETWEEN GUADELOUPE and Martinique in the middle of the Lesser Antilles horn, Dominica remains one of the Caribbean's last unspoiled islands: its primal rain forests undeveloped, its black-sand beaches seemingly unmapped, a pristine reef flung just off the coast. The latest eco-luxury retreat follows that barely-there spirit; Secret Bay appears to emerge from the green vastness—from overhead, you might even miss it. Designed by Venezuelan architect Fruto Vivas, the four wood-and-glass stilted villas are composed of native hardwood with floor-to-ceiling windows. Two secluded beaches and a hidden sea cave, not to mention a chef at your disposal for private meals in your bungalow, eliminate any need to leave the property. But, should you need to expand your horizons, hire a local guide with Shore Trips to take you in a skiff up the Indian River from nearby Portsmouth; you'll row through a dramatic landscape of gnarled mangroves and dense jungle scattered with ghost crabs. The journey ends near the volcanic Morne Diablotins, where a ramshackle bar offers generous glasses of ice-cold beer.

Relaxing by the infinity pool in a Secret Bay villa.

GUIDE

STAY
Secret Bay
Portsmouth; 767/445-4444;
secretbay.dm. **$$$$**

DO
Shore Trips
888/355-0220;
shoretrips.com.

CARIBBEAN FOOD

An epicurean tour of the islands

The beach
at Grand Case,
in St. Martin.

Blues Bar & Restaurant chef Itel Cicilia in Curaçao. Above: Foie gras and plantains at Martinique's Le Brédas.

WITH FRESH LOCAL ingredients, exotic spices, and cooking influences from around the globe, the Caribbean has finally landed on the gastronome's map. Here are 12 islands, from Anguilla to Trinidad, whose most inspiring restaurants are working incredible wizardry in the kitchen right now.

Anguilla This tiny British territory is at the forefront of the region's transformation from culinary backwater to foodie paradise, with a mix of laid-back barbecue joints and chic hotel restaurants.
WHERE TO EAT Smokey's at the Cove has a lineup of char-grilled meats that could give the pits of Memphis or Kansas City serious competition. The no-frills, open-air café sits on an uninhabited beach with vistas of neighboring St. Martin. Order the rack of lamb or honey ribs and unwind with a knockout rum punch, made with a pinch of cinnamon.

Barbados You can find flying-fish sandwiches at any beachside shack here, but lately the national dish is moving up the Barbados food chain. Bajans love their specialty marinated in lime, doused with hot sauce, battered in egg, and served steaming hot—along with other sea-to-table dishes that attract dozens of celebrity chefs to the annual Barbados Food & Wine and Rum Festival each November.
WHERE TO EAT When the master cooks are on the island, you'll find them feasting on Thai-inflected seafood such as yellow-curry-and-pineapple swordfish at the Cliff. The three-tiered, torchlit terrace occupies a spectacular post atop a coral stone outcropping on the Platinum Coast.

Cayman Islands Banking isn't the only thing they do well on this western Caribbean archipelago. The area also offers a unique food culture with roots that stretch back more than 300 years, to the buccaneers who settled

caribbean + latin america

93

St. Lucia's Grand Piton mountain. Left: Shrimp-and-cucumber ceviche at Dove Restaurant, in Tortola.

on the islands. "Old Caymanian" cuisine is an eclectic mix of British, Jamaican, and Central American influences, and its spicy sweetness is addictive.
WHERE TO EAT At Vivine's Kitchen, patrons line up for specials such as stewed turtle and curried goat, scrawled on a blackboard. The dishes are often accompanied by cassava cakes and served on the low-key terrace of the husband-and-wife owners' house.

Curaçao With a population made up of more than 50 nationalities, Curaçao's culinary heritage runs the gamut from French and Dutch to Brazilian, Indonesian, and Japanese. Staples include *yuana* (stewed iguana) and *kokada* (coconut patties).
WHERE TO EAT On the tip of a weather-worn pier, Blues restaurant focuses on mouthwatering fusion dishes: New Orleans–style jambalaya; lemony black tiger shrimp; lobster bisque. Pair them with sundowners and listen to the local take on jazz, playing in the background.

Grenada The Island of Spice has long produced cloves, nutmeg, and cinnamon for export. Grenadian kitchens use the seasonings for plates like ginger pork,

curried mutton, crayfish broth, and stir-fried rabbit.
WHERE TO EAT Spiky-haired Brit Gary Rhodes kicked off the celebrity-chef rush to the Caribbean a decade ago when he opened his namesake restaurant at the Calabash hotel. On the menu: citrus-*souscaille*-topped prawns and grilled snapper and lobster with chayote and orange bouillabaisse.

Jamaica Along with reggae and Red Stripe, jerk has become a Jamaican national icon. Originally conceived by runaway slaves, the dish is made of meat marinated in a piquant sauce, then slow-cooked over a pimento-wood fire. Chicken and pork are the standard, but mutton, beef, and even fish are often used, too.
WHERE TO EAT On an island known for its roadside jerk stalls, the best is Scotchies, in Montego Bay, packed with dreadlocked natives and beachgoers hanging out on refashioned kegs under thatched-roof pavilions.

Martinique Foie gras and green bananas? Only here, where French haute cuisine marries Creole cooking in restaurants that look as if Bogart and Bacall might have romanced there in *To Have and Have Not*.

Many of the top spots are set in French-colonial villas and plantation houses.

WHERE TO EAT Martinican chef Jean-Charles Brédas is evangelical about all things locavore. His signature platters at Le Brédas rotate every few weeks; try the lychee duck breast, presented on a colorful ceramic plate.

Puerto Rico The region's *cocina criolla* combines Spanish, American, and indigenous cultures. *Lechón asado* (roast pig on a spit) is an island-wide passion, while the use of peppers in both classic and nouvelle dishes is an art form mastered by the best chefs.

WHERE TO EAT At his 23-year-old Pikayo restaurant, Wilo Benet employs homegrown techniques to whip up some of San Juan's most exciting delicacies, such as Portuguese octopus with shallot escabeche and serrano ham.

St. Lucia Locals flock to the towns of Gros Islet and Anse La Raye on Friday nights for "jump ups" that blend food, drink, and music. Barbecued seafood is served along with breadfruit, sweet potato, or blackened corn.

GUIDE

EAT

Bistrot Caraïbes
Grand Case, St. Martin;
590-590/290-829;
bistrotcaraibes.com. **$$$**

Blues Bar & Restaurant
Willemstad, Curaçao;
599-9/461-4377;
avilahotel.com. **$$$**

Chaud Restaurant
Port of Spain, Trinidad; 868/
623-0375; chaudkm.com. **$$$**

The Cliff
St. James, Barbados;
246/432-1922;
thecliffbarbados.com. **$$$$**

Dasheene at Ladera
Soufrière, St. Lucia; 758/459-
6618; ladera.com. **$$$**

Dove Restaurant &
Wine Bar
Road Town, Tortola; 284/494-
0313; thedovebvi.com. **$$$**

Le Brédas
St. Joseph, Martinique;
596-596/576-552. **$$$$**

Pikayo
999 Ashford Ave., San Juan,
Puerto Rico; 787/721-6194;
wilobenet.com. **$$$**

Rhodes Restaurant
at Calabash
St. Georges, Grenada;
473/444-4334;
calabashhotel.com. **$$**

Scotchies
North Coast Hwy.,
Montego Bay, Jamaica;
876/953-3301. **$**

Smokey's at the Cove
Cove Bay, Anguilla;
264/497-6582;
smokeysatthecove.com. **$$$**

Vivine's Kitchen
Gun Bay, Grand Cayman;
345/947-7435. **$$**

WHERE TO EAT To sample a more refined version of the St. Lucian feast, head to Dasheene at Ladera, overlooking the iconic green Pitons. Chef Nigel Mitchell uses organic produce from nearby plantations for centuries-old island recipes: roasted conch with pickled vegetables; plantain gratin with coconut rum sauce.

St. Martin The isle of St. Martin offers two for the price of one: delicate French cuisine on the north side, heavier Dutch dishes in the south.

WHERE TO EAT Waterfront dining is abundant in villages like Grand Case, where Lyons, France, transplants and brothers Thibault and Amaury Mezière turn out French classics (sautéed frog's legs; escargot) at Bistrot Caraïbes. Try the island's own homegrown libation, guavaberry liqueur, cane sugar, and a rare berry harvested from bushes that grow in the central highlands.

Tortola Once primarily a jumping-off point for the other isles in the British Virgin Island chain, mountainous and verdant Tortola has been getting a second look from the sailboat set.

WHERE TO EAT In Road Town, chef Travis Phillips turns out the island's best haute cuisine at his Dove Restaurant & Wine Bar, a 1912 gingerbread-trimmed cottage scattered with antiques. The crowd pleasers: ginger lime and coconut mussels; red-wine raspberry duck breast and the tiramisu ice cream. Come evening, sun-kissed patrons enjoy barrel-aged whisky Manhattans and wine from a robust collection on an outdoor patio shaded by a mango tree.

Trinidad More than 40 percent of Trinidadians are of South Asian origin, which means that the Indian cuisine is especially good here. But immigrants from Africa, Europe, South America, the Middle East, and China have also enhanced the epicurean experience.

WHERE TO EAT Chef Khalid Mohammed is Trinidad's prodigal son: an alum of the prestigious French Culinary Institute, he returned home after stints in New York and Miami to open the critically acclaimed Chaud Restaurant, in Port of Spain. Don't miss his hearty "kitchen sink" platter: short-rib and steak *ragù* with mushrooms, tomatoes, and Pecorino Romano, poured over tortiglioni pasta. ✦

TULUM, MEXICO

A bohemian beach destination captures the spotlight

The view of
the Caribbean
from the
Tulum ruins.

Biking along Tulum's main road. Right: A pool at one of Be Tulum's suites.

EXPENDIO DE MEZCAL

ALL AND TAN AND YOUNG and lovely, the girl in the red bikini and cork sandals steps through a craggy passage in the walls surrounding the 1,000-year-old ruins of Tulum. She might be the girl from Ipanema. Or perhaps Ixtapa or Ibiza. All eyes are on this beauty, whose carefree glamour hardly looks out of place, even in this ancient sacred site.

Once a sleepy beach outpost, Tulum has become a fashionable yet decidedly low-key escape on a bohemian Grand Tour that might take in Marrakesh, Goa, and Phuket. During the past decade, stylish expats have set up shop, working with native craftsmen to build chic yet authentic Mexican hotels and produce small accessories lines, while adventurous chefs have drafted the fire of habaneros into a global cuisine with Italian, Asian, and Middle Eastern accents.

As an aspiring beach bum, I have sampled much of the Mexican shoreline, but Tulum's emerging reputation for New Age character and cool-hunter cachet made me long to return. Carved out of jungle

less than 50 years ago, Tulum exists in a time warp, one in which the countercultural idealism of the late 1960's dovetails with 21st-century notions of ecotourism and sustainability. Here, recycling means using benches from a van as theater seats for outdoor movie screenings. Solar panels provide electricity, and nighttime lighting is so low that you might need to ask for a flashlight at check-in.

If you can find a desk clerk, that is. Direct calls to Tulum hotels are annoyingly futile. Even the most expensive resorts communicate only by e-mail. I was to land in the evening on one of Virgin America's direct flights from Los Angeles to Cancún and needed to rent a car to drive the 75 miles south to Tulum. Amansala,

A colorful local bus. Right: The beach bar at Be Tulum.

The Tulum ruins. Left: A room at Encantada.

a fitness-focused spot famous for its Bikini Boot Camp, sent me a message assuring me that a late check-in was no problem; there would be someone to greet me at reception. When I arrived, there were two blondes—lovely Labradors sprawled on the wooden walkway, lolling in the early-May heat.

"*¿Dónde está la recepción?*" I venture hopefully to a passerby.

I am directed to the restaurant, where a lissome young lady, radiant with yoga-blissed serenity, swipes my credit card—an all-too-rare occurrence in a largely cash-only economy where merchants accept both pesos and dollars.

"There are no locks on the doors," she informs me, "only latches on the inside." But there are security boxes, she adds, "and the dogs know who's staying here and who doesn't belong."

Apparently, the dogs couldn't detect my distinctly fish-out-of-water scent. This, however, is what happens whenever I visit a vortex of altered consciousness, particularly one that is endlessly raved over; it takes a while for my L.A.-bred cynicism to subside. Fortunately, I am able to meet up with my designer friends John Powell and Josh Ramos, who've driven in for the weekend from Mérida to spruce up a rental villa on a private beach in Tulum's Sian Ka'an Biosphere nature preserve. We dine on smoky wood-fired pork at Hartwood Restaurant, where the soundtrack is 1970's rock, the waiter wears a T-shirt that reads SLACKER, and the chef/co-owner Eric Werner is a bearded Brooklynite who formerly cooked at Peasant, in Manhattan. The meal is sumptuous; the conversation boisterous; the you-are-here decompression complete.

Drifting off to sleep in my bed, cocooned by mosquito netting, it hits me: if Tulum and I are going to get along, I'll have to accept it like that sweet but flaky friend—not altogether reliable, but absolutely irresistible.

The thump of LMFAO's hit "Sexy and I Know It" wakens me, booming from an early morning exercise class I have no intention of joining. Amansala's founder, New Yorker Melissa Perlman, sends me to Mateo's Mexican Grill, her brother's restaurant, for breakfast. As a worker in this environmentally aware mecca applies some kind of varnish to a table, giving me a wicked contact high, I order coffee and *huevos divorciados* (eggs with *salsa roja* and *salsa verde*).

Mateo's is on the touristy northern end of the beach, across the street from the waterfront, on what is known as the jungle side. This densely packed area is where Tulum's first resorts were built, and it's home to roadside stands selling colorful string hammocks, embroidered quilts, and other souvenirs. Nearby, a local with gray dreadlocks and Gaultier shades hawks handmade jewelry and carved obsidian on a folding table. In Mixik, a Mexican handicrafts store, I stumble upon a stash of Jamaican lobby cards for 1970's movies. At 50 pesos (around $4) each, I greedily snap up a half-dozen. The cashier carries the credit card machine to the window, trying in vain to get a Wi-Fi signal to post the transaction. Cash it is, then.

Heading south leads to what I call Tulum's "zona yoga," a string of rustic cabanas, spas, and om-sweet-om

■ 'What more do you need when you have jungle, beaches, and architecture that still remains shorter than the tallest palm tree?'

resorts. In its center, adjacent to such boutiques as the beach dress shop Josa Tulum and new cafés comprising the style-centric section of town, Tulum-inaries Italian designer Francesca Bonato and her husband, Nicolas Malleville, an Argentine model for Burberry and Gucci, established a fashion beachhead with Coqui Coqui Tulum Residence & Spa. Their arrival brought an international network of beautiful people—Jade Jagger and Sienna Miller are regulars—and the couple transformed the rough-hewn limestone beach house into an intimate inn 10 years ago. Coqui Coqui's cool, dimly lit concrete guest rooms have a vampire glamour also reflected in the mostly black lobby, which serves as a shop selling a collection of beautiful leather jewelry and silk rebozo shawls and unisex scents such as agave and a mint-lime mixture called Menli.

In Tulum, luxury and earthiness coexist, but the coin of the realm is spirituality. It is a place known for on-site shamans, and the swankest hotel in town, Be Tulum (where the Argentinean-style rooms have limestone walls, freestanding tubs, and air-

conditioning), offers something even more ambitious: for $100, the in-room menu promises that a holistic card-reading will "recess your inner wisdom and clarify your paths." Seeking a more hands-on experience, I stop at a roadside kiosk for a massage in a *palapa* and a take-home jar of Dijon-colored Mayan Clay, which claims to relieve sunburn, eye bags, insect bites, and depression. "Mix it with honey if you put it on your face, then wash it off in the ocean," the salesperson advises. The idea just makes me hungry.

At Casa Jaguar, where Euro-house lounge music provides a mellow backdrop for conversation, my friends and I enjoy cocktails that combine mezcal with hibiscus, cinnamon, and orange. We are joined by Jiri Filipek, a Bangkok-born former Manhattan fashion and home-décor retailer, who has set up Passage to Culture, an insiders' concierge and tour company for Tulum visitors. "It's like the Wild West here in a way," she says of her new home. "If you have a dream and ambition, you can re-create your life."

That's certainly true for David Graziano, who left New York, where he opened the clubs RDV and Kiss & Fly, to wear sandals all day long. After breakfast at Ahau Tulum, his 20-room resort across from Casa Jaguar, he shows me a newly finished suite, a soaring two-story villa with a sleeping loft made from reclaimed timber and a massive hand-painted Asian lantern hanging from the woven A-frame ceiling. In his short time here, Graziano has witnessed Tulum's coming-of-age as a beach destination. "Simplicity and nature are the new luxury. What more do you need when you have a jungle, white-sand beaches, and architecture that still remains shorter than the tallest palm tree?"

Ahau Tulum's beachfront. Opposite: The bar at Hartwood Restaurant.

I spend an afternoon at the ruins, a five-minute drive north of downtown, taking in the carefully restored relics of a civilization that thrived in the 13th through 15th centuries. The reconstructed temples are jaw-dropping—even from the distance imposed by the ropes that guard them from tourists—and pique my curiosity. What kind of people once lived here? Lisa Meschi, the American proprietor of the oceanfront inn Encantada, tells me the theory that the locals have. "The ruins you see were their getaway from the larger cities and hectic lifestyle."

On a boat trip through the Sian Ka'an Biosphere Reserve's Muyil lagoon, drifting through the waters of a canal the Maya dug thousands of years ago, I realize the natural wonders of the area still serve much the same purpose. Tulum may be a global style destination, but its simplest pleasures remain timeless. +

Adapted from "Next Stop: Tulum," by David A. Keeps.

GUIDE

Turns out he was right. Settling into an easy routine—swimming, eating, and napping the days away—I begin to appreciate Tulum's allure. It is rustic yet cool, small and easy to navigate. I leave the beach for the pueblo, or downtown, where the main road has shops selling jaguar heads and woolly versions of Mickey Mouse and the only English the vendors know seems to be, "How much do you want to pay?"

There are also ice cream parlors and restaurants like Los Aguachiles, a recent arrival from Cancún. Eric Werner from Hartwood is picking up a to-go order when I visit, and recommends *los figurines* (lettuce wraps with fresh seafood) and *aguachidos*, an extra-spicy northern take on ceviche with cucumber, pickled red onion, purple cabbage, and a habanero salsa that the menu says is "grate for killing a hangover."

STAY

Ahau Tulum
Km 7, Crta. Tulum-Boca Paila; 521-984/167-1154; ahautulum.com. **$$**

Amansala
Km 5.5, Crta. Tulum-Boca Paila; 521-984/100-0717; amansalaresort.com. **$**

Be Tulum
Km 10, Crta. Tulum-Boca Paila; 877-265-4139; betulum.com. **$$**

Coqui Coqui Tulum Residence & Spa
Km 7.5, Crta. Tulum-Boca Paila; 521-984/100-1400; coquicoquiperfumes.com. **$$**

Encantada
Km 8.7, Crta. Tulum-Boca Paila; 650/212-6782; encantadatulum.com. **$$**

EAT

Casa Jaguar
Km 7.5, Crta. Tulum-Boca Paila; 521-984/155-2328; casajaguartulum.com. **$$**

Hartwood Restaurant
Km 7.6, Crta. Tulum-Boca Paila; hartwoodtulum.com. **$$**

Los Aguachiles
Avda. Tulum at Avda. Palenque; 521-984/802-5482; losaguachiles.mx. **$$**

Mateo's Mexican Grill
Km 5.2, Crta. Tulum-Boca Paila; 521-984/114-2676; mateosmexicangrill.us. **$$**

DO

Passage to Culture
521-984/129-1774; passagetoculture.com.

Sian Ka'an Biosphere Reserve
Crta. Tulum-Boca Paila; cesiak.org.

SHOP

Josa Tulum
Km 7.5, Crta. Tulum-Boca Paila; 521-984/115-8441; josatulum.com.

Mixik
Km 5, Crta. Tulum-Boca Paila; 521-984/871-2136.

MEXICO CITY

For decades, the Mexican capital's status as a destination for the arts drifted under the radar, despite a repository of homegrown talent and historical gems. Now experimental exhibits and a flourishing modern art scene have cemented the city's place as an essential stop on the global cultural pilgrimage tour. Below, eight spots not to miss, from the classic to the cutting-edge.

Anahuacalli Museum

In the southern part of the city, Diego Rivera's pyramid of volcanic rock houses the artist's quirky collection of pre-Hispanic works. Crisscrossing stone staircases connect a labyrinth of tomblike rooms displaying carved animal figurines and Teotihuacan masks, while an upstairs studio contains Rivera's sketches for his murals and portraits. *150 Calle Museo; Coyoacán; 52-55/5617-3797; museoanahuacalli.org.mx.*

Antiguo Colegio de San Ildefonso

This 18th-century former Jesuit school is known for its placid porticoes lined with satirical works by José Clemente Orozco, a 20th-century Mexican muralist. As paintings, they are emotionally wrenching; as critiques of society, they are scathing, portraying aristocrats as fat grotesques and Law and Justice as conniving criminals. *16 Justo Sierra, Centro; 52-55/5702-2991; sanildefonso.org.mx.*

Casa Luis Barragán

The former residence of the great Mexican Modernist has remained untouched since it was built in 1948. Barragán created intensity by distilling light, color, and structure to their purest essence: a long wall pops with pink, for example, while a window is positioned to align its shadow with the opposite wall. *12-14 General Francisco Ramírez, Daniel Garza; 52-55/5515-4908; casaluisbarragan.org (by appointment).*

Hilario Galguera

Located in the San Rafael district, Hilario Galguera's namesake gallery embodies the city's thriving contemporary movement. The space highlights international stars such as Damien Hirst—who struck up a friendship with Galguera at a chance social gathering—as well as Mexican artists like Bosco Sodi and Daniel Lezama. *3 Francisco Pimentel, San Rafael; 52-55/5546-9001; galeriahilariogalguera.com.*

Labor

Owner Pamela Echeverría used to spend rollicking nights at this former run-down pool hall and live music venue across from Casa Luis Barragán. Now she hosts experimental shows in the refurbished gallery of soaring ceilings and polished concrete. The wildly creative programming ranges from workshops and lectures to screenings of documentaries by emerging filmmakers. *5 General Francisco Ramírez, Daniel Garza; 52-55/6304-8755; labor.org.mx.*

Museo del Juguete Antiguo

What started as an obsession became a multigenerational labor of love. Japanese-Mexican architect Roberto Shimizu began accumulating vintage toys in 1955; his son oversees the collection of more than 45,000 pieces (most of them manufactured in Mexico) in a place wedged between auto-body shops south of Centro. The overabundant, tongue-in-cheek displays of toy soldiers, Barbie dolls, and *luchadores* (freestyle wrestlers) promise to induce pangs of joyful nostalgia. *15 Dr. Olvera, Doctores; 52-55/5588-2100; museodeljuguete.mx.*

Museo Nacional de Antropología

Among the pre-Columbian treasures in this 1964 Modernist landmark is the Piedra del Sol, a monumental stone disk whose carvings reveal the mathematic sophistication of Aztec beliefs. But there are other, quieter riches: a jadeite mask from Palenque; a frescoed Toltec vase; an armored vest made, exquisitely, from seashells. *Paseo de la Reforma, Chapultepec Park; 52-55/4040-5300; mna.inah.gob.mx.*

Museo Tamayo

A 2012 remodeling and expansion put Museo Tamayo on the cultural map as a world-class venue for modern art, with rotating exhibits by prominent artists such as Pierre Huyghe and Michael Stevenson. Design junkies rave about the well-curated gift shop, which stocks Mexican and international decorative objects, architecture books, and exhibition catalogues. When you're finished browsing, head to the sun-filled terrace for lunch overlooking Chapultepec Park. *51 Paseo de la Reforma, Miguel Hidalgo; 52-55/5286-6519; museotamayo.org.*

Anahuacalli Museum's volcanic-rock façade. Right: A mural by Fernando Leal at Antiguo Colegio de San Ildefonso.

Admiring a painting in the Museo Tamayo. Left: A gallery at Museo del Juguete Antiguo.

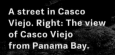

A street in Casco Viejo. Right: The view of Casco Viejo from Panama Bay.

PANAMA CITY

The capital's colonial district takes center stage

Plaza Francia. Right: The penthouse suite at Casa del Horno.

Developer K. C. Hardin sitting in a Canal House Hotel suite. Left: A pulled-pork tortilla at the Tántalo Hotel.

THE CASCO IS HAPPENING but it hasn't quite happened. Mention Panama at any cocktail party in my fashion-barometer hometown, East Hampton, New York, and people all say the right things; they make sure you know they know it's a hot destination. But very few of them have made the five-hour trip from New York, and although *Sports Illustrated* came to shoot its 2012 Swimsuit Issue, models aren't exactly herding here yet. How long can this innocence last?

The Casco, the southwestern tip of Panama City, overlooks the Pacific entrance to the canal, where huge container ships hover like shoppers on Black Friday. It's just three avenues wide and nobody uses addresses. Architecturally encyclopedic, designated a UNESCO World Heritage site in 1997, it could easily be the setting for the next photo series by Robert Polidori. It's erotic like Havana, moldering like New Orleans, world-weary like Cuernavaca, Mexico, and just dangerous enough, like Miami's South Beach in its early years—all of this seasoned with a dash of *The Night of the Iguana*. The booming city beyond couldn't be more different, with its Singapore skyline and Dubai aspirations (*Forbes* magazine once described it as "Monaco with bananas"). Since the handover of the canal to Panama in 1999, and even more so after 9/11, Panama City has become a stomping ground for South Americans, a place for them to get all the Carolina Herrera and Hermès they want without being kidnapped or waiting hours to be fingerprinted in Miami passport control. In five days I never went to their part of town, but they showed up in the Casco at night to play.

The neighborhood is small, but it's quite a show. In a 15-minute walk from your hotel you can see grand old houses carefully restored as luxury condos; squatters on filthy sofas watching brand-new flat-screen TV's in abandoned buildings; the presidential palace; crumbling pastel façades held together by makeshift scaffolding; trees growing through former ballrooms; endless construction sites; and streets populated by (along with working-class Panamanians going about their day) surfers of all ages, expats of many nationalities, birders, eco-tourists, barefoot children, trust-fund brats, and street vendors napping in fetal position under folding tables off of which they sell Panama hats (asking price: around $20).

"You see that woman in costume? It's not a costume." K. C. Hardin is pointing out a Kuna woman wrapped in the traditional bright sewn-textile panels they sell around the neighborhood as everything from ankle bracelets to sofa pillows. An American in his late thirties, Hardin used to be a heavy-duty corporate lawyer until he came to Panama on a surfing trip. After a six-year leave of absence, he finally admitted he was never going back. He's a real estate developer now, using his sharp legal teeth to polish up the Casco while keeping it from becoming one more could-be-anywhere stop on the global fabulousness circuit.

He isn't alone in this, and here it gets complicated: Hardin's partner in the real estate firm Conservatorio is Ramón Arias, also a lawyer, who moved into a run-down apartment in the Casco nearly 20 years ago, when most people of his class wouldn't even walk there. Arias hired Hildegard Vásquez, then a newly minted architect who'd come home to Panama, to renovate his family residence. "By the time I was done, I was married to him and pregnant," Vásquez says, sitting behind her desk at Hache Uve, now the leading preservation architects in the country. Hardin got married, too, to Patrizia Pinzón, who now has a desk at Arco Properties, which markets the buildings that Conservatorio develops as well as real estate throughout the Casco. And who's at the desk behind Pinzón? Hardin's mother, Clara Keyes Hardin, who moved down from Santa Fe, New Mexico. It's one big family with one big mission.

Authentic is the team's favorite word as they slowly and strategically try to improve and preserve a living, working neighborhood, and also get us to come visit. The key, they say, is not to displace all the locals. Along with stylish hotels and apartments, they're building affordable housing, a travel agency, a bakery, restaurants, artists' residences, a hostel, and a community center. Their hotels employ mostly neighborhood people trained by a local foundation. Pinzón and Clara Keyes Hardin don't so much sell real estate as pick and choose ideal neighbors, putting off the house flippers and finding sympathetic young Panamanians, South Americans who want a break from glitz, and Americans and Europeans looking to reinvent themselves in a place where luxury condos cost only about $300 per square foot. As Pinzón explains, "You want people who embrace the neighborhood as it is, not ask, 'When will it be finished?'"

"There's always somebody who came before you," Vásquez says. "The moment you see that, you understand the big picture." History, however, is a big disconnect in Panama—a country that was once as subjugated to the United States as any colony, even if it technically wasn't one. (For most of the past century, Panamanians couldn't even enter the Canal Zone without an American host.) "Our history is happenstance. It's not history," Vásquez says. "Mostly people here want new. Miami is Mecca."

Conservatorio's first hotel, the Canal House—a cool, dark refuge from the heat that feels like a rich man's residence—has only three guest rooms. Daniel Craig stayed there while filming *Quantum of Solace* in 2007, went back to England, and, without even being asked to, raved about it in the press, giving the Casco a big boost. Their second hotel, Las Clementinas,

where I stayed, has six huge, high-ceilinged suites and a lot of stairs; you don't so much feel you've checked in as moved in. Neither hotel relies on the usual hip-hotel tricks; both have more of a Graham Greene atmosphere. If I'd gotten any more into it, I would have bought a bottle of seven-year Havana Club, taken a glass from the bathroom, and let the barely revolving ceiling fans hypnotize me until I passed out.

Other developers are in the game, too. Casa del Horno is a small hotel with a lot of gorgeous stonework and a Milanese sleekness. Tántalo Hotel is positioning itself as the party place, with a huge bar in the lobby and another on the roof and each room designed by a different Panamanian artist. A French-style hotel under construction is lurching along—nothing moves fast in Central America.

The next big opening will be Conservatorio's American Trade Hotel. The Casco's largest, at 50 rooms, the property is also its most architecturally ambitious, spanning four major historic buildings; and the

GUIDE

The rooftop bar at the Tántalo Hotel. Opposite: Patrizia Pinzón at home in Casco Viejo.

most strategically located, in the neighborhood's center. It could be the equivalent of the Delano igniting South Beach. "Every great city has an iconic hotel that embodies the city," Hardin says. The concept seems like a natural: a lobby that's the crossroads of the city that's the trade crossroads of the world, a magnet for a mythical guest whom Hardin calls the Cosmo-tropico-latino. You know this smoothy. You see him in Nespresso bars all over the world, stirring his single for 20 minutes.

It's all a bit ambitious, but this earnest bunch never quits. "Everything worthwhile is Sisyphean, don't you think?" Hardin says. Panama can be a dodgy country. The team has had its share of threats. Right now they're fighting with the city over a proposed expressway around the Casco—a sure way to kill any neighborhood. But I wouldn't bet against them.

With the opening of the nearby Museum of Biodiversity, designed by Frank Gehry, and bigger and more amenity-rich hotels, people will surely be coming to the Casco in greater numbers in the next few years. The most demanding of the Four Seasons crowd may want to hold off until then, but for everybody else, this is a time that travelers will look back on wistfully. At some point the rough edges are going to be smoothed out. The disarming Panamanian custom of shaking your hand—your driver and your bellman stick out an arm, and you think they're reaching for your bag—will probably give way to more distanced, classic hotel training. The day will come when you'll have to fight for a reservation at Ego y Narciso, where you can now take all the time in the world ordering plate after plate of ceviche under the full moon. There won't always be bars like La Casona, down a dark, dead-end street in a derelict old building, where you can drop in for a mojito with a hundred other people if you're still up at 4 a.m. You can come now, or you can wait for the Assouline book. ✦

Adapted from "Casco Viejo Rising," by Stephen Drucker.

ECUADOR

A journey into the country's interior, from Quito to the jungle

Achuar Indian beadwork. Opposite: A view of Plaza de San Francisco, in Quito, from Casa Gangotena.

A Mashpi Lodge suite. Left: The hotel's "sky-bike," suspended from cables in the trees.

Plaza de San Francisco. Right: Roses at Hacienda San Agustín de Callo, in Lasso.

112

B Y THE TIME I ARRIVED back in Quito, the raw egg a shaman had smashed over my head in her house in Peguche was hardening into an uneven spiky gel, and, like some disoriented punk rocker, I walked the streets of the Ecuadoran capital, preparing my excuses. The high altitude, I reasoned, had impaired my judgment, not to mention I'd lost my itinerary, which was at this point a blessing, considering my journey was about to take me directly toward an erupting volcano, down the so-called river of piranhas, and into the care of a man who went into tourism at the suggestion of a tree.

The sun dipped behind the jagged Andes, and I stepped into the Plaza Foch, in Quito's hippest neighborhood, reeking of unknown potions. An after-work crowd fanned out from the corner restaurants. Cigarette men in ski caps paced the sidewalk, offering me their trays. VIVA ASSANGE, read a graffito along a metal wall. I sat down at an outdoor bar to ponder what I'd gotten myself into.

F or many travelers, Ecuador is something of a mystery. Bordered by larger neighbors—Colombia to the north, Peru to the south and east—and the Pacific Ocean along its western coast, the Oregon-size country is perhaps better known for attractions outside its mainland borders: the Galápagos Islands, 600 miles offshore, which account for a majority of the country's tourist visits; and, recently, Julian Assange, the Australian Wikileaks founder, who took up residence in Ecuador's London embassy, and whom Ecuador's firebrand president, Rafael Correa, granted asylum. Such publicity illustrates a basic challenge. "Sometimes we meet with travel agents and they don't even know where Ecuador is," says Oswaldo Muñoz, a diplomat, hotelier, and longtime tourism-industry leader. That may be changing, however. In the past few years, a concerted effort by public and private developers has gotten under way to turn Ecuador's mainland into an ecotourism player, taking advantage of the country's diverse topography—soaring mountains, tropical jungles, and pristine coastline—and the richness of its indigenous cultures.

D espite the enticing sight of a hipster in a fedora hurrying a string bass across the street, I didn't stay in Plaza Foch for long. Itching from the nettles the shaman had smacked me with, I hailed a cab and was soon ascending and plunging down the narrow, roller-coaster streets of old colonial Quito, heading toward Casa Gangotena, the stateliest hotel in town. A palatial space with Egyptian-marble floors, soaring ceilings, and a postcard view of the city from its balcony overlooking historic Plaza San Francisco, the hotel is owned by Roque Sevilla, a conservationist and former mayor of Quito who fought for the inalienable rights of nature article. As I emerged from my cab, I prayed the sulfurous odor accompanying me would go unnoticed by Sevilla's staff.

Sevilla's job description had induced me to request a meeting. A tall, Harvard-educated mensch with a thin mustache and a balding, oblong, Quito-shaped head, he had made a small fortune in insurance and mobile phones and, after his stint as Quito's mayor, bought the country's largest tour company, Metropolitan Touring, in 2001. After opening the solar-paneled Casa Gangotena—one of the most beautiful colonial buildings in the country— to international acclaim, he created the country's highest-profile new property, the eco-friendly Mashpi Lodge, deep in the Chocó jungle. Now his modest goals are to connect all of Ecuador with a network of trails, help get the country to a zero-carbon footprint by 2025, and introduce to the jungle an *E.T.*-like bicycle that will allow visitors to Mashpi to fly overhead and, as he put it, "see the jungle the same way as would a toucanet."

As an economist, Sevilla believes that tourism is more valuable than exploiting oil. "People ask me, 'Is there a strategy?'" Sevilla said, as if anticipating my question, while I took a seat at a long table in his spare, downtown office the following week.

caribbean + latin america

113

"But there is a strategy. It's not just an idea." He grabbed a marker and bounded over to a framed slab of glass that hung like a painting on the wall. On it were rudimentary sketches of buildings, and he enthusiastically added a coastline and a mountain range, with arrows pointing in the direction of the wind. "Why did I decide to invest only in Ecuador?" he asked me, but I only nodded, still in a food coma from the 32-course breakfast buffet I'd just finished in Gangotena's baroque dining room. "I'm interested in protecting a specific kind of environment."

did have some notion of what he was talking about. I'd driven with a guide to Mashpi a few days earlier, up into the Andes, through one-road towns where whole feathered chickens hung from the backs of motorcycles, cows stopped traffic, and church days were determined by the availability of itinerant pastors. Eventually we turned down a gravel road, which I was sure was narrower than my vehicle, and descended deeper and deeper into the dense, tropical Chocó.

■ Ecuador's mainland has become an ecotourism player, taking advantage of the country's diverse topography and the richness of its indigenous cultures.

Ecuador proudly proclaims itself "number four in the world for birds," and, of the 1,600-plus species found in the country, 900 reside in the Chocó; no place on the planet is denser with species of orchid. The area was months away from being razed for timber in 2001 when Sevilla bought it. He spent the next 11 years fending off squatters (some of whom now work for Sevilla as guides and forest wardens) and persuading the government to agree to a unique development deal. Of the $8.5 million he spent on Mashpi, the government financed nearly a quarter, which will be sold back to the public as shares.

Not surprisingly, Mashpi isn't your typical eco-lodge. Built with steel beams and glass, it looks like a modern loft building in SoHo, complete with spa and

hot tub. When I arrived, the soaring, glass-enclosed dining room—where my dinner that evening was interrupted by the thud of two herons banging into the 40-foot-high window—was buzzing with the bird and insect set. (A bee man was also on hand.) Designed as a research base as well as a tourist destination, Mashpi employs a staff biologist and hosts scientific projects such as one in a giant round butterfly tent in the jungle. A gondola, which opened in May 2012, carries guests a mile and a quarter over the forest to other trails. I traipsed out to another spot in the jungle to the self-powered sky-bike prototype, which beckoned on a cable overhead. I stepped up, strapped in, and began pedaling into the air, thrilled until I noticed the ground dropping off precipitously below and I had to cry out for a guide's assistance to backpedal to safety.

Crushed by the realization that I would never truly experience the world as a toucanet, I fell into a minor depression, sensing forces I couldn't control. Then my driver spoke up. "I know a shaman," he said. "An Otavalo woman."

Clemencia lived in Peguche, a small mountain village outside the northern town of Otavalo, and, after making an appointment, we hit the road. The Otavalo Indians, with the highest literacy rate in the country, are often cited as exemplars of progress, having managed to preserve their traditions and still enjoy a good standard of living. Otavalo's food and crafts markets are the most famous in Ecuador, and I killed time trolling the rows of vegetable and spice stalls, where women in gray hats sat behind tubs of fresh garlic and small men hurried past, carrying stalks of the hallucinogenic plant ayahuasca on their shoulders like baseball bats. There were no gringos in sight, and, smiling, I pointed my iPhone at a woman selling meat. But she cursed and threw a handful of shelled nuts in my face.

We got back in the car and drove to Clemencia's small cement home. A rotund woman wearing jeans and a feather hat, she had three packs of Lark cigarettes open on her table. The dirt-floored room was damp and lit only by candle. "Don't take this too seriously," she said in Quechua and Spanish, as my driver interpreted. "And this hat? I just wear this for show."

Before I could stop her, I was shirtless and rubbing a long candle all over my body, which she then placed on

The courtyard at Casa Gangotena. Below: A page from a bird-watcher's guidebook at Mashpi Lodge.

her mantel and lit. A black sediment appeared on it and the flame, compared with the other candles around it, was minuscule. Clemencia, obviously stunned, stared at it with her arms on her chest. "You," she said at last, "are almost one hundred percent stressed."

For the next hour, she spit in my face, blew fire on my chest, and spanked me with prickly branches, invoking the spirit of the mountains. "Dance with me," she said, leading me around a straw mat. Then she hugged me and said I was moving through life with the parking brake on. I looked at my candle. The flame was soaring. So long as I didn't bathe until morning or consume pork, fish, or caffeine for three days, I was to be healed.

W e may have to change our plans," my driver said as we sat in traffic leaving Quito the following morning.

"I was thinking the same thing," I said, fresh from a shower and tired of the road construction and our snail's pace.

"I mean tomorrow," he said. "Tungurahua is still erupting. We may have to take another route."

An hour later, we pulled into Hacienda San Agustín de Callo, built on a 600-year-old Incan ruin, in the high plains below the snowcapped Cotopaxi volcano. I was overcome with exhaustion and fell asleep in my claw-foot bathtub next to one of three fireplaces in my suite. My living-room library held 12 volumes of large leather books featuring press clippings about Galo Plaza, the uncle of San Agustín's proprietor, Mignon Plaza.

A dashing, erudite woman with reddish-brown bangs and dark nail polish, Plaza tells me about her family. They are the Kennedys of Ecuador. Her uncle and grandfather were both presidents. Other family members were prominent artists, writers, and matadors. Over the years, Ecuador's volatile politics and economy chipped away at the family fortune, and she opened her family estate to guests 15 years ago. "I never dreamed of being a hotel person," she said as we drank Argentinean Merlot by candlelight in an ancient Incan ceremonial room. "But I was obsessed with restoration. That's how I got money to fix the house."

My driver had called Clemencia to clarify my fish restriction—it forbade only swimming fish, not shellfish—and, relieved, I dug into my plate of shrimp

The living room at Hacienda San Agustín de Callo. Left: Textile vendors in Quito. Opposite: In the jungle near Kapawi Ecolodge.

in olive oil, quinoa croquettes, and *locro,* a traditional potato-and-grated-cheese soup served with fresh avocado. Plaza suggested I stay for a month, but since I had only one more day, I went horseback riding with Martín, the hacienda's head rancher and one of Ecuador's finest bullfighters. We galloped through rolling farmland, stopping at a pasture owned by Plaza's brother, where about 40 small bulls were grazing. "They're being raised to be in the ring," Martín said. "They can't have any human contact until they are four years old." There was one big bull nearby. "What about that one?" I said. Martín nodded in deference. "He was pardoned," he said, a rare case in which the crowd votes to let a bull go. "He was too brave."

Oil and the environment have clashed in this region for decades, and, as I was assisted into a long canoe upon landing in an Amazon basin airstrip, I wondered what was in the murky water. "This is the Kapawari," my boatman said, "the river of piranhas." I remained quiet the rest of the way, the *Jaws* theme song playing in my head as the sun beat down.

When we landed at a wooden dock, I was greeted by Ángel Etsaa, an Achuar Indian wearing face paint, who escorted me down a walkway to a village of bamboo huts and hammocks on stilts in the river. "Welcome to Kapawi," he said, speaking at a clip that suggested he'd never owned a calendar.

The Kapawi Ecolodge & Reserve is an experiment in sustainable ecotourism. Five years ago the original developers gave it back, as agreed, to the Achuar, who

GUIDE

STAY

Casa Gangotena
Oe 6-41 Calle Simón Bolívar and Calle Cuenca, Quito; 593-2/400-8000; casagangotena.com. **$$$**

Hacienda San Agustín de Callo
Lasso; 593-2/290-6157; incahacienda.com; all-inclusive. **$$**

Kapawi Ecolodge & Reserve
593-4/228-5711; kapawi.com; all-inclusive. **$$$$$**

Mashpi Lodge
N45-74 Av. De Las Palmeras at De Las Orquídeas, Quito; 593-2/298-8200; mashpilodge.com; all-inclusive. **$$$$$**

operate it and make up 80 percent of the staff. Meager profits flow back into the surrounding Achuar communities, which have been able to build schools; they allow lodge guests to visit. But with oil exploration continuing in the area and only 15,000 Achuar left on the planet, I couldn't help pondering whether the place would be some kind of Atlantis in the near future, and I headed straight to the tiki bar and ordered a beer and browsed the bookshelf, torn between *The Birds of Ecuador* and *Coups and Cocaine*.

Etsaa took me to the boat again, and we headed downstream toward the larger Pastaza River, which eventually flows into the Amazon on its way toward the Atlantic Ocean. Howler monkeys moseyed across branches above us. A trio of pink river dolphins frolicked nearby.

Etsaa hardly seemed a hotel man, and I asked how it was that he'd gone into the business. He pointed to a tree. "This tree?" I said. It had a thick trunk and branches that towered above the jungle.

"The spirit of the jungle is called Arutam," he said, "and it is especially found in the kapok tree." At the age of 18, he went to a kapok near his village, two hours away, and did a tea ceremony, in which he fell asleep, hoping to receive a message. And he did. "Arutam told me, 'Someday you will be a leader, work for your people, and receive guests,'" Etsaa said. He interpreted this to mean he was destined for tourism, and got special permission from his community to leave for school in Quito. Four years later, he returned, and he is now the administrator of Kapawi.

We took out our balsa-wood rods, about a foot long, and some thin nylon string. Onto the hooks went raw cow meat. We cast out and waited for the piranha. I had a bite, but no catch. Etsaa too. We moved to another location, where a shirtless man and his son waited with their lines in the water. "Anything?" Etsaa called out to him in Achuar. Nope.

Finally we went back empty-handed, and as I lay in bed that night, I wondered what the tree would say to me if I asked. ✦

Adapted from "True Adventures in Ecuador," by Julian Rubinstein.

LIMA, PERU

An art scene blossoms

WITH CONTEMPORARY GALLERIES and a boho-chic vibe, Lima's seaside Barranco neighborhood is fast emerging as the city's art hub. Take Wu Galería, a light-filled studio accessed through a wrought-iron gate and run by historian Frances Wu. The space showcases a mix of budding Peruvian and international artists specializing in diverse forms of media—drawing, sculpture, and installation. In 2012, native son and fashion photographer Mario Testino made a splash with the opening of the nonprofit MATE Asociación Mario Testino in a restored 19th-century villa. Along with masks and books by regional artisans, the vast cultural center houses the largest collection of his work. From there, head to Galería Lucía de la Puente for modern compositions by local stars, including Joaquín Liébana and Patrick Tschudi. A private passageway in the gallery will soon lead to the Arts Boutique Hotel B, a former retreat of the aristocratic Garcia Bedoya family built in 1914. True to its location at the center of the city's creative district, the creamy Belle Époque mansion is a veritable treasure trove of Latin American paintings, antiques, and 18th-century statues.

GUIDE

STAY
Arts Boutique Hotel B
301 San Martín; 51-1/206-0800; hotelb.pe. **$$$**

DO
Galería Lucía de la Puente
*206 Paseo Sáenz Peña;
51-1/477-0237;
gluciadelapuente.com.*

**MATE Asociación
Mario Testino**
*409 Avda. Pedro de Osma;
51-1/251-7755; mate.pe.*

Wu Galería
*129 Avda. Sáenz Peña;
51-1/247-4685;
wugaleria.com.*

SANTIAGO, CHILE

Chile's largest city gets a polished new edge

The Santiago
skyline after
a rainstorm.

FOR DECADES, SANTIAGO SAT in the ever-looming shadows of its pulsating sister cities, Rio de Janeiro and Buenos Aires, primarily serving as a gateway to the rest of Chile. Not anymore. Artists are transforming boulevards into street-art havens, and leafy avenues are now the playground for progressive chefs and sophisticated designers. In the Bellavista district, the 15-room Aubrey is Santiago's first true boutique hotel, decorated with chic Tom Dixon lamps, floor-to-ceiling windows, and dark wood paneling. It's a 10-minute drive north to the Museo de la Moda, South America's only fashion museum. Set in a revamped 1960's mansion, the building has a 10,000-piece collection that spans four centuries (don't miss the light-blue jacket worn by John Lennon in 1966). Santiago's food scene is heating up, too, with the spotlight on Chile's rich culinary traditions. To experience its distinctive blend of Andean and Asian cuisine, check out Ox, for dishes such as crisp Chilean sausage and tender Wagyu beef. Or book a table at the W Santiago's buzzy NoSo restaurant; you can't go wrong with corvina in fennel confit, paired with a Chilean Sauvignon Blanc.

GUIDE

STAY
The Aubrey
299-317 Constitución;
56-2/2940-2800;
theaubrey.com. **$$**

EAT
NoSo, W Santiago
3000 Isidora Goyenechea;
56-2/2770-0000;
starwoodhotels.com. **$$$**

Ox
3960 Nueva Costanera;
56-2/2799-0260; ox.cl. **$$**

DO
Museo de la Moda
4562 Avda. Vitacura;
56-2/2219-3623;
museodelamoda.cl.

SÃO PAULO, BRAZIL

This high-energy mega-metropolis has rapidly developed from a town known for meat-centric *churrascarias* into a cauldron of food creativity. Family-run restaurants paying homage to age-old recipes; hotbeds of experimentation—it's all here, with the bonus of Brazilian authenticity.

Attimo

Chef Jefferson Rueda's bistro, designed by architect Naoki Otake, combines Italian specialties with rural ingredients from his hometown of São José do Rio Pardo. The result? Creative dishes like sweet-potato gnocchi with pig's ear, and pork sausage corn *pamonha* (tamale). The unconventional pairings are served in a minimalist dining room of ivory marble and stainless steel with white cheese-grater walls and an artful stone staircase—it's no wonder that locals are praising it as São Paulo's most intriguing arrival. *341 Rua Diogo Jácome, Vila Nova Conceição; 55-11/5054-9999; attimorestaurante.com.br.* **$$**

D.O.M.

A required stop for foodies (including chefs Alain Ducasse and Ferran Adrià), D.O.M. specializes in imaginative plates that flaunt native Brazilian flavors, prepared by the pioneering Alex Atala. The former punk rock DJ presents his courses in a minimally designed space in the hills of the elite Jardins district. On the menu: coconut cubes ornamented with edible ants, and a banana-lime dessert scented with the floral *priprioca* root, previously used only in perfume. *549 Rua Barao de Capanema, Jardins; 55-11/3088-0761; domrestaurant.com.br.* **$$$**

Epice

Two massive wooden doors mark the entrance to the intimate, French-inspired Epice, opened by 33-year-old Alberto Landgraf, whose previous stints include Pierre Gagnaire in Paris and Gordon Ramsay in London. His whimsical dishes play with textures and flavors: a deceptively simple squash entrée is presented raw, as a cream, and in gnocchi all at once; pork belly arrives atop a bed of garbanzo beans sprinkled with paprika and morsels of Spanish chorizo. *1002 Rua Haddock Lobo, Jardim Paulista; 55-11/3062-0866; epicerestaurante.com.br.* **$$**

ICI Brasserie

The latest venture from local chef Benny Novak is a lively spot in the glass-encased JK Iguatemi shopping mall. Inside you'll find French phrases scribbled across mirrors and blackboards, slick floors made of concrete, and two open-air kitchens. There are charcuterie boards and veal sausages, but the burger topped with Emmentaler cheese and caramelized onions is a standout. Pair it with a glass of the namesake pilsner, ICI 01, from the nearby Colorado Brewing Company. *2041 Avda. Presidente Juscelino Kubitschek, third floor, Vila Olímpia; 55-11/3078-1313; icibrasserie.com.br.* **$$**

Maní

A white stucco farmhouse, a tree-shaded courtyard, and an enchanting series of small parlor lounges make Maní, in the quiet Pinheiros district, an unlikely sanctuary for avant-garde cooking. But Brazilian chef and ex-model Helena Rizzo and her Catalan husband, Daniel Redondo, are die-hard epicureans. The alums of El Celler de Can Roca, one of Spain's temples of molecular gastronomy, give classic regional dishes a seriously modern spin. Order the pork carpaccio *feijoada*, followed by the slow-cooked eggs topped with pupunha (palm heart) foam. *210 Rua Joaquim Atunes, Jardim Paulistano; 55-11/3085-4148; manimamoca.com.br.* **$$**

Mocotó

In the ramshackle working-class neighborhood of Vila Medeiros, sophisticated Paulistas come to sample chef Rodrigo Oliveira's northern-Brazilian dishes, such as crisp *torresmos* (fried pig skins) and rich *mocofava* (cow-hoof soup with sausage). Don't let the wait outside discourage you. Savor the block-party vibe with a glass of cachaça from the nearly 350-bottle collection. *1100 Avda. Nossa Senhora do Loreto, Vila Medeiros; 55-11/2951-3056; mocoto.com.br.* **$$**

Tordesilhas

Chef Mara Salles still uses the recipes she learned growing up in the Pernambuco countryside at her laid-back restaurant on nightlife-heavy Rua Bele Cintra. The rustic ambience (wooden tables; glass food jars lining the walls) sets an authentic feel for flavor-packed meals seasoned with colorful varieties of *conserva de pimento* (pickled chiles). Try the tender duck braised in *tucupi,* a spicy cassava broth, and house-made ice creams in traditional flavors including tangy *cupuaçu* and creamy tapioca. *465 Rua Bela Cintra, Consolação; 55-11/3107-7444; tordesilhas.com.* **$$**

Epice's lunchtime crowd. Left: The citrus-tree-shaded entrance to Maní.

Sautéed octopus in a manioc cream at Tordesilhas. Left: Chef Rodrigo Oliveira (right) at his restaurant, Mocotó.

COQUETÉIS
ENERGETICO: CATUABA, JURUBEBA,
PÓ de GUARANÁ e MARAPUANÃ,
GARAPA DOIDA: CACHAÇA, MELADO de
CANA, SUCO de ABACAXI e LIMÃO.
MAMULENGO: CACHAÇA, LICOR de CANA,
CHOCOLATE e LEITE CONDENSADO

CAIPI
CAIPIRINHA: CACH
CAIPIROSKA: VOD
CAIPIRISSIMA: R
CAIPIRÉ: SAQU
CANGIBRINA: CACH

BUENOS AIRES

Latin America's culture center heats up

THE ENERGY IS PALPABLE in Buenos Aires, where forward-thinking hoteliers, chefs, and gallery directors have injected the city with innovative projects, each one more modern than the last.

Check in to the stylish Hub Porteño, an ll-suite Belle Époque gem in tony Recoleta whose well-connected owner, Gonzalo Robredo, is on hand to unlock the best the city has to offer—be it a meet-and-greet with a famous polo player or a mansion tour with a noted interior designer. A short taxi ride south, the cathedral-size Faena Arts Center is a must-do for contemporary art fans. Colorful works by visual artists such as Cuban duo Dagoberto Rodríguez and Marco Castillo (known together as Los Carpinteros) have filled a raw gallery space that has floor-to-ceiling windows looking out on the waterfront neighborhood of Puerto Modero.

Come evening, crowds fill the open-air bars scattered among the barrios for pre-dinner cocktails. Join the locals and head to one of the many *puertas cerradas* (underground supper clubs) that have popped up across the city. The most sought-after table is Paladar Buenos Aires, in the Villa Crespo barrio, where chef Pablo Abramovsky serves fresh market ingredients while his sommelier wife curates wine pairings. Not ready to turn in? Sharpen your milonga moves at the Centro Región Leonesa dance hall. This is, after all, the birthplace of tango.

GUIDE

STAY
Hub Porteño
*1967 Rodríguez Peña;
54-11/4815-6100;
hubporteno.com.* **$$**

EAT
Paladar Buenos Aires
*Acevedo and Camargo;
no phone; paladarbuenos
aires.com.ar.* **$$**

DO
Centro Región Leonesa
*1462 Humberto Primo;
54-911/4147-8687.*

Faena Arts Center
*1169 Aimé Paine;
54-11/4010-9233;
faena.com.*

An outdoor courtyard at Hub Porteño, in Recoleta.

A view of the
Lisbon cityscape
from Elevador
de Santa Justa.

EUROPE

CORNWALL, ENGLAND

Secret gardens and windswept beaches

A view of St. Mawes from the Hotel Tresanton.

Porthgwidden beach, in St. Ives. Above: A guest room at the Tresanton.

IGHT COMES SOFTLY to St. Mawes in late July, like an illustration out of a children's book. The sky is a dark navy, pinpointed with stars, and the moon hangs comically low, casting St. Mawes Castle—built by Henry VIII in the 16th century as part of a defensive chain of fortresses—in a lunar glow. Falmouth Bay shines to our left just past a tiny curve of sand as my sister and I walk back to the Hotel Tresanton along Lower Castle Road after dinner in the village. During the day the cerulean sky is marked with big puffy clouds; the water is a blue-green with patches of turquoise, filled with bobbing sailboats and their colorful sails; and the scrawny beach is host to energetic families outfitted with towels, pails and shovels, and sun lotion. Now all is quiet except for the sound of clinking halyards and an occasional dog barking. Along the way we pass palm trees, originally imported from China, and a row of attached cottages painted in pastel shades that front the water and have winsomely nautical names such as Seaward, Bay Cottage, and Tavern Rocks. My favorite one, after much study, is Seacliffe Warren: it is covered with vines, like the house in *Madeline*, and has two thatched-roof bay windows paned with bottle glass. Finally we come upon the sign DELIVERIES TO THE KITCHEN OF HOTEL TRESANTON, which signals we have arrived at the cluster of higgledy-piggledy whitewashed old buildings that make up our destination.

There are places that speak to you unexpectedly, exerting a lure beyond the geographical, calling up a vision of who you might be in a different setting than you've known, living an alternate life to the one you lead. One such place for me, ever since I first laid eyes upon it eight years ago, is the southwestern tip of England: Cornwall, where the country narrows into a shape approximating the human foot, the air smells briny, and the climate is uncharacteristically warm. I had come here to search out the lighthouse that played such a key role in *To the Lighthouse*, my favorite of

Virginia Woolf's novels. Although that novel is set in the Hebrides, it is based on Woolf's memories of blissful childhood summers spent at St. Ives, on the Cornish coast, and the lighthouse she writes of is the Godrevy, situated on an island of its own at the head of St. Ives Bay. It was on that trip that I became enamored of the narrow, winding (and mostly two-way) roads overhung with foliage and the bursts of wildflowers that mark the landscape, as well as the shimmery quality of light the area is known for. I loved stopping in the cozy pubs that dot this part of England, even in a slip of a village like Portloe; looking at the art galleries in St. Ives and Newlyn; and watching the ornery seagulls as they flapped around the beaches, letting out their indignant cries. It was also on that trip that I discovered the timeless allure of St. Mawes, a gentrified fishing village about 1½ hours east of St. Ives in the lush section of Cornwall known as the Roseland Peninsula, and

the casual glamour of the Tresanton, a 30-room hotel owned by Olga Polizzi.

Polizzi, the daughter of hotelier Lord Charles Forte, is director of design for the Rocco Forte chain of international hotels run by her brother; the Tresanton is one of two properties (the other is the Endsleigh, in Devon) that she owns. She was introduced to St. Mawes by her husband, the writer William Shawcross, who vacationed here from boyhood on, and in 1997 she began a two-year redesign and restoration of a former sailing club that would become the Tresanton. The memories of my stay here, in an airy room with a large terrace that seemed like it might have belonged in a particularly tasteful but not too "done" summer house, as well as a wish to see if St. Mawes still beckoned in the same way, had brought me back for a week's stay at the hotel. Last time I was here I actually daydreamed about moving to the village, trading in the overstimulated atmosphere

of Manhattan for something more spare and close to nature, a place less dependent on the hum of the present moment. It was the sort of town, as I was told repeatedly, where "everybody knows what everybody is doing," which appealed to me after the steadfast anonymity of the city. I sensed that there might be an undertone of desolation to this removed part of the world, especially during the winter months, but even that seemed appealing to me. I saw myself writing for hours at a desk overlooking the water, then stopping to take a walk and perhaps get a cup of coffee at one of the sleekly designed food emporiums. I could envision myself making a few friendships among the locals, who managed to combine an air of affability with a kind of dignified reserve. I was curious to see if the relaxed charms of the area would hold up on a second visit—or if they had grown mythic once I was back on my familiar urban turf.

This visit I booked the Garden Room in Rock Cottage, a building slightly behind the main one that you get to by way of a short path that is illuminated with wall lights and lanterns at night. Done up in Polizzi's trademark declarative style, it has exquisite black-and-white hand-printed wallpaper in a pattern of palm fronds and birds, as well as touches of color via pillows, blankets, and a strategically placed Fontana Arte orange-framed mirror from the 1950's. The room is smaller than the one I stayed in years earlier and lacks a view of the water, but more than makes up for it with the enchanting private garden it opens out on. It is possible to sit in this garden of a summer morning or late afternoon, as I did with my sister, who flew from Jerusalem to meet me, and feel like you have arrived at just the spot—one that radiates a spirit of *"luxe, calme, et volupté"*—that you have dreamed of being in. We have tea here once or twice,

europe

131

and one morning we take our breakfast here, although most days we choose to have our eggs, fresh-baked croissants, and coffee at the hotel's sparkling white restaurant with an unobstructed view of the water.

On one of our first days my sister and I pass a little blond girl gardening in the front yard of a cottage on Lower Castle Road with a man who appears to be her grandfather—and I feel in an instant that this sort of poignant, small-town scene is precisely what I have been nostalgic for. We have come back from several hours of poking around the village, with its single pharmacy, post office, Barclays and Lloyds banks, and an old-fashioned-looking "Fashion Centre" with a sign in the window declaring all swimwear now 5 pounds. We also stopped in to check out the tiny St. Mawes Butcher, which closes at 2 p.m. on Sunday and carries haslet, the pork meat loaf, as well as ox tongue, black pudding, and an array of local cheeses with such names as Cornish Crumbly, Miss Muffet, and Smuggler (a mature cheddar). Farther along, there are various stands selling fish-and-chips and the ubiquitous "cream tea." Down at the bottom, there is a kind of mini-mall, where we stop in at the Square Gallery, which carries locally made art and handcrafted objets and is run by a lovely woman named Cathy Talbot. I get into a discussion of the charms of St. Mawes with Cathy, who has lived in nearby Falmouth with her husband and four children since 1997. "It's a leveling place," she points out, "because everyone wears flip-flops and the seasons have stretched out. People seem to leave whatever's happening elsewhere behind when they come here. And the generations visit together, providing a sense of continuity."

The reality behind the picturesque image is, of course, less idyllic and more complicated, as is always true. Cornwall, once a robust fishing and mining area, no longer has much industry other than tourism since its stock of pilchards—a variety of sardine—dried up and the tin and copper mines shut down. There are still jobs to be had in the china clay industry (although a lot of the work is now done in Malaysia) and there is talk of reopening the tin mines. Meanwhile, St. Mawes, with its natural beauty and pacific spirit, has become a second-home haven for wealthy Londoners and other Europeans, which contributes to the ever-rising cost of living. One grumpy longtime resident complained to me

Glendurgan Garden, in Mawnan Smith. Above: A cottage in St. Mawes.

about how the rich and famous visitors to the area had pushed the price of dinner in town "up to 50 quid."

Upon the recommendation of Olga Polizzi, I engage Charles Fox to be my driver and guide for two days. Fox is a garden designer and artist whose family has lived in the area since the early 17th century and whose great-great-grandfather created Glendurgan, one of Cornwall's finest gardens, which was given to the National Trust in 1962 (and about which Fox has written an excellent memoir). He takes me hither and yon, pointing out the sights as well as all manner of flowers—from bluebells and primroses to campion, honeysuckle, and valerian (the late poet laureate John Betjeman's favorite). After visiting the St. Just in Roseland Church, which harks back to the 13th century and is still in use, with beautifully maintained gardens and a cemetery, we drive all the way to Mousehole, in far southwestern Cornwall, where we pull up at a small hotel called the Old Coastguard that overlooks the English Channel. Outside on the terrace, while we wait for our drinks under a sun that is blessedly temperate, I notice three generations at the next table—a father with two children and their grandfather—playing board games. To my eye, it looks impossibly harmonious and old-world, as if the Internet had never been invented and the extended family hadn't yet yielded to the isolated nuclear version.

There is more to see: Penzance, where we check out Penlee House Gallery & Museum, built in a converted Victorian house, which features work by artists from the area, including Walter Langley, Lamorna Birch, and others of the Newlyn School, as well as an exhibit of the plein-air paintings of Dame Laura Knight. We also make a quick stop at the Abbey, a blue 17th-century town house converted into a hotel and owned by the former model Jean Shrimpton that feels like a step back into the world of *Brideshead Revisited*. Then we're off to the quaintest little stretch of beach hidden away in Polkerris, a blink of a village on the harbor; just above the beach is the Gribbin Gallery, which carries, among other local art, some striking wooden carvings by David Moore. At my request, Fox makes a detour to Mevagissey, a little town that I remember fondly from my prior visit, where we pause for refreshments at a beachside hotel, Trevalsa Court. At his insistence, just when I feel I've exhausted my sightseeing capacities, we make a last-minute dash for the nearby Lost Gardens of Heligan. Fox gives me a hurried but expert tour of the restored working gardens of this centuries-old estate, where more than 200 varieties of fruits and vegetables are grown and which also includes a subtropical garden filled with exotic plantings from around the world.

And then, inevitably, although time here does indeed seem to stretch out and pass more slowly, the week is up. After a last drink at the Tresanton bar, my sister and I reluctantly pack for our return trips home. I find myself once again deeply, almost magnetically attached to this place and am not surprised to read, midway through our stay, that Cornwall is officially rated as "one of the best places to live in the country," coming in second from the top according to Prime Minister David Cameron's first annual "happiness index." I wonder whether I would be happier here as well, or whether my vision of St. Mawes is simply a sustained daydream, abetted by props courtesy of the Tresanton. What I know for sure is that one of these days I'll be lured back, for another glimpse of the water and sky and the sound of seagulls cawing. ✦

GUIDE

Adapted from "English Seaside Paradise,"
by Daphne Merkin.

europe

LISBON

Portugal's second-oldest city remains one of the Continent's most culturally vibrant destinations. From the opulent Manueline architecture of its storied cathedrals to new-age art institutions and performances of traditional fado, Lisbon's artistic bounty is a seamless mix of the ancient and the up-and-coming.

Calouste Gulbenkian Museum
Housed on a former estate, the late Armenian oil tycoon's exhaustive private collection is considered by many to be the finest accumulation of 19th-century relics in the world. Expect to see a vast array of works, such as Egyptian, Greek, and Roman antiquities; medieval illuminated manuscripts; and Lalique jewelry and glass.
45a Avda. Berna; 351/217-823-000; museu.gulbenkian.pt.

Castelo de São Jorge
The country's first king, Afonso I, captured this 12th-century crenellated citadel on the highest hill in Lisbon from the Moors in 1147; it later became the center of his kingdom. Visit the archaeological ruins in the adjacent courtyard before climbing the castle ramparts for sweeping vistas of the Alfama district.
Castelo de São Jorge;
351/218-800-620; castelodesaojorge.pt.

Jardim Botânico d'Ajuda
Explore the shaded lakes and steep hills of Portugal's centuries-old botanical garden, overlooking the Belém neighborhood and the Tagus River. Originally built for King Dom José I's grandsons in 1768, the park's upper terrace has greenhouses full of bamboo, bougainvillea, and beds of colorful orchids, while the lower level is crowned by a Baroque fountain with carved serpents and sea horses.
Calçada da Ajuda;
351/213-622-503; jardimbotanicodajuda.com.

Mosteiro dos Jerónimos
A monument to royal power during Lisbon's Age of Discovery, this 500-year-old monastery is perhaps the world's best example of ornate Manueline architecture. Its gabled limestone façade stretches the length of the Praça do Império square; the inside blends motifs from the sacred to the maritime. Spend an afternoon taking in the cloisters, chapels, and tombs, where great figures in Portuguese history (poet Fernando Pesoa; explorer Vasco da Gama) were buried.
3 Praça do Império; 351/213-620-034; mosteirojeronimos.pt.

MUDE (Museu do Design e da Moda)
In the stark, raw space of a former bank in Baixa, you'll find some 200 design objects once owned by art collector Francisco Capelo. The exhibits, which range from Art Deco and Modernism to Pop art and postmodernism, include contemporary furniture by Gio Ponti and Studio 65 (keep an eye out for the iconic Bocca sofa, or "Marilyn Lips") and vintage couture by Balenciaga, Vivienne Westwood, and Yves Saint Laurent (to name a few).
24 Rua Augusta;
351/218-886-117; mude.pt.

Museu Coleção Berardo
A 2007 addition to Belém's sprawling cultural center, the Berardo has a 900-plus inventory of modern paintings, sculptures, and videos dating from the early 1900's (Picasso; Marcel Duchamp) to 2002 (Albuquerque Mendes; Robert Silvers).
Praça do Império; 351/213-612-400; museuberardo.pt.

Palácio dos Marqueses de Fronteira
This 17th-century palace is one of the best places to see displays of azulejo tiles (its walls depict detailed hunting scenes and religious episodes). Leave time for a stroll through the 14-acre grounds, with their perfectly manicured hedges and Della Robia–inspired sculptures.
1 Largo da São Domingos de Benfica; 351/217-782-023; fronteira-alorna.pt.

Sé Cathedral
As legend goes, ravens once protected the body of Vincent of Saragossa—patron saint of Lisbon—after his death in the early fourth century and followed him by boat to the Romanesque church here. The site has since been built and rebuilt in a mishmash of styles, with little of the cathedral's original structure remaining. But historians shouldn't fret: the excavation site is open for public viewing, and Saint Vincent's casket, along with other artifacts, can be found in the Upper Treasury.
Largo da Sé; 351/218-866-752; patriarcado-lisboa.pt.

Tasco do Jaime
Don't leave town without going to a live concert of fado—the country's own guitar-based music characterized by mournful, melancholic rhythms. Most clubs are tourist traps, but this 22-year-old taverna in Graça is the real deal. Singers perform spontaneously, and locals often stand up to join in.
91 Rua da Graça;
351/218-881-560.

The view from Castelo de São Jorge. Left: An exhibit at MUDE.

The Jardim Botânico d'Ajuda. Right: A room inside Palácio dos Marqueses de Fronteira.

IBIZA, SPAIN

The quiet side of a legendary party island

Atlantis, a former quarry on the island's western coast.

T'S GETTING CLOSE TO SUNSET, and a bit chilly, but I have
no desire to leave. A structured landscape of medieval cisterns
and fruit trees, Es Broll de Buscastell, the site of an ancient
freshwater spring, reminds me of nothing so much as the Garden
of Eden. It's absolutely still, fragrant with pine, and the cool
water is perfect for a lazy dip. Though I've been coming to Ibiza
for nearly a decade, this is my first time at Es Broll, a brilliant
suggestion from English friends who have summered on this
Mediterranean island long enough to know its secrets.

Think of Ibiza and you likely imagine mega-clubs and all-night
rave parties. And indeed, if you stay in Platja d'en Bossa or Sant
Antoni de Portmany, that may well be a big part of your experience.
Yet what is really extraordinary about this island is how much
variety exists—and cohabits peacefully—within its compact area.
Ibiza is many things, many places in one, with an almost
immeasurable variation of atmospheres that range from urban
to pastoral, high-test to utterly restful.

To find the Ibiza of refined relaxation, my boyfriend, Stephen,
and I head for the low-key western and northern parts of the
island. Santa Gertrudis de Fruitera, located near the center of the

island, is our usual jumping-off point. This
gorgeous town, with its pedestrian-only
center, is full of boutiques and restaurants,
some quite traditional. We've spent
many happy afternoons at Bar Costa, a
comfortable meeting spot for locals that is
home to what may be the island's best
jamón ibérico on toasted *pan con tomate.*
Another favorite—for boldface names
including Jade Jagger and Jean Paul
Gaultier—is the bustling terrace of Macao
Café, which serves excellent Italian dishes.
Santa Gertrudis, with its selection of
clothing, jewelry, leather goods, and home-
décor shops, as well as a wonderful bookstore
called Libro Azul Ibiza, is inevitably where
I find myself on a last-minute jaunt for gifts.

The village atmosphere of Santa
Gertrudis seems positively electric compared
with that of the hamlets farther north.

The evening after my reluctant departure from Es Broll, we went to Sant Mateu d'Albarca for an early (these things are relative) dinner around 11 p.m. and ate simple grilled meats in the shadow of an adobe-like church that dates back to the 18th century. Not far off is Santa Agnès, a one-horse town with an old-school grocery next door to Can Cosmi, ground zero for the island's best Spanish potato omelette, known as *tortilla de patata*. Across the street is Sa Palmera, where I can't get enough of the gazpacho—ideal takeaway for beach picnics— and roasted lamb shoulder. Nearby is the leather shop Cas Sabater, owned by a graceful German, Manfred Postel, who displays his grandmother's circa-1920's handbags alongside his own sandals, belts, and eyeglass cases.

To drive between towns is to encounter a landscape that is ancient and majestic. The windmills and prickly pears of the south give way to pine forests; terraced hills with olive, fig, and almond trees; and the occasional carob or pomegranate bush. I haven't visited in winter yet but hope someday to see the almond trees in bloom, one of the reasons Ibiza is known as the *isla blanca.* Myriad stone walls divide the red earth, and whitewashed estates called fincas, some many centuries old, dot the scenery. All this sits under an impossibly blue sky, which at twilight turns a shade of lilac-silver.

Our hotel, the family-owned Es Cucons, is near Santa Agnès, an easy bicycle ride from town along the narrow Camí des Plá de Corona. This is one of the loveliest countryside hotels on the island, with 15 rooms around a tranquil swimming pool. Stephen, our friend Ian, and I wait patiently as the *sangría de cava* is prepared

from scratch, with time for the fruit to macerate, but it is worth it; they also serve fresh watermelon and mint juice.

Friends who live on the island—owners of the chic Hotel Los Jardines de Palerm—take me to the far western coast of the island to discover another hidden treasure, the seaside quarry known as Atlantis. This is a massive excavation of cliff where the stone was taken out to build the walls of Ibiza's Dalt Vila, one of two remaining walled citadel towns in the whole of Europe. It's a steep hike down, but the rewards are great. We swim in a Mediterranean that time has forgotten, salty and clear and silent. On the climb up, we see the sun set beyond Es Vedrà, an offshore rock formation reputed to be the home of the island's patron goddess, Tanit.

Another day, we opt for an athletic session on the water, renting kayaks near Port de Sant Miquel to explore the grottoes and deserted beaches of the area. From here it's not far to the cliffside luxury of Hotel Hacienda Na Xamena. Along the way we spot a field of colorful tie-dyed fabrics drying in the sun at Original de Ibiza, an impromptu shop that recalls the island's hippie past.

Later that afternoon, we reverse course to the south and stop off at the seaside lounge at Cap d'es Falcó. Here, on white-draped beds at the water's edge, my friends and I enjoy cocktails and tapas, then drive back along the island's famous salt pans as they reflect the lights of the airport across the flats. We have found the quiet heart of Ibiza. ✦

Adapted from "Secret Ibiza," by Henry Urbach.

GUIDE

STAY
Es Cucons
*110 Camí des Plá de Corona,
Santa Agnès; 34/97-180-
0453; escucons.com.* **$$$**

Hotel Hacienda Na Xamena
*Urbanización Na Xamena,
Port de Sant Miquel;
34/97-133-4500;
hotelhacienda-ibiza.com.*
$$$$

**Hotel Los Jardines
de Palerm**
34 Can Pujol d'en Cardona,

*Sant Josep de sa Talaia;
34/97-180-0453;
jardinsdepalerm.com.* **$$**

EAT AND DRINK
Bar Costa
*Plaça de l'Església,
Santa Gertrudis de Fruitera;
34/97-119-7021.* **$**

Can Cosmi
*1 Plaça de Corona, Santa
Agnès; 34/97-185-5020.* **$**

Cap d'es Falcó
Platja d'es Codolar,

*Sant Jordi de ses Salines;
34/66-433-1269;
capdesfalco.es.* **$$$**

Macao Café
*8 Carr. de la Venda des
Pobles, Santa Gertrudis
de Fruitera;
34/97-119-7835.* **$$$**

DO
Dalt Vila
Portal de ses Taules, Ibiza.

Es Broll de Buscastell
Sant Antoni de Portmany.

SHOP
Cas Sabater
*3 Plaça de Corona,
Santa Agnès;
34/97-180-5051;
cas-sabater.com.*

Libro Azul Ibiza
*1 Carr. de la Venda de Parada,
Santa Gertrudis de Fruitera;
34/97-119-7454;
libro-azul-ibiza.com.*

Original de Ibiza
Port de Sant Miquel.

The pool at the hotel Es Cucons. Left: A breakfast of eggs and *jamón ibérico* at Hotel Los Jardines de Palerm.

A stone ruin overlooking the Mediterranean. Right: Bar Costa, in Santa Gertrudis de Fruitera.

A lookout point designed by Antoni Gaudí in L'Eixample with views of La Sagrada Familia.

BARCELONA

Exploring Spain's style hub

IT'S NOT AS THOUGH BARCELONA just cropped up on the radar—the city has been a European center of design and culture for years. But a fresh harvest of innovators in architecture, fashion, and hospitality are reenergizing the Catalan capital. Take Hotel Ohla, in the Gothic quarter, where eyeball-like orbs dot the 18th-century façade; an all-black lobby welcomes you at check-in; and the Scandinavian-inspired rooms are done up in slick blond-wood furnishings and chocolate-toned Formica walls. Then there's the hotel's Michelin-starred Saüc restaurant run by up-and-coming chef Xavi Franco. Here, heavy regional dishes are given the gastro makeover: cod brandade is presented with mushrooms and truffled egg yolk; coastal fish comes with toasted sea urchins. Farther east, the bohemian El Born barrio has emerged as a gathering place for the city's creative entrepreneurs. Wander its pedestrian-only streets, filled with one-off boutiques. Our favorites: La Clinique, for limited-edition sneakers, and Mutt, where the city's cognoscenti shop for hard-to-find art and architecture books.

GUIDE

STAY
Hotel Ohla
49 Via Laietana;
34/93-341-5050;
ohlahotel.com. **$$**

EAT
Saüc
49 Via Laietana;
34/93-341-5050;
ohlahotel.com. **$$$$**

SHOP
La Clinique
7 Caller dels Mirallers,
no phone;
lacliniquefinestore.com.

Mutt
15 Carr. de Comerç;
34/93-192-4438; mutt.es.

The interior
of Merci.

142

PARIS

An emerging neighborhood in the City of Light

PARIS'S COOL CROWD HAS BEEN creeping north to the Haut-Marais, a tangle of tiny streets that runs from the Picasso Museum to the Place de la République. Blame this migration on Bonpoint founder Marie-France Cohen, who opened her multi-brand fashion and décor shop, Merci, in an old wallpaper factory in 2009. Ever since, fashionistas have been flocking to the low-key, formerly working-class area to gaze at Merci's wildly creative displays of housewares, fragrances, and clothing. Foodies are drawn to the neighborhood too, for casual restaurants like the pizzeria Grazie, owned by Cohen's son, Julien, or the wonderful food stalls along Rue Charlot at the Marché des Enfants Rouges, Paris's oldest food market.

Even some of the neighborhood's trendiest boutiques seem to have a natural connection to cuisine: they're often located in old *boulangeries*, like the Isabel Marant store on Rue Saintonge. Instead of *pain aux raisins*, the large vitrines feature Marant's chiffon dresses and coveted wedge-heeled sneakers. Fashion and food also convene at the Hôtel du Petit Moulin, another former bakery. The 17 rooms are decorated by Christian Lacroix, each with a different color scheme and blown-up copies of the designer's couture sketches. The quintessentially French finishing touch: the toiletries are from Hermès.

GUIDE

STAY
Hôtel du Petit Moulin
29/31 Rue de Poitou, Paris; 33-1/42-74-10-10; hotelpetitmoulinparis.com. **$$**

EAT
Grazie
91 Blvd. Beaumarchais; *33-1/42-78-11-96; graziegrazie.fr.* **$$**

Marché des Enfants Rouges
39 Rue de Bretagne; 33-1/40-11-20-40; lestaminetdesenfants rouges.com.

SHOP
Isabel Marant
47 Rue Saintonge; 33-1/42-78-19-24; isabelmarant.tm.fr.

Merci
111 Blvd. Beaumarchais; 33-1/42-77-00-33; merci-merci.com.

A market on
Rue du
Marché, in the
Provençal
town of Vence.

PROVENCE

France's original culinary paradise

Small boats near
Port de l'Olivette, on
Cap d'Antibes.
Right: Sunbathing
on the coast.

WHEN MY MOTHER AND FATHER fell in love, in the summer of 1967, they took off for Provence. They were in Switzerland at the time, and both 21 years old. A few days after they met, an impromptu Mediterranean weekend vacation seemed like the thing to do, and so they boarded a train to Cassis, a pretty fishing village east of Marseilles. They arrived in the evening. My mother decided they would sleep on the beach, and she tossed my father's too-heavy American suitcase under a bush near the train station with an energetic flourish. My mother was Swiss, and fearless. She had packed a small tent, which they pitched near the water after walking through town and along the length of the beach. They shared a baguette and a bottle of wine. That night, when the mosquitoes came, they lit cigarettes and smoked furiously inside the tent, which my mother insisted was the standard European method of fighting them off.

I think of my parents in their smoky tent as I stand in the shallow water in front of Plage Keller, on the Cap d'Antibes. The bohemian romance of the French Riviera of 1967 seems a lifetime away—

my lifetime, in fact, since I was born in 1968—but the freewheeling, sybaritic mood remains. There is the sheer physical beauty of the place, the infinite gradations of blue sky and blue water in the distance, the golden, glowing sunlight and air, the extra-attractive people in their bathing suits, the sound of laughter and ice cubes melting in the heat. The whole scene takes on the sudden, nostalgic glamour of an old Polaroid or an Instagram shot.

But the glamour is real, not a special effect. The drive to the beach had taken us past the grand villas of the superrich hidden away among the trees. Villa America, Sara and Gerald Murphy's 1920's outpost— where they entertained the likes of Picasso, Hemingway, and Scott and Zelda Fitzgerald—was a few minutes' walk away, and so was the iconic Hôtel du Cap. At Plage

Keller, meanwhile, athletic waiters from Le César adjusted our bright-yellow beach umbrellas, tracking the sun throughout the day, and took orders for drinks and lunch. My wife, Yumi, and friends sprawled on our chaise longues drinking Badoit and reading Gillian Flynn and Hilary Mantel novels. We were on vacation. We were in Provence. It's funny how a place can insert itself into your life, seemingly by accident, and then take on mythical powers of attraction. I have been coming to the Côte d'Azur repeatedly over the past several years, sometimes for vacation, sometimes for work, and the more I come here, the more I want to come back.

I am not the only one, needless to say. In my family, it was my great-aunt, the writer M.F.K. Fisher, who led the way. She had come to France for the first time in the late 1920's, living in Dijon with her first husband, and she made a career out of writing about food and life—and quite often, France—seducing American readers with her descriptions of oysters, or freshly picked green beans, or of sitting alone at a café, happy, drinking a glass of vermouth. In the late 1950's she went to Provence with her sister Norah—my grandmother—and their children, whom she enrolled in local schools. (This was an epic voyage that I grew up hearing about from my father and uncles—they had traveled by ship from California.) M.F. loved Provence. She and Norah came to France often, and for months at a time. In the fall of 1970, the sisters rented an apartment not far from Plascassier, where Julia Child and her husband, Paul, had built their vacation house. Contemplating her future in a letter to a friend, M.F. wrote: "I know, at this far date in my life, that I was meant to live and if possible to die on a dry, olive-covered hillside in Provence." This was not to be, however.

The trip that fall of 1970 was a fateful one, not only for my great-aunt, but for the entire American food establishment. They were all there in Provence together that fall and winter, more or less coincidentally: Julia Child, James Beard, Richard Olney, Simone Beck, the Knopf editor Judith Jones, and M.F.—the people behind the seminal cookbooks and food writing of the era. They ate and drank and cooked together (and talked and sniped and gossiped, too), and they were all, in one way or another, rethinking their attachments to France, where they had each fallen in love with food and cooking to begin with.

A street scene in Vence. Above: Fresh goat cheese at Au Poivre d'Âne, also in Vence.

I have been writing a book about this historical moment, about the American love affair with France and how it came to an end—or at least, how the terms of the relationship, in the realms of food, taste, and snobbery, had changed rapidly in the late 1960's. The unquestioned authority of French haute cuisine was waning; the American counterculture, with its co-op vegetable gardens and homemade bread, was on the rise. And as it turned out, the casual, rustic cooking of rural French bistros and Provençal home kitchens had an outsize role to play in inspiring the modern American food revolution, from Chez Panisse to every farm-to-table menu in the land.

This is why I've been coming to Provence again and again: to untangle the strands of cultural and culinary history that made it so influential for Child, Beard, my great-aunt, and the others—a place where food and life intertwined so easily, and indeed still do.

■ Provence is made for cooking. The markets, fruit-and-vegetable stands, butchers, fishmongers, bakeries, and cheese shops all have the best stuff imaginable.

On this trip, I had rented a house in the hills near St.-Jeannet, a tiny town outside Vence. The massive stone former olive-oil mill, Le Moulin de la Cagne, was built in the 1700's and set on a steep, terraced hillside that fell away into a gorge. The owner of the house was a Dutch flower-bulb impresario, and the gardens were appropriately grand, full of rare and spectacular plants, otherworldly blooms, and enormous cacti. There was a grape arbor above the outdoor table where we ate every meal; there were mulberry, olive, lime, grapefruit, plum, and kumquat trees; there was a mossy pool for a collection of carp. We hung our laundry to dry instantly in the heat on the upper terrace, and swam in the pool on the lower terrace. Farther below was a large vegetable garden, where we picked tomatoes and cucumbers.

Every night at exactly eleven o'clock, the sprinkler system would activate. It was a very thorough, drenching, professional sprinkler system, one befitting a Dutch flower man. He had forgotten to mention it, and so on one of the first nights we were there, we found ourselves frantically clearing wine glasses and stowing chair cushions as the sound of the hissing, spraying water grew louder and louder, surrounding us. We escaped inside. The timing and coordination of the various sprinklers was fiendishly complicated, I learned, and could not be changed. And so we got used to the late-evening water.

The garden sparkled in the morning, lush and green. Towering above the house, above the village of St.-Jeannet, was a small, bare mountain—the Baou de St.-Jeannet. It was craggy and beautiful, like a smaller Montagne Ste.-Victoire in a Cézanne painting, and had some of that flinty hardness. This is the essential duality of Provence, I thought as I stood in the garden and looked up at the cliff. The softness and the toughness. The wild, fertile abundance, and the austere, unforgiving stone; the unbelievable richness and perfection of the tomatoes and peaches, but also the dry prickliness of rosemary bushes and thistles. Two sides of the same lovely coin.

Provence is made for cooking. The markets, fruit-and-vegetable stands, butchers, fishmongers, bakeries, and cheese shops all have the best stuff imaginable: large crates of peaches and nectarines, all just ripe, sell for a few euros. Your average supermarket chicken was mind-bogglingly delicious. Staples like wine and bread were transcendent. The local bakery, Aux Suprêmes de St.-Jeannet, didn't look like much. It was set just off the main roundabout in the center of town, in a little shopping area next to a pharmacy and gift shop. But inside was that amber smell of all French bakeries, the smell of butter and flour being fired into golden-brown croissants at high heat. In the morning, a long, fast-moving line led past trays of petits fours—tiny éclairs; apple tarts; Mont Blancs—toward the bins of baguettes in front. I came every day, and felt a little more French each time, rattling off my order and then driving the mile or two to the house with my window rolled down.

A slightly longer drive was required to get to the food shops in Vence, a larger town with a well-preserved medieval center that has narrow streets opening onto squares lined with cafés, and plenty of kitschy Provençal gift shops, but plenty of real food shops, too. There were greengrocers in small spaces with cement floors, and specialty markets selling cheese and wine. I found a butcher whose store, Boucherie Centrale, was built into the exterior wall of the old town. He was an icon of French bourgeois contentment, a portly man in a bloody apron slicing off large pieces of his house-made terrines of pâté, dispensing sausages and cooking advice, steaks, pork chops, and legs of lamb.

L ike M.F. and Beard, who in 1970 had embarked on numerous art excursions, we stopped at the Matisse Chapel, in Vence, a beautiful building designed by the artist in the late 1940's and containing his stained-glass windows, murals, and other works. And in St.-Paul de Vence, the next town over, at the Fondation Maeght, a strange, Brutalist-looking cement structure surrounded by lawns, trees, and sculpture gardens that was built in the mid 60's by Paris art dealer Aimé Maeght. There were Giacomettis, Chagalls, Calders, and Braques. The ocean was a few blocks away. We wandered the alleys in the direction of the Grimaldi Castle, built on the ramparts surrounding the city, and the sudden looming-into-view of the Mediterranean was almost shocking. It sparkled, bright blue. The Grimaldi now houses a small Picasso museum. This was where the artist worked for a little over a year just after World War II, producing dozens of paintings and drawings, including the famous *La Joie de Vivre*. The museum also has numerous colorful ceramics with his designs and drawings. The aesthetic of this art—all of it, at the Matisse Chapel, the Maeght Foundation, the Picasso museum— was sunlit, happy, vigorous, and bold; it was Provençal.

Back at the house in St.-Jeannet, we cooked with Child, Beck, Beard, Olney, and M.F. in mind, re-creating the communal atmosphere and sense of hedonistic possibility in the kitchen, embracing the pleasure of the land itself—the tomatoes, the crates of peaches. When my friend Kathie Alex came to lunch one day, toward the end of our trip, I felt the past connecting to the present. I'd met Kathie on previous trips here, while researching my book: she is a former student of Simone Beck's and the present owner of La Pitchoune. The Childs had built that house with the understanding that it would belong to the Beck family after they died, and the Becks eventually sold it to Kathie. She teaches cooking classes in the house, where Child's kitchen remains unchanged—her kitchen utensils still hanging on the walls.

I made an onion tart—the onions cooked very, very slowly, with lots of thyme; Yumi made a large green salad and a small white-bean-and-tuna salad. We cut up baguettes and sliced tomatoes and cantaloupes. We opened a rosé. We were ever-so-slightly nervous, cooking for a real cook, but of course we needn't have been. The atmosphere and philosophy and ingredients of Provence conspire to make this sort of outdoor lunch party a grand, sunny, rosé-tinted success. We ate and talked for hours.

By the time Kathie started teaching cooking classes, in the 1990's, the original generation of American pioneers had retired or passed on, leaving a booming food culture behind. M.F. died in 1992, in Glen Ellen, California, where I grew up visiting her as a kid, and where she served family lunches on the veranda. Now Kathie was pondering her future—who would take over Julia's La Pitchoune kitchen when she retired?— and we were serving lunch, keeping traditions alive. We toasted our meal, and the history all around us, the people who came before us, and Provence, of course. Then we unpacked the pear tart from the St.-Jeannet bakery, maybe the best pear tart ever made, and raised our glasses again. ✦

Adapted from "Return to Provence," by Luke Barr.

GUIDE

STAY
Hosted Villas
800/374-6637;
hostedvillas.com;
from $1,300 per week.

EAT
Le Novella
40 Blvd. d'Aguillon;
Antibes;
33-4/93-34-73-29. **$$**

DO
Fondation Maeght
623 Chemin des Gardettes,
St.-Paul de Vence;

33-4/93-32-81-63;
fondation-maeght.com.

Musée Picasso
Château Grimaldi,
Place Mariejol, Antibes;
33-4/92-90-54-20.

SHOP
Aux Suprêmes de St.-Jeannet
Quai du Peyron, St.-Jeannet;
33-4/92-11-02-09.

Boucherie Centrale
26 Ave. Marcellin Maurel,
Vence; 33-4/93-58-01-03.

Late afternoon at Plage Keller, on Cap d'Antibes.

Piazza del Popolo,
in central Rome.

ROME

An art capital gets a contemporary face-lift

THE ETERNAL CITY'S DRAMATIC physique, from its majestic antiquities to its sinuous Baroque curves, has been thrown into even higher relief by a modern makeover sweeping the city's museums and galleries. A booming contemporary art scene has piqued the attention of the international creative set, spearheaded by the reopening of the 1883 Palazzo Delle Esposizioni after a five-year renovation. The nearly 32,800-square-foot building has rotating exhibits of works ranging from Helmut Newton nudes to black-and-white landscape photos of Rome in the 1970's. In the Flaminio neighborhood, the cantilevered Zaha Hadid–built MAXXI National Museum of XXI Century Arts proposes a more resolutely avant-garde agenda: first-rate artists such as South African William Kentridge and American Kara Walker share space with architecture retrospectives highlighting heavyweights like Carlo Scarpa. Modernity is also celebrated at smaller galleries across the city. Gagosian's first European outpost outside London, housed in a circa 1921 former bank, has been a fixture in Rome since it opened in 2007. Here, top talent including Takashi Murakami and Rachel Feinstein are giving the historic city 21st-century appeal.

GUIDE

DO
Gagosian Gallery Rome
16 Via Francesco Crispi;
39-06/4208-6498;
gagosian.com.

MAXXI
4A Via Guido Reni; 39-06/322-
5178; fondazionemaxxi.it.

Palazzo Delle Esposizioni
194 Via Nazionale; 39-06/489-
411; palazzoesposizioni.it.

CAPRI, ITALY

Hedonistic pleasures on the Tyrrhenian Sea

Swimming at La Fontelina beach club, on Capri.

THIS FOUR-SQUARE-MILE SPECK off the Sorrento Peninsula, with its limestone cliffs and waterfront villas, fully embraces the concept of *la dolce vita*. For proof, just look to the bronzed afternoon crowds, with their gleaming Gucci sunglasses and designer bathing suits, stretched out on the rocks and sipping Prosecco at La Fontelina beach club (it makes for an indulgent, voyeuristic lunch). From the main port, a funicular railway whisks visitors to Capri town, where you'll find shops like 100% Capri (specializing in crisp linens) and Dsquared (whose eclectic designs include Grecian-style silk dresses and neon tees).

But here, it's not just about how you look; it's where you stay. Check in to the J.K. Place Capri, a whitewashed retreat that puts a modern spin on nautical chic: round porthole-style interior windows, white sofas, and ocean-blue walls. (Book room No. 2 for its roomy terrace overlooking a stretch of white sand.) At sunset, join well-heeled Italians for a nightly *passeggiata* along Capri's dimly lit streets before settling in at an outdoor bar on the island's main piazza to watch the action unfold.

GUIDE

STAY
J.K. Place Capri
225 Via Provinciale Marina Grande; 39-081/838-4001; jkcapri.com. $$$$

DO
La Fontelina
Località Faraglioni; 39-081/837-0845; fontelina-capri.com.

SHOP
Dsquared
81 Via Camerelle; 39-081/838-8235; dsquared2.com.

100% Capri
29 Via Fuorlovado; 39-081/837-7008; 100x100capri.com.

A painting by
Petrus Norbertus
von Reysschoot
at Maison d'Hôtes
Hôtel Verhaegen.
Opposite: A view at
dusk over the
Leie River in Ghent.

FLANDERS, BELGIUM

Three cities steeped in age-old artistic traditions

Cristina Van Steenbergen-di Resta, an owner of Antwerp's International 14. Right: A guest room at Maison d'Hôtes Hôtel Verhaegen.

Mustard jars at Yves Tierenteyn-Verlent, a shop in Ghent. Left: Plantin-Moretus Museum's interior garden.

NLESS YOU ARE A DIAMOND dealer on business flying from New York, you are likely to arrive in Antwerp, as I did, by rail. Likely too you will be traveling via a larger city, because Antwerp—as opposed to Paris or Amsterdam or London, from which it's an easy train hop—is considered a second-string destination on the European hit list.

From the high-speed-train tracks, escalators lifted me past a bold new gridded superstructure by architect Jacques Voncke into the glorious cathedral of the original turn-of-the-20th-century station. The contrast was revelatory. Here in a nutshell was the palette and soft light, the deep tradition and smart modernity that I would see again and again over the next few days as I made my own accelerated loop through the trinity of cities—Antwerp, Ghent, and Bruges—that anchor the northern region of Belgium known as Flanders.

On trips to Paris, I know what I'll find: elegance, beauty, a certain feminine delicacy. But Brussels, the seat of the European Union, is a peculiar hybrid of international bland and haute guildhall, its avant-garde stylishness tucked into corners. Could it be that I would discover a purer form of Belgian interior style in an area half the size of Maryland—the golden triangle of Flanders?

What I was seeing out the taxi window was not promising. Drab postwar buildings, in-fill for wide swaths of Antwerp that had been leveled by bombs during World War II, supplanted the spectacle of the train station. But my hotel itself, the Julien, was all-redeeming. Only good things could lie behind double doors of such chic taupe and perfect gloss. In the white foyer, an antique settee upholstered in natural linen and a simple domed light fixture were the only adornments. Modern sectionals in pale gray wool cozied up to the twin black-marble fireplaces of the parlor. Even on this dim afternoon, natural light penetrated deep into the interior.

The Flemish have a gift for taking a space not much larger than an air shaft and transforming it into a sanctuary. At Julien, the public rooms had no views to speak of, but sitting in them was a pleasure thanks to walls of gridded glass opening onto small courtyards. At breakfast, it was not the passing trolleys outside that drew my attention but the scene opposite: a tiny courtyard, white-walled and gravel-floored, with the elegant skeleton of a single bare tree emerging from asymmetrical waves of evergreen hedges. Such a painterly hand with plant material could only be credited to the influence of local landscape designer Jacques Wirtz.

What Wirtz is to landscape design—a game changer with far-reaching influence—another Flanders native son, Axel Vervoordt, is to interiors, only tenfold. For 30 years, Vervoordt has defined Belgian style. Fourteen years ago, he bought a former distillery a short drive from Antwerp's center that he turned into showrooms, offices, and exhibition spaces and renamed Kanaal. The large, spare rooms of the brick warehouses and concrete silos, where contemporary art and unusual antiques mix with farm tables and oversize slipcovered sofas, encapsulate his vision in its most elevated form.

Vervoordt's work can also be experienced at a trio of places tucked into Vlaeykensgang, an easily missed alley just off the pedestrian Oude Koornmarkt. At his namesake gallery, the cool black stone floors and whitewashed walls form a monastic setting for works by the likes of Anish Kapoor. Serene in a softer way is Sir Anthony Van Dijck Restaurant, designed by Vervoordt in the 1980's. That the look—roughly plastered walls; scrubbed pine tables—still seems current is testament to the designer's trust in simplicity and natural materials.

Even though Vervoordt has moved ahead, not all of his countrymen are with him. Belgian style as represented by his earlier Van Dijck restaurant suits the Flemish, whose interiors reflect a fundamentally conservative nature—stylish but never flamboyant. It's a sensibility embodied by Flamant, the Flemish equivalent of Restoration Hardware. The Flamant brothers opened their first shop in Antwerp 30 years ago, bringing well-made, well-priced, modern interpretations of antique pieces to the bourgeoisie. I bought candles in a soft taupe that recalled the shades of beige and gray dominating contemporary Flemish interiors. An echo of the pallid light captured by painters, the palette is refined—though to some it's simply dull.

"I'm so tired of the Flanders style. I feel like I'm looking at rooms through panty hose." This comment was made to Cristina Van Steenbergen-di Resta by a friend, but it could have been the decorator's own lament. Her shop, International 14, was a star among the emporiums I explored along Kloosterstraat, the spine of Antwerp's antiques district. A rare straw hat, circa 1820, was treated as sculpture; brilliantly colored taxidermy parrots were sprinkled amid handsome Swedish cupboards. "In the 16th and 17th century, it was all the rage to collect odd items from around the world and display them in *verzamel* cabinets," Van Steenbergen-di Resta said. "I think of the room as a cabinet, and the decoration and people who live there as the collections that bring the story to life."

Knowing what to enhance and when to leave well enough alone is a hallmark of Flemish style, as I discovered anew at the Maison d'Hôtes Hôtel Verhaegen, a 50-minute train ride away in Ghent. To

their listed 18th-century *hôtel particulier*, Jan Rosseel and Marc Vergauwe brought their own high intelligence, treating the architectural shell as the treasure it is while adding wit and comfort. Shapely modern lamps offset boiserie and paintings by 18th-century Flemish artist Pierre Norbert van Reysschoot. Striped carpets complement the original herringbone-wood and black-and-white marble floors. If it is possible to be both taut and lush in decoration, then Rosseell and Vergauwe are masters. Rare are the places where one can experience the art in *l'art de vivre*. Rarer still are the times that I arrive at a hotel and want to abandon the rest of my itinerary. So I stepped away from Hôtel Verhaegen only long enough to gather excitement about my return.

Once the most important center for wool and cloth in medieval Europe, Ghent wears its historical significance lightly. A few blocks from the guesthouse, I came across a contemporary design store, Surplus Interieur; Ghent's best art and architecture bookshop, Copyright; and Dille & Kamille, a Belgian-Dutch chain of orderly, tin-bin bazaars of kitchen and bath accessories. At the Design Museum Ghent, I took in

GUIDE

STAY

Exclusive Guesthouse Bonifacius
4 Groeninge, Bruges; 32-50/490-049; bonifacius.be. **$$**

Hotel Julien
24 Korte Nieuwstraat, Antwerp; 32-3/229-0600; hotel-julien.com. **$$**

Maison d'Hôtes Hôtel Verhaegen
110 Oude Houtlei, Ghent; 32-9/265-0760; hotelverhaegen.be. **$$**

Maison Le Dragon
5 Eekhoutstraat, Bruges; 32-50/720-654; maisonledragon.be. **$$**

St. Jacob B&B Brugge
20 Oude Zak, Bruges; 32-50/677-399; stjacobs.be. **$**

EAT

Rock-fort
15 Langstraat, Bruges; 32-50/334-113; rock-fort.be. **$$$**

Sir Anthony Van Dijck Restaurant
16 Vlaeykensgang, Oude Koornmarkt, Antwerp; 32-3/231-6170; siranthonyvandijck.be. **$$$**

DO

Axel Vervoordt Gallery
16 Vlaeykensgang, Oude Koornmarkt, Antwerp; 32-4/7788-8060; axel-vervoordt.com.

Design Museum Gent
5 Jan Breydelstraat, Ghent; 32-9/9267-9999; designmuseumgent.be.

Groeninge Museum
12 Dijver, Bruges; 32-50/448-743; museabrugge.be.

Kanaal
15-19 Stokerijstraat, Wijnegem; 32-3/355-3300; kanaal.be.

Plantin-Moretus Museum
22–23 Vrijdagmarkt, Antwerp; 32-3/221-1450; museumplantinmoretus.be.

St. Bavo Cathedral
1 Bisdomplein, Ghent; 32-9/269-2045; sintbaafskathedraal.be.

SHOP

Copyright Art & Architecture Bookshop
8B Jakobijnenstraat, Ghent; 32-9/223-5794; copyrightbookshop.be.

Dille & Kamille
15 Hoornstraat, Ghent; 32-9/233-9112; dille-kamille.be.

Flamant
50 Meir, Koetshuis VH Paleis OP Denmeir, Antwerp; 32-3/226-7760; flamant.com.

Frederiek van Pamel
3 Eiermarkt, Bruges; 32-50/344-480; frederiekvanpamel.be.

International 14
13 Minderbroedersrui, Antwerp; 32-4/7297-0340; international14.com.

Surplus Interieur
9 Zwartezustersstraat, Ghent; 32-9/223-5294; surplusinterieur.be.

Yves Tierenteyn-Verlent
3 Groentenmarkt, Ghent; 32-9/225-8336; tierenteyn-verlent.be.

Belgian masterpieces such as an 18th-century wooden chandelier by J. F. Allaert and the tubular 1930's furniture of Gaston Eysselinck. I stood in rapture before the panels of the van Eyck brothers' Ghent Altarpiece in St. Bavo Cathedral, and in dismay at the ugly (if necessary) climate-controlled glass box that encases it. I stopped in at Yves Tierenteyn-Verlent—not so much for the tangy traditional mustard made fresh several times a week, but for the original 1860 interior.

Half an hour away by train and less than half the size, Bruges felt more packed than Ghent and far more touristy, the streets leading off the Markt choked with lace and chocolate shops. To meet the needs of so many visitors, Bruges has exploded with small guesthouses where you can dial into any period look. I chose to stay at St. Jacob, a 19th-century building transformed into a contemporary B&B with four smart white rooms. Emmanuel Vanhaecke and his sister, Lyne, run two charming others that step further back in time: Maison Le Dragon and Exclusive Guesthouse Bonifacius. Stay at the latter and you are practically on the Groeninge

Museum's campus; the high-breasted hearth and leaded-glass bay windows of Bonifacius's breakfast room, overlooking the canal, are just a courtyard away.

The diverseness of Bruges was what held my interest. One moment I could be immersed in the shadows of low-ceilinged rooms and the rich textures of cobblestoned courts. The next I would be admiring Frederiek van Pamel's way with mixing Asian artifacts, branches, leather, and zinc in his floral shop.

At tiny, rocking Rock-fort I nabbed a counter stool and watched the chefs turn out fried liver with jam. My head was filled with images of the trip, so many of them beautiful, unexpected, even contradictory. What made Flanders such a satisfying place to visit was not the ease of train travel or the accommodations, which were some of the chicest I have ever encountered, but its identity. Flemish style is stealth style, Flanders the land of under-promise and over-delivery. Flanders is only small if you're not looking. ✦

Adapted from "New Masters," by Heather Smith MacIsaac.

europe

AMSTERDAM

Welcome to the new Amsterdam, where an exciting marriage of dining and design has taken root. Here, the Masters are progressive chefs, homegrown ingredients adorn every platter, and Europe's most singular urban eating experiences are just a quick tram ride beyond the central canal zone.

Bolenius

This light-filled spot was a labor of love for chef Luc Kusters and his partner Xavier Giesen, the dapper host who mans the dining room. The dishes are inspired by the restaurant's urban kitchen garden—improbably planted under the post-postmodern skyscrapers of the Zuidas quarter. Borage and tarragon flowers decorate a shocking-green cube of lettuce gelée. Cauliflower is bewitched into a trompe l'oeil risotto highlighted with herring roe. Even pickled onion—an Amsterdam tavern classic—gets a conceptual makeover as a liquid-nitrogenated sorbet in a cone infused with cinnamon, nutmeg, and cloves. To top it off: a Willy Wonka extravaganza of Dutch caramels, waffles, and marshmallows.
30 George Gershwinlaan; 31-20/404-4411; bolenius-restaurant.nl. **$$$**

Brasserie & Lounge

Housed in a late-19th-century neo-Gothic bank building now known as the Conservatorium Hotel, Brasserie & Lounge celebrates the triumphant homecoming of local culinary hero Schilo van Coevorden from stints in Japan, Dubai, and Marbella, Spain. Now *le tout Amsterdam* is clamoring to taste his nuevo-Spanish bravura applied to indigenous ingredients. Farmhouse goat yogurt? It's dolloped with Adriaesque beet sorbet and gilded with Dutch caviar. *Gado gado?* Amsterdam's Indonesian favorite gets reinterpreted as a witty collage of tiny fried eggs, shrimp crackers, schmears of peanut sauce, and pickles accenting the crisp fried sweetbreads.
27 Van Baerlestraat; 31-20/570-0000; conservatoriumhotel.com. **$$$**

Eye Bar-Restaurant

At the creamy-tile-and-glass Eye Film Institute, the museum's curatorial spirit carries over to the restaurant's simple lunch menu served on a terrace overlooking the zany silhouette of the IJ-Dock complex, a mixed-use building that includes the Palace of Justice and luxury apartments. A baguette from famous organic bakery Vanmenno joins with silky salmon smoked over beech and oak wood by the boutique Baykow smokehouse. The elegant veal *kroketten* hail from the Holtkamp patisserie. For dessert, try the lemon-meringue tart and the fruit-studded apple cake from rival bakery Kuyt.
1 IJpromenade; 31-20/589-1402; eyebarrestaurant.nl. **$$$**

Merkelbach

In the 17th century, wealthy burghers built summer residences in idyllic Frankendael Park to escape the canal's clutter and stench. Now the only period *buiten* (garden manor) remaining is the stately Huize Frankendael, where Merkelbach occupies the coach house. A meal is an especially appealing tableau: a glass of rosé at a patio table; a picture-perfect salad of pink and yellow heirloom beets assembled by Slow-Foodie chef Geert Burema; ravioli filled with velvety cauliflower purée and dressed in dusky chanterelles and rich country butter.
72 Middenweg at Frankendael Park; 31-20/665-0880; restaurantmerkelbach.nl. **$$$**

REM Eiland

Even in this city of swoon-inducing waterside settings, REM Eiland turns heads. Back in the mid sixties this former oil rig of cubical steel, rising 80 feet on stilts, was repurposed into a pirate TV broadcasting station; it's since become the ultimate dining attraction in the emerging Houthaven port district. Under exposed ductwork at tables refashioned from scaffolding wood, a stylish crowd orders charcuterie and seafood platters from the brasserie menu. Pair them with a glass from the affordable wine list, such as a Barbera from Piedmont.
45-2 Haparandadam; 31-20/688-5501; remeiland.com. **$$$**

Riva

The young, worldly Australian chef at Riva fries up a peppery soft-shell crab, dishes out a sassy hoisin-glazed quail, and slow-cooks a seriously soulful goat-meat *crépinette* in a space done up with burnt-orange leather banquettes arranged under ceiling panels that evoke a river current. Take your croissant-and-butter pudding out to the deck and watch as the lighting gets moodier, the river grows glossier, and the regulars unmoor their boats on the Amstel River and sail home.
1 Amstelboulevard; 31-20/760-2030; caferestaurantriva.nl. **$$$**

Brasserie & Lounge. Left: Chef Geert Burema in front of an installation by Dutch artist Lotte Geeven at Merkelbach.

REM Eiland, a restaurant on stilts in Amsterdam. Right: Lobster with golden berries at Bolenius.

HAMBURG, GERMANY

Old-world grandeur refashioned

A building in the warehouse district. Opposite: Sunset over Hamburg Harbor.

The Hamburg Rathaus, or town hall. Left: An evening view of the arcades along Alster Lake.

A ship in Hamburg Harbor. Right: The lobby of the 25hours Hotel, in HafenCity.

A *WASCHECHTE HAMBURGER* is not something you eat. It's a person born and bred in Hamburg, and it was a few such dyed-in-the-wool locals who put the city in perspective for me. Hamburg may be the richest city in Germany, but it is not a city that shows off, like Munich; it is quieter than Berlin but more sophisticated, too—a publishing and manufacturing center. The country's leading news publications, including *Der Spiegel* and *Die Zeit*, are based downtown. Airbus planes are assembled here. In the western suburb of Blankenese, once a fishing village, are the discreet villas of the wealthy.

These days, the city is changing. There's the new Elbe Philharmonic Hall: architects Herzog & de Meuron's stunning building, well under way, looks like a glowing glacier landed on a dark-brick harborside warehouse. The concert hall is an icon as alluring as any siren architecture of our time. And like the Sydney Opera House or the Guggenheim in Bilbao, this building draws attention to a city unaccustomed to being stared at or visited from far and wide.

The philharmonic is in HafenCity, once a customs-free port zone you had to show your passport to enter, now the site of Europe's largest urban development project. Almost 50 new buildings have gone up, about a third of the total planned, by some of the world's most talented architects: Rem Koolhaas designed a monumental floating geometric ring that is to be a science center. Richard Meier and David Chipperfield have conceived office buildings, and Zaha Hadid is in charge of a "promenade link" to the old city. There is a also a chic boutique hotel, the 25hours.

M y first long walk in Hamburg led me past a string of museums from the Deichtorhallen to the Kunsthalle. The day I visited there was a dense veil of mist that dissolved only to reassemble more evenly and thickly, and I felt like the character in *Wanderer Above the Sea of Fog* by Friedrich: a figure in tails, holding a stick, standing on a rock and looking out onto an expanse of sea-foam, as ominous waves break over a nebulous landscape.

The sea was not far from where I was. A tributary of the Elbe River travels 65 miles to the North Sea from Hamburg, and the tides are such that a sailboat can come back upriver even on windless days, making it a natural harbor. But the expanse of water closer to me was Alster Lake. Its reflective presence in the center of town gives Hamburg an uncanny atmosphere. The Neuer Jungfernstieg, an elegant street that runs along the Alster, is lined with furriers, jewelers, and high-fashion boutiques. This is affluent Europe in the form of a civil, contented society, built on the city's merchants and harbor. The luxury brands on the nearby Neuer Wall street were familiar—Cartier, Bulgari, Mont Blanc— but along a canal by the Rathaus, or town hall, I came across a small Syrian café with just five tables: the Salon de Thé Saliba. Its windows were decorated with neat rows of dates stuffed with walnuts and baklava alternating with tangerines.

The Rathaus, designed by seven architects in the historicist neo- Renaissance style and completed in 1897, was one of the few grand buildings left standing after World War II. It has a central tower and wings covering 50,000 square feet. The parliamentary chamber, with wooden panels and leather benches and tall windows, reeks of European civility.

Steps away is one of the city's liveliest establishments: Café Paris. Despite its name, this is a venerable Hamburg institution. At a little after 12 I sat at a table by the back wall of the delicately ornamented Jugendstil room. It is full of shimmering glazed tiles, and two cupolas set into the tall ceilings are frescoed with pastoral scenes—young men with bales of hay and crates of apples; a bare-chested woman accompanied by two cupids. By a quarter to one, the hall was packed with a young crowd, consuming plates of steak tartare, bucketfuls of mussels with fries, and boiled beef with horseradish, all at a furious rate. I decided that sitting here watching the crowd was the most fun to be had in Hamburg.

amburg once belonged to the Hanseatic League, which regulated trade along the northern coast of Europe in the Middle Ages. Later, the city welcomed the rule of Kaiser Wilhelm I, but retained the privileges of a free harbor. Today, Hamburg offers a stately beauty without grandiosity—since there were never any princes or kings, there are no palaces to be seen. Instead, there are understated residential streets like the Ise Strasse, in Eppendorf, rising and falling like a well-paced breath, and lined with well-proportioned turn-of-the-20th-century houses whose façades are mostly white, pale gray, or the color of custard.

One of Hamburg's oldest neighborhoods is St. Pauli, an entertainment and red-light district that originally catered to sailors. Here, women still sit in shop windows waiting to be chosen, as in a similar district in Amsterdam. Hamburgers are proud of St. Pauli. Nikolaus Hansen, editor of the publishing house Arche/Atrium, told me the red-light district was so socially acceptable that he remembers driving through it with his grandmother when he was a kid. In the early 1960's the Beatles lived in Hamburg and played in several of the clubs in St. Pauli—Lennon once performed a set in his underwear. Nowadays, the Reeperbahn, also known as "sinful mile," is geared toward tourists, and an order of orange juice might come with a lap dance.

One afternoon, I sat at the Café Leonar, in the nearby Grindel neighborhood. Grindel is a genteel, whitewashed, fin de siècle residential area that had a Jewish population of thousands before World War II, before many of them left and most of those remaining were killed in the Nazi camps. Some of the names of the dead are engraved on individual square brass plates, which were set into the sidewalks by the artist Gunter Demnig.

So what is so Jewish about the Leonar? Not so much the "Israeli hummus" or the fact that bagels can be had. Perhaps the fact that there are so many newspapers to choose from, and even a few books. This is a serene place where one can read and think. If a cell phone dares to bleep, its owner heads for an enclave between the front door and a heavy velvet curtain to answer in whispers.

I contemplated the city's illustrious intellectuals: art historian Aby Warburg, whose collection was relocated to London; Heinrich Heine, whose descriptions of Hamburg are some of the most vivid and who once said that there was not enough holy water in the world to wash the Jew out of him; Arthur Schopenhauer, whose family lived in a house on a canal here in the 1790's.

here are many canals in Hamburg, and many bridges—more, they say, than in Venice and Amsterdam put together. The 17 brick warehouses of the Speicherstadt, with entrances from the water and from land, were built at the turn of the last century.

On my last day, I walked through the botanical garden and came upon a small Japanese garden with a few low thatched-roof wooden constructions. From there I proceeded to the architect Fritz Höger's 10-story Chilehaus—a building shaped like the prow of a ship

GUIDE

Furniture for sale at Richard, on Wexstrasse. Right: The bar at Café Paris.

and made of dark bricks with white window frames. In the arcaded ground floor is a fabulous store called Manufactum. High-quality handmade objects were for sale there, such as feather shuttlecocks for a bamboo badminton set, a genuine ostrich-feather duster, and three-winged boomerangs made of Finnish birch. In another downtown design shop, Richard, I found a selection of modern and antique furniture. Then it was time for tea in the high-ceilinged drawing room of the Fairmont Hotel Vier Jahreszeiten, overlooking the lake.

The editor Nikolaus Hansen took me to dinner that night. We went to his favorite restaurant, Engel, on the Elbe River. You drive along the Elbchaussee and reach a point where the ferry docks. Up the stairs, and seemingly suspended over the water, is a room with only 12 tables. The space is long and narrow so that you see the river close up or across the width of the restaurant. The décor is simple—white tablecloths; wooden tables and floors that are rocked by the docking of ferries. The menu is what you'd expect—grilled fish, shrimp, or filet. Over a leisurely meal Hansen told me what it had been like to grow up in Hamburg.

Before reunification Hamburg was hemmed in by the sea and by the nearby border with East Germany. To go to West Berlin took many hours, between police formalities on one side and the other. "From 1950 to 1990, when the Wall came down, more than a thousand people were killed at the border—in the middle of civilized Europe," Hansen said. "When I was a kid there were no tourists, and after nine the city was dark. But the city changed, became more extroverted after the war. Still, it kept its unexcited temper."

It's funny how the day appears to last different lengths of time in different parts of the world. In New York City it lasts about 12 minutes, divided into morning, afternoon, and evening, with four minutes for each. In Hamburg, the day seems multiplied by three and is steeped in the kind of time to stop at a café and read a newspaper or a book. After a few days in this quietly old-fashioned and architecturally futuristic little capital of contentment, I could see just what Hansen meant about Hamburg's "unexcited temper." ✛

Adapted from "The New Old Hamburg," by Gini Alhadeff.

europe

The living room
and library
at Stockholm's
Ett Hem.

STOCKHOLM

Uncovering the city's design gems

SWEDEN'S CAPITAL IS A SWEET juxtaposition of modern and medieval, where high-design hotels and avant-garde buildings share the cityscape with cobblestoned alleys and soaring church spires. Nowhere is this mix of nostalgia and newness so appealingly expressed than in the boutique-lined streets of posh Östermalm. At Svenskt Tenn, there's a beautifully curated selection of contemporary housewares and furniture, along with signature Josef Frank botanical prints from the 1960's. For more blue-chip style, browse the colorful glass vases and bowls by Alvar Aalto at Modernity. Around the corner, edgy local label Acne Studios looks to the future of Swedish fashion: racks are filled with sleek conceptual knitwear and asymmetrical leather jackets.

The city's forward-thinking aesthetic extends to hotels as well. In the Larkstaden district, the 12-room Ett Hem, designed by London-based Ilse Crawford, has interiors layered in Midcentury furniture from Scandinavia (Georg Jensen candlesticks; Gotland sheepskins), with art from the owner's personal collection. Don't miss breakfast in the glass conservatory, where chairs are draped in reindeer pelts and blazing fires in *kakelugns* (traditional Swedish stoves) keep guests toasty during the cold winter.

GUIDE

STAY
Ett Hem
2 Sköldungagatan,
Östermalm; 46-8/200-590;
slh.com. **$$$$**

SHOP
Acne Studios
2 Norrmalmstorg,
Östermalm; 46-8/611-6411;
acnestudios.com.

Modernity
6 Sibyllegatan, Östermalm;
46-8/208-025;
modernity.se.

Svenskt Tenn
5 Strandvagen, Östermalm;
46-8/670-1600;
svenskttenn.se.

europe

VIENNA

The Austrian capital has always possessed a colorful narrative, one starring extravagant emperors, visionary artists, and world-renowned musicians (Mozart; Beethoven). Its rich past is on view at Vienna's many historic landmarks, but a wave of renovated museums and galleries has fueled the city's latest cultural renaissance. Here's where to experience the best of old and new.

Academy of Fine Arts Vienna

Only 1,300 students attend the Academy of Fine Arts, one of Vienna's most prestigious schools, founded in 1688 by court painter and Austrian baron Peter Strudl. The campus spans over eight acres and includes a museum that displays Hieronymus Bosch's famous *Last Judgment* triptych and the country's largest selection of Romantic drawings.
3 Schillerplatz; 43-1/588-161-818; akbild.ac.at.

Albertina

At this Neoclassical palace built in 1744, the 21 Hapsburg staterooms are decorated in gold-and-silver alloys, and the walls are filled with masterpieces by da Vinci, Cézanne, and Raphael. Another highlight: the Wedgwood Cabinet room, noted for its intricate porcelain reliefs.
1 Albertinaplatz; 43-1/534-830; albertina.at.

Belvedere

You could spend an entire day wandering the French gardens dotted with statues and fountains at Prince Eugene of Savoy's 18th-century summer retreat, but save time to explore the two Baroque palaces, with paintings by Renoir, Monet, and Oskar Kokoschka.
27 Prinz-Eugen-Strasse; 43-1/795-570; belvedere.at.

Leopold Museum

One of the most beloved art havens in the MuseumsQuartier is the Leopold, designed by Berlin-based Ortner & Ortner architects. The boxy white structure showcases Gustav Klimt gilded paintings and the world's largest compilation of Egon Schiele oil canvases. Three nights a week, the glass-encased roof terrace hosts a party with live DJ's that lasts until morning.
1 Museumsplatz; 43-1/525-700; leopoldmuseum.org.

MAK

Works of art across all media dating back to the Middle Ages—glass; ceramics; textiles; metal—are on display at the Museum of Applied Art. After exploring the galleries, hit the café-restaurant Österreicher im Mak, run by chef Bernie Rieder. His menu of local comfort food, such as pork goulash and veal schnitzel, is the perfect complement to the museum's three floors of arts and crafts.
5 Stubenring; 43-1/711-360; mak.at.

MUMOK

In this charcoal-hued lava cube, 20th-century paintings (Picasso; Giacometti) share space with unique works embodying 1960's Actionism (naked bodies; animal carcasses). There's also an assortment of Pop art, including Andy Warhol's *Orange Car Crash* and Roy Lichtenstein's *Red Horseman*.
1 Museumsplatz; 43-1/525-000; mumok.at.

21er Haus

The Belvedere is now home to this glass-and-steel archetype of Modernist architecture. Inside the purple-lit neon shell, you'll find a serious collection of postwar Austrian art, from avant-garde exhibitions to conceptual retrospectives. If you're a film buff, leave time for a lesson in motion picture history at the cinema, based on architect Karl Schwazer's original from the 1958 Brussels Expo.
1 Arsenalstrasse; 43-1/795-5770; 21erhaus.at.

Wiener Prater

In addition to claiming one of the world's most famous Ferris wheels (which reaches 212 feet high), these 62 acres of grounds offer dozens of other diversions: running and biking trails, pony-riding stables, a museum highlighting the park's history (don't miss the vintage carousel horses and an old fortune-telling machine), even Austria's biggest disco. Consider it Europe's answer to Coney Island.
Prater; 43-1/729-2000; praterservice.at.

Wiener Staatsoper

In the city that gave birth to Mozart's *Cosí Fan Tutte*, classical music continues to weave itself into Vienna's everyday fabric. At the Staatsoper, Dominique Meyer, the former general director of the Paris Opera, curates an array of world-class programs. Wander the main hall, one of the only parts of the opera house spared during World War II bombings, to view original 18th-century frescoes. Then have a cocktail in the gold-leafed Tea Salon, where Viennese royalty once entertained their guests.
2 Opernring; 43-1/890-5397; staatsoper.at.

Wiener Staatsoper. Left: Locals lounging in the MuseumsQuartier's courtyard.

The Ferris wheel at Prater amusement park. Right: A gallery in the Leopold Museum.

KITZBÜHEL, AUSTRIA

An Alpine resort town embraces style and history

Kitzbühel at nightfall. Opposite: Riding a ski lift in the Austrian Alps.

Krapfen (pastries) at Café Praxmair. Right: Kitzbühel tourists from Bavaria.

Walkjacken (wool sweaters) at Hans Frauenschuh. Left: The view from Hahnenkamm mountain.

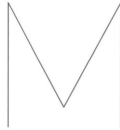

MIDWINTER DUSK FALLS as gently as snow on the mountain village, its timbered buildings huddled beneath the towers of twin medieval churches. Shop windows spill their light onto snow-dusted sidewalks as I make my way through the archway of the town's ancient gate, then pause to let a team of carriage horses clip-clop past. Stepping quickly through the winter cold, I slip down a pedestrian passageway, hang a right on a narrow cobbled street, and soon arrive at Hans Frauenschuh, a shop built in the traditional Austrian farmhouse style, with long wooden balconies on the upper floors and a pitched roof now laden with snow. A friend who grew up in the village has insisted that I drop in: this, she promises, is the real Kitzbühel.

As I step inside and shake off the cold, the shopkeeper, Elisabeth Frauenschuh, greets me from behind a sturdy table with cast-iron legs. The air is rich with the smells of traditional Austrian materials: deer leather; chamois; boiled wool; loden. Elisabeth walks me around the store, inviting me to run my fingers over the intricate stitching on a pair of boys' lederhosen, the lumpy wool of the handmade house slippers, the soft deer leather of a *Janker* jacket. The store, she tells me, was founded by her father, Hans. "As a young boy he was orphaned and grew up on an uncle's farm in great poverty," she says. Determined to improve his lot, he worked hard tanning hides, expanded his business, and raised a big family. Today his six children run four companies between them, including one that designs, manufactures, and retails Austrian-made clothes in 120 stores across Europe and the United States. A few blocks away, Elisabeth's sister Theresia runs another store, Frauenschuh, that's stocked with high-tech ski pants and sleek down parkas of the company's own design, all set in a blindingly contemporary space with blond-oak floors and buckskin-covered walls.

As Elisabeth shows me a pair of boiled-wool socks knitted by the wife of a shepherd, a gnomelike figure with tousled white hair emerges from the back room, looking comfortably chic in sandals and a loden cardigan. It's Hans himself. "He's retired, officially," Elisabeth says, "but he still shows up at work every day at seven a.m."

The Frauenschuhs are emblematic of Kitzbühel, a place that's at once profoundly traditional and utterly stylish. This mountain village has played host to some of the world's wealthiest and most celebrated figures for more than a century. Even as it evolves to keep pace with the fashionable Europeans who buy houses here now, it maintains its down-to-earth, mountain-folk spirit—a rare balancing act, especially among Alpine ski resorts of such lofty renown.

You can't talk about Kitzbühel, of course, without talking about skiing. Set in an immense bowl, the confluence of three Alpine valleys, the village is surrounded by icy crags that rise above a precipitous white landscape. Kitzbühel was among the first wave of winter resort towns to introduce the sport of skiing to the public, back in the days when Britain was an empire and Russia had a czar. These days, the resort offers a vast amount of widely varying terrain, linking together a chain of peaks that stretches 15 miles from north to south. Is it cutting-edge? Not exactly. The lifts that bind it all together are a pastiche, from ancient T-bars to a supermodern cable car that spans peaks two miles apart. This hodgepodge means that you can't cover nearly as much ground as you could at one of the mega-resorts back home, and when I first set out on the pistes I wondered if the resort's proprietors were taking the sport seriously enough. Then I remembered: this is Austria. If that's the way they want to do it, maybe that's the way it should be done.

And if the Austrians know skiing, they *really* know après-ski. They basically invented it. From the turn of the last century until the 1950's, Kitzbühel's old Grand Hotel was the ne plus ultra for international celebrities, including Edward, Prince of Wales, and Wallis Simpson. Later, the action shifted to the Hotel Zur Tenne, an intimate inn stitched together from three adjacent houses in the heart of the medieval city. Though its history dates back to the reign of the Holy Roman Emperor Charles V, all that was overshadowed by the gamboling of Frank Sinatra, Kirk Douglas, and Bob Hope. The scene may be quieter today—at night, the lobby bar is thronged with a tanned and immaculately attired crowd, chatting away and cheerfully smoking cigarettes—but it's still a place where the celebrated feel at home. The day after my visit, Hugh Grant was scheduled to check in, and a few days later Arnold Schwarzenegger and the Begum Aga Khan stopped by.

Today a pair of newcomers are vying to take the Tenne's crown. The Grand Tirolia Kitzbühel, a few miles outside town, was built at staggering expense by Yelena Baturina, the billionaire wife of the former mayor of Moscow. The five-story hotel blends modern and rustic with impeccable self-control: stacked stone is left rough-edged; unadorned wood has been laid out in simple planes. The crown jewel is its flagship restaurant, Petit Tirolia, which was elevated to national prominence by its founding chef, Munich-born Bobby Bräuer, who was named the top chef in Austria by Gault Millau in both 2011 and 2012, but who left the kitchen in the hands of his replacement, 31-year-old Steve Karlsch, a protégé of star German chef Tim Raue.

GUIDE

The other new jet-set magnet, the Kempinski Hotel Das Tirol, is set along the flank of a forested mountain six miles south of town. A glowing oblong of metal, wood, and stone, this quietly opulent world-within-a-world opened at the end of 2011. My room contained a wood-burning fireplace and chairs upholstered in faux animal skins from a medley of species. From the lounge chairs on my balcony I could see the steaming outdoor swimming pool. The suite flirted with opulence but remained in good taste.

Craving that feeling of connection that comes from immersing oneself in a community that has accreted over the centuries, I found myself drawn back into town. Strolling the oval of streets that once defined the village's inner keep, I ducked into Café Praxmair, a coffee shop where the owner's daughter, who happens to look like a Chanel model, served me a fluffy jam-filled confection called a *Faschingskrapfen* that is only available during the Carnival season. A few doors down, I stumbled upon Haderer, a shoe shop that has been owned by the Haderer family for three generations. One of the shopgirls handed me a men's brogue, a beautifully

Outside the Panorama Alm mountain lodge. Left: A room at the Kempinski Hotel Das Tirol. Opposite: Alternative transportation in Kitzbühel.

crafted piece of leather so meticulously burnished that it seemed to glow, and informed me that, if I wanted, the cobblers in the downstairs workshop could have a pair finished for me in six months. By now the sunlight was beginning to fade, so I hopped over to the tiny nearby village of Aurach, where Hallerwirt, an inn built of hewn logs, has been welcoming guests since the 18th century. Even in Kitzbühel, the Filzer family's three-century-long ownership counts as particularly enduring. After I'd sipped a glass of local Huber beer in the wood-paneled *Gaststube,* the current innkeeper took me into a banquet room to show off a painted chest that has been in the family since 1492.

The ultimate Kitzbühel experience, of course, would subsume all of its wonderful idiosyncrasies at once: the cozy historic charm and the grand Alpine vistas, the simplicity of the mountain folk and the glamour of the international wealth cloud. And so, on my last day, I set out on a cross-country-skiing odyssey, working my way from mountain to mountain until I reached a distant peak called Zweitausender. From there it was a quick trip to the doors of the Panorama Alm restaurant, set in the most dramatically sited of the many rustic *Hütten* (cabins) scattered among the mountains.

The restaurant is a traditional Alpine cabin with rough-hewn timbers and roaring fireplaces. If it weren't so busy, I'd have tried to get a table in one of the little nooks inside, but as it was, I was content to hit the more casual café, get a well-roasted half-chicken, and find a spot on the deck. It was a bit surreal to sit in the cold air and warm sun, surrounded by jagged peaks, and be sonically bathed in the up-tempo Europop playing over the P.A. system. But I hardly noticed, absorbed as I was in people-watching. Who were those people over there, with their leopard-print snow pants and fuchsia shells—a Frankfurt banker and his trophy wife? A pair of boldfaced names from a country with an illegible alphabet? Before I could discern any decisive clues, they had clomped off into the snow. I glimpsed them later from my chairlift, two dots of impossible brightness, gliding down the shoulder of a hill and disappearing into the shadows of the mountain beyond. ✦

Adapted from "Alpine High," by Jeff Wise.

SLOVENIA

A land of castles, waterfront hotels, and pine forests

Lake Bled, in northwestern Slovenia, with the town of Bled in the distance and, in the foreground, Bled Island and the Church of St. Mary.

Ljubljana's iconic
Triple Bridge.
Left: The courtyard
at Antiq Palace
Hotel & Spa.

The village of
Goče, in western
Slovenia. Right:
Biking near
the University of
Ljubljana.

MAY LIVE TO REGRET committing this piece of advice to print, but you should go to Slovenia and you should go soon, because eventually this all-but-unknown country, with its medieval villages, onion-dome spires, idealistic love of the arts, and vigorous wines will no longer be hidden in plain sight.

From its borders, clockwise from the north, you can step into Austria, Hungary, Croatia, and Italy. It has Alps and wind-raked valleys, cobblestoned streets and modern highways wending through vineyards and farms. Slovenia is a place where a meandering car can suddenly be overtaken by a buzzing burst of touring cyclists in Day-Glo—it's like finding oneself in a school of tropical fish—and then in a beat they're gone, around the bend, heading for the next vowel-deprived village. Trbovlje, Krško, Črnomelj—in Slovene, even nearby Trieste, Italy, is spelled without a single, solitary vowel: Trst. Slovenia is also a place where anything resembling a river in anything resembling a town after dark in summertime will likely as not have great arcing bouquets of fireworks over it, accompanied by the sounds of artillery. Desk clerks, when asked, cannot come up with the occasion. Festival, anniversary? "We just like fireworks," one confides.

Slovenia was once part of Yugoslavia, which itself was created out of numerous Big Bangs and was, from the end of World War II to the 1990's, held together under the firm but practical rule of a marshal, Josip Broz Tito, and his successors. Yugoslavia, though far from being an anti-Western country, and far from being an exclusively Socialist state, was part of the Eastern bloc, and when the Soviet Union and the other European Socialist countries began to fall in the late 1980's, and Tito himself was no longer alive, Slovenia was the first state within Yugoslavia to successfully declare its independence. There was a brief war, which lasted only 10 days, with very few casualties. Soon, of course, all that remained of Yugoslavia was in tragic turmoil, suddenly consumed by the worst kind of identity politics, with Serbians, Croatians, and Bosnians swirling in an orgy of so-called ethnic cleansing.

Yet Slovenia remained remarkably peaceful in this brutal period, and its preference for tranquillity and civility is evident as soon as you enter the country. In 10 days, my girlfriend and I didn't hear a raised voice, or see an untended garden. In fact, gardening seems like the national pastime, with cascading riots of blooms in every yard, on every balcony, foaming over the sides of ceramic pots and sprawling up walls and over trellises, all carefully groomed into one civil- and civic-minded aesthetic. How is it that every single garden exhibits this elegantly controlled chaos of color, that every stack of firewood looks like some kind of tongue-in-groove wooden puzzle that a genius child put together?

It may simply be that it's literally a way for a country that has been pressed like a flower between the leaves of a heavy book to bloom again.

LJUBLJANA

In 1895, when Ljubljana was still a part of the once-powerful Austro-Hungarian Empire (note to American and Chinese oligarchs: all things must pass), the city suffered a major earthquake, and the most historic and picturesque sections of this small city that exist now were in fact built or rebuilt in the early 20th century. The leading architect of the time, Jože Plečnik, remains a revered figure in Slovenia; he designed the monumental Church of St. Francis, the bustling central market, the great university's immense library, and the city's emblematic and always busy Triple Bridge, a graceful pedestrian-only cement trident across the narrow Ljubljanica River. His sometimes avant-garde, early modern style can be seen all over the city.

The Slovenes' reverence for Plečnik is rivaled by the high esteem in which they hold their great national poet, France Prešeren, whose Romantic lyrics, written in the mid 19th century, have been a spring from which the roots of Slovenia's national identity have been nourished—in secret during times of subjugation and openly now in this time of autonomy and independence. Plečnik and Prešeren have an ideal meeting place in Ljubljana, where a statue of the poet stands a few yards from the Triple Bridge. Cross the water and you see, along the waterfront, an overwhelmingly Slovenian crowd enjoying beers, coffees, wines, gelati, and pizzas in one another's company on a wine-woozy summer afternoon.

One *trg* (square) leads to the next—past a fair-trade children's clothing store for idealistic young couples, galleries showing local artists, a shop devoted entirely to locally harvested salt and several others to gelato—until we are on Stari Trg, one of the most beautiful streets in Ljubljana. Following the wave-patterned sidewalk around the corner we're at Gornji Trg and the Antiq Hotel, which was not very long ago a carpentry shop, and which is now firmly and delightfully exploring its own Mitteleuropa personality, with rattling teacups, floral carpeting, handmade

■ Ljubljana Castle has magnificent views of the city below, its spires, its practically motionless canal, and its sense of people holding their collective breath while the storms of history pass over.

lace (a Slovenian specialty), steep staircases that would befit Dr. Caligari himself, and hallways full of sudden right turns and unexpected windows. Our room's windows open up to the hotel's back garden. It is here that we discover our first Slovene to raise his voice. But in all fairness, it needs to be pointed out that this shrieking lad is not quite two years old, and he seems to be conversing with a butterscotch-colored house cat that could double as an ottoman.

It is also here that we discover we have neglected to pack our powerful sleeping pills. We make a stab at sleep au naturel and end up instead back outside sitting along the water, watching random fireworks above and a group of folk dancers below, on a platform just higher than the Ljubljanica. After that, gelato, and a late-night stroll across the Dragon Bridge, adorned at its corners with queasily realistic dragons, their scales, claws,

and ribbed wings the perfect metaphor for first-night-in-a-foreign-country insomnia.

We keep walking along the intermittently marked path from the city center, and in about 15 cardiovascular, birdsongy early-morning minutes, there it is, the city's most prominent landmark: Ljubljana Castle, built in the ninth century, rebuilt in the 16th, and variously used as a home for ruling nobles, a jail, a poorhouse, and a military fortress.

There's a lovely outdoor café up top, and a stall offering free books and magazines to anyone who wants to loll in the sun and read. But most of the people here have hiked up for the magnificent views of the serene city below, its spires, its practically motionless canal, and its strong sense of a people holding their collective breath while the storms of history pass over.

Having failed to sleep at one Antiq Hotel we seek to change our luck by checking in to the rather more luxurious (yet equally offbeat) Antiq Palace Hotel & Spa. Once a palazzo built for a wealthy and well-placed Austrian family as their in-town residence, when the Austrians fled Ljubljana during World War I, the majestic and graceful stone structure was converted into an apartment house. But as the years passed, the space eventually became derelict, and would remain so until two locals purchased it a few years ago and transformed it into a showcase for their taste, a living example of their idea of comfort, intimacy, and luxury.

With its thick walls and high ceilings (most of them still bearing the original frescoes), the hotel stays warm in the winter and cool in the summer, and the rooms themselves are immense and eccentrically homey in their décor. In its public spaces, the hotel is a mix of courtyard and columns, whitewashed walls and Art Deco sconces. The winding, narrow street was built near one of the walls of Emona, as the city was called in its ancient Roman incarnation. Now the street is home to one of the city's great music schools, and guests at the Antiq Palace can dine in the courtyard with background music supplied by students honing their skills a few hundred feet away.

The sounds of music not only fill the courtyard, but also come pouring through the open French windows of our suite after dark. A block from the hotel in the newly restored Congress Square (designed by the ubiquitous Plečnik), 1,100 musicians and singers are

rehearsing for a gala performance of Mahler's massive Symphony No. 8, with teams of technicians setting up the stage and the sound system, and trumpeters accustoming themselves to their places on the stone balconies of the buildings that line the square.

Valery Gergiev, the Russian conductor, and an orchestra and chorus made up mostly of Slovenes and Croatians carry the impromptu audience of passersby, diners and drinkers, and wide-awake travelers through a spellbinding performance that captures the reach and ambition of this profound work. Much better than sleeping, even if sleeping were an option.

PTUJ

From Ljubljana to Ptuj is an easy drive on well-marked roads through luscious farmland, crops cultivated at 60-degree angles, pole beans as tall as two men, fields of corn, and a steady procession of small towns, each one pinned to the landscape by a church spire. Ptuj straddles the Drava River, green as grass, but clear enough to show the vigorous webbed feet of the mallards etching chevrons as they move upstream.

The town itself is a medieval maze of one-way streets, where women in capri pants somehow are able to nimbly negotiate the ankle-snapping cobblestones in defiant high heels. Here, too, the cafés are full of conversation, relaxing, smoking, talking—miraculously immune to the fiendish tirade of Europop music, songs consisting of a techno beat with random American phrases repeated over and over, a cringe-inducing and increasingly common misrepresentation of our culture.

Despite its susceptibility to this manufactured madness, Ptuj is also the home of several serious schools of music, and as we walk along the Drava watching the lazy life of the river, from an open window wafts the sound of a fledgling string quartet.

Ptuj has been open for business since the Stone Age. It has been home to Celts, Magyars, Slavs, and various Hapsburgs, whose double chins and imperious stares are on display in supposedly flattering portraits housed

A swimming class
on a pier in Piran.
Left: Piran's seafront.
Opposite: St. George
Cathedral, in Piran.

in the town's great castle. Room after room of these vain faces are putting us on edge, not to mention their finery and table settings on display in glass cases and, most challenging of all, depictions of *The Odyssey* with cavorting noblemen and their girlfriends woven into tall tapestries. It's possible we need a nap.

BLED

The landscape between Ptuj and Bled has the beautiful, utilitarian contours of a sailor's knot, and we drive, winding our way through vineyards, up and down steep roads lined with limestone that is piebald with moss. Our resting place, on the edge of Idrija, is the Hotel Kendov Dvorec, a graceful manor decorated with handmade lace and a Princess Grace type of Catholicism—cherubs lolling on tabletops and pedestals indoors and out. Vaguely ecclesiastical Muzak whispers from unseen speakers.

Early the next morning, we leave the Hotel Kendov and drive to Bled. Pronounced just like it looks, there's the town Bled and the Lake Bled and then the Vila Bled, where we're staying. If you believed in vampires, this is where they would have their country home, and yet it's

the opposite of gloomy: a sun-drenched town clustered around a brilliant blue lake, at the center of which is a fairy-tale island with a church, set upon in the summer months by boats bearing brides and their grooms.

We hike straight up the side of a cliff to Bled Castle, which turned 1,000 in 2011 and presides over not only the lake and the town but also what seems like the entire vast blue and green region, the views from its parapets and stone stairways sweeping and majestic. There's a museum that tells the history of the region, a chapel, a Gutenberg printing press, a restaurant, and an herbal gallery.

Going back down the same way we came, we then take a turn around Lake Bled. As always, the trail is perfectly groomed but doesn't lose its path-through-the-forest quality. The luxury lakeside hotels make their presence known mostly in understated ways— brass-plated names on ivy-covered fences and boat landings accessible only by key.

The Vila Bled served as a summer residence for the Yugoslav royal family and then for Tito, and the hotel staff is happy to show us through his quarters, a maze of polished oak cabinetry and floors with an

incongruous number of coat hooks and a wall of sheer curtains overlooking trees and lake. A mural in the villa's music room depicts the revolution, culminating in a mother with a child on her shoulder—a kind of socialist-realist Madonna and Child—muscles rippling, eyes radiating joy and purpose, waving a banner with a red star, an iconography that seems both thrilling and sad, coming as it does in this building at the end of a long columned driveway and a parking lot dotted with late-model German cars.

PIRAN

The oval-shaped and marble-clad Tartini Square in Piran, a medieval town on the tip of the Slovenian seaboard, is home to St. Peter's Church and is surrounded by alleys opening onto alleys opening onto stairways and small, ancient-looking shops—parking is on the edge of all this, so it's only unmotorized traffic through the cool stone streets. Five minutes' walking in any direction and the sea, or the Gulf of Piran, is visible. Although there are most certainly better dining establishments down the intriguing streets of Piran, we go for the waterfront promenade, where we can

watch the sunset and people at the same time. The air turns a dark blue and a jazz combo starts up two doors down from our chosen spot.

Our hotel is a couple of miles away, in Portorož: the Kempinski Palace, an opulent establishment overlooking a more traditional and touristed beachfront. At a late breakfast on the formal dining-room terrace, the buffet tables are laden with food as photogenic as the other diners. The house-baked cereal—dark wheat twigs; cashew quarters; crumbly granola—makes muesli look like Captain Crunch. We're slowly being schooled in the Slovenian aesthetic, just in time to leave.

We have, of course, finally been sleeping through the night. We attribute that luxury to having become accustomed to the bucolic mysteries of the place. And now it's time to go home. For me, heading home is one of the greatest pleasures of travel, but today my heart is heavy, and it takes me a few moments to realize why.

For the most part, when we travel we are always there a bit after the fact, chasing the thing that has already occurred. So much of traveling is doing what other travelers have done, but Slovenia, perhaps more than any place we have ever visited, belongs to us. Yes, it is a secret place, but it cannot remain so for much longer. ✦

Adapted from "Secret Slovenia," by Scott Spencer.

GUIDE

STAY

Antiq Hotel
3 Gornji Trg, Ljubljana; 386-1/ 421-3560; antiqhotel.eu. **$**

Antiq Palace Hotel & Spa
10 Gosposka Ul., Ljubljana; 386-8/389-6700; antiqpalace.com. **$$**

Hotel Kendov Dvorec
2 Na Griču, Spodnja Idrija; 386-5/372-5100; kendov-dvorec.com. **$$**

Hotel Mitra Ptuj;
6 Prešernova Ul., Ptuj; 386-2/ 787-7455; hotel-mitra.si. **$**

Kempinski Palace Portorož
45 Obala; 386-5/692-7000; kempinski.com. **$$**

Vila Bled
26 Cesta Svobode, Bled; 386-4/579-1500; vila-bled.com. **$$**

DO

Bled Castle
11 Cesta Svobode, Bled; blejski-grad.si.

Church of St. Francis
Bolniška Ul., Ljubljana; slovenia.info.

Ljubljana Castle
1 Grajska Planota, Ljubljana; ljubljanskigrad.si.

Ptuj Castle
1 Muzejski Trg, Ptuj; ptuj.info.

Off the coast
of Hvar.

HVAR, CROATIA

The jet set's newest escape

HVAR IS THE LATEST OF THE international playgrounds, heir to that noble lineage running from Cannes and Capri through St. Bart's and South Beach. The island is so relentlessly gorgeous it makes your eyes ache: the harbor edged with bougainvillea, the exquisitely aged Renaissance façades, the nonstop parade of caramelized torsos. You could spend a month in tiny Hvar Town and never tire of the daily routine. At the morning market, Claudia Cardinale look-alikes rub shoulders with locals shopping for figs. As the sun climbs higher, breakfast seamlessly merges with lunch. Try the buttery spaghetti with lobster at Macondo, on a narrow cobblestoned alley off the main square. Come twilight, the crowd congregates at Carpe Diem, a waterfront club whose long arched stone patio is occupied by well-heeled revelers dancing until the wee hours. If you left your mega-yacht in St.-Tropez, hole up at the nearby Adriana Hvar Spa Hotel, with nine spacious purple-and-cream suites that overlook the boat-filled marina.

GUIDE

STAY
Adriana Hvar Spa Hotel
Fabrika; 385-21/750-200; suncanihvar.com. **$$**

EAT
Macondo Groda
Hvar Town; 385-21/742-850; open April–October. **$$**

DRINK
Carpe Diem Riva
Hvar Town; 385-21/742-369; carpe-diem-hvar.com; open May–September.

europe

ODESSA, UKRAINE

Waxing nostalgic in the Pearl by the Black Sea

The Odessa waterfront at night. Above: The Odessa National Theater of Opera & Ballet. Opposite: Cookies and marmalades on display at Café Kompot.

ISTORY NEVER FEELS musty or dead in Odessa. Partly that's because this flamboyant Black Sea port, geopolitically in Ukraine but with a soul and esprit all its own, is such a young city, just over two centuries old. But mainly it's because Odessites gossip about historical personages as if they had all shared a Soviet communal apartment.

"*Our* duke!" proclaims a vendor of sailor shirts, gesturing at the gray Neoclassical statue. We're on Primorsky Boulevard, the acacia-lined promenade fronting the city's seaside heights. *Our* duke is, of course, Armand-Emmanuel du Plessis, Duke de Richelieu—a relative of the famous French cardinal, exile from the French Revolution, and, as the city's mayor between 1803 and 1814, the man credited with the splendid emergence of this "Pearl by the Sea."

"Our duke had to flee France," Comrade Sailor Shirts confides, luridly. "On account of an arranged marriage...*to a hunchback dwarf!*"

His transhistorical scandal-mongering delights me. Suddenly the statue's stony gaze under his laurel wreath turns a lot less aloof.

My mother and I sit on a Primorsky bench, doing what the locals do—cracking sunflower seeds. Nearby, on the iconic granite Potemkin Steps, my boyfriend, Barry, is gleefully "re-enacting" the famous close-ups from *Battleship Potemkin,* Sergey Eisenstein's 1925 masterpiece of cinema (and propaganda fabrication) about a shipboard mutiny. We've been in Odessa only a few hours and already our heads are spinning. But that's why we've come: to soak up the outsize lore of this vibrant, garrulous port variously known as Southern Palmyra, Babylon on the Black Sea, or "Odessa-Mama" to its inhabitants. After St. Petersburg (Peter the Great's northern window on Europe), sunny Odessa (Catherine the Great's southern window on Europe) is the most mythologized place in Russian cultural history, the birthplace of some of last century's greatest musicians, writers, humorists,

The Presidential Suite at Hotel Bristol. Right: Taking in the sun at Odessa's Big Fountain beach.

The Potemkln Steps. Left: A fishmonger at Privoz Market.

and gangsters. Even if it has formally "belonged" to Ukraine since 1991.

My mom and I bring with us our own Odessa issues. Though born here in 1934, Mom grew up in Moscow, and only knew her native city from her 1970's seaside vacations with me. Ah, our un-idyllic Odessa Augusts, bivouacking on flimsy cots with mom's local relatives. In the concrete courtyard of their communal-apartment block, giant underwear flapped, drying, while neighbors fried smelly fish on their Primus stoves. As a kid I regarded Odessa with imperialist Muscovite condescension—and wild curiosity. The Odessites seemed piratical and operatic. They spoke a strangely accented Russian, and gave directions in negatives: *See our gorgeous, glorious opera house? Well, you don't want to turn there.* At Langeron beach we'd spread our meager towels, squeezed amid reddened Socialist flesh. Mom would smear my frail Moscow body with healing mineral Odessa mud, and there I'd lie, pining for our cold northern capital.

And yet after my mom and I emigrated to America in 1974, I found myself missing Odessa. The *myth* of Odessa. Now, strolling here again, I recognize Odessa-Mama, and don't. The new Southern Palmyra seems like another freshly dolled up semi-globalized post-Soviet city of around one million, with the requisite Max Mara boutiques and smiley youths herding at a chain called Top Sendvich. Signs are in Ukrainian now. The Soviet grime and provincial inferiority have been covered up with fresh, blazing pastels—pistachio, custard, sky blue. But still. Off wide, arrow-straight avenues, laundry flaps in crumbling courtyards and melon-bosomed matrons shriek at their husbands: "Moron! DON'T nauseate into my ear!" And once again Mom and I gape at the fantastical trove of architectural detail: lascivious caryatids bare their breasts to the pungent Black Sea breezes; Atlases writhe under the weight of preposterously ornate porticoes. The taste for such flamboyant eclecticism was set in the mid 19th century, when Odessa was so flush from its status as a grain-shipping free port that its *bindiuzhniki* (draymen) rolled cigarettes from 10-ruble bills. The local populace was eclectic from the start. Greeks, Russians, Italians, Armenians, French, and especially Jews—all flocked to the rollicking port seeking their fortunes. The center's

Neoclassical layout? The work of a Dutch engineer. The cakelike neo-Baroque opera house? Built in the 1880's by the Viennese architects who designed the Vienna State Opera. Even the Potemkin Steps were a British job.

Odessa has a Greek Street, an Italian Boulevard, and a French Boulevard. But "the queen of all streets," to quote one native son, is Deribasovskaya—named after José de Ribas, a Neapolitan (of Irish and Catalan stock) who in 1789, while in the service of Catherine the Great, conquered the dusty Ottoman fort that would become Odessa. We watch the action on the cobblestones below from the second floor of Café Kompot. Belles in stilettos; *bêtes* in black leather jackets; oldsters in panama hats—everyone eventually ends up here at Kompot, the grand café named after the idyllic fruit compotes of our Soviet summers. The bi-level space is a canny mash-up of U.S.S.R. nostalgia and flea-market chic. At our antique wooden table we chase spoonfuls of bracing *solianka*, a meat soup zesty with capers and olives, with shots of devilishly warming horseradish-and-honey vodka. "Just like my grandma's!" Mom moons over the plump *syrniki* (farmer-cheese patties).

Kompot's co-owner, local restaurant czar Savely (Savva) Libkin, stops by. Fiftyish, wiry, and dapper, Libkin exemplifies your post-Soviet *biznesman,* but with savvy *and* soul. Like me, he grew up in a crammed Soviet apartment with a grandfather who "didn't have one bad word for Stalin." In 1993, "still pre-*koka-kola,*" he opened Odessa's first pizza chain, then graduated to far more stylish concepts such as Kompot, the nostalgic Dacha, and the haute-rustic Steakhouse nearby. "Moscow?" he snorts. "The poor can't afford it; the rich spit on it." Libkin himself jets to Paris or Piedmont, Italy, on eating research trips. And yet hearing him talk about old Odessa's Jewish cuisine you can practically taste the garlicky wallop of his grandmother's *kotleti* (Soviet burgers) or picture his grandpa laboring over *forshmak*, the iconic local chopped herring. Libkin espouses a mission: "To return Odessa cuisine to the Odessites."

His hipster daughter, a fashion photographer living in Tokyo, turns up. "Papa," she says, "I need a severed head for a photo shoot."

"*Nyet problem,*" Papa replies. "Human or animal?"

We bid them good luck and zoom off to the opera. From our orchestra seats, the interior of the recently restored theater resembles a red-velvet-lined hatbox inside of which a delirious prankster has exploded a bag of gold dust. Plaster angels throw their limbs from high perches. How opera-crazy are Odessites? So crazy that moms used to name their girls Traviata (never mind the connotation in Italian). On tonight's bill is *Iolanta*, a Tchaikovsky caper about a blind princess. The soprano shrieks; the tenor bleats; but still I'm overcome with emotion. This is the building where my grandfather proposed to my grandmother. Anna Pavlova, Enrico Caruso, and Sarah Bernhardt all roamed this stage. During World War II bombardments, radio bulletins began with, "The opera house is still standing."

Next day, we're off in Libkin's black Audi for a tour of the famous Privoz Market, which dates from the early 19th century. Libkin laments recent modernizations—"all that's left is the cheating"—but I'm fascinated by the cacophonous sprawl. On teeming sidewalks Moldovan gypsies hawk potions (herbal Viagra, anyone?). Inside the vintage meat hall, Mom and I swoon first at the pristinely preserved Stalin-era artwork of Soviet "abundance," then at the porcine extravagance: kielbasa garlands, mosaics of quivering headcheese, fat-studded blood pudding sold by hulking dames in outrageously frilly aprons. The produce aisles resound with endearing Odessa vernacular. "*Rybonka*, my little fishie! Stop touching my cucumbers already. They won't get any harder!"

That night we have an ecumenical seder at Libkin's best restaurant, Dacha. On leafy French Boulevard, which is lined with 19th-century summer houses, he has restored a cream-colored mansion set in a rambling garden of poplar and fruit trees. The warm twilight is scented with apple blossoms; Soviet sixties pop wafts moonward. Waiters greet customers with herbal vodkas, garlicky house-made pickles in wooden tubs, and Ukrainian *lardo*.

"*Oy gevalt*! My childhood, I'm gonna faint," an old matron gulps, touring the cozy rooms decorated with sentimental knickknacks from Soviet apartments.

"In Odessa we had like a hundred nationalities," declares Sasha, the suave service manager. "Our passion for feta, a Greek legacy. Roasted peppers, a Moldovan touch. Grilling from the Armenians; borscht, *vareniki* dumplings, and stuffed cabbage from the Ukrainians." Dacha's stuffed cabbage is succulent and petite as a pinkie. And here are the Jewish specialties we've been promised: velvety hand-chopped *forshmak* of fat herring; poached rooster suspended in flavorful aspic. We finish with majestic *kambala*, the meaty, snow-white Black Sea turbot sizzled on an iron griddle.

On our last day we diet on museums—and cultural myths. Our morning perambulation takes us past a tawny-yellow Neoclassical building. Anxious kids haul cello and violin cases inside. This is the Stolyarsky Music School, I realize—a legendary production plant of young virtuosi named after the early-20th-century violin instructor Pyotr Stolyarsky. Frenetic Paganini passages soar from a Stolyarsky window, and I think of another Odessa virtuoso: Isaac Babel, the magician of the Russian short story. Born in the Jewish neighborhood of Modolvanka in 1894, Babel captured Odessa's brash *kolorit* (atmosphere) in compressed, pungent prose that's electric, almost violent, with metaphor. A "factory that churned out child prodigies," Babel wrote, hinting at Stolyarsky, "of Jewish dwarfs in lace collars and patent-leather shoes."

Reminiscences about Babel draw us to the Odessa Literary Museum, founded in the late 1980's, near the Opera. Inside the powder-blue 19th-century palace, sumptuous rooms host displays on Odessa's cultural eras and the writers who were either born or wrote here. The green hall dedicated to Pushkin is the museum's crowd-pleaser. Pushkin spent a year of political exile

GUIDE

EAT

Café Kompot
*20 Deribasovskaya Ul.;
380-48/237-6801;
compot.ua.* **$$**

Dacha
*85 Frantsuzky Bul.; 380-48/
714-3119; dacha.com.ua.* **$$**

Steakhouse
*20 Deribasovskaya Ul.;
380-48/234-8782;
steak.od.ua.* **$$**

DO

**Migdal Shorashim
(Jewish Museum)**
66 Nejinskaya Ul.,
*apartment 10;
380-48/728-9743;
migdal.ru.*

Odessa Literary Museum
*2 Lanzheronovskaya Ul.;
380-48/722-3370;
museum-literature.
odessa.ua.*

**Odessa National Theater
of Opera & Ballet**
*1 Tchaikovsky Per.;
380-48/740-5147;
opera.odessa.ua.*

Privoz Market
*Privoznaya Ul.;
ukraine.com.*

in Odessa in the 1820's, immortalizing the city in the "Odessa stanzas" of his verse novel, *Eugene Onegin.* Immortal, too, is the gossip: how Pushkin cuckolded the regional governor, who got him back by giving the poet the assignment of making a survey of locust infestation.

The Soviet century had a different plague in store for writers and poets. We halt before the museum's most chilling artifact: the signature wire spectacles of Isaac Babel. The writer had worn glasses since childhood. The NKVD (the KGB's predecessor) came for him in 1939, torturing and then killing him. The last photo of Babel shows him in captivity, battered and—so piercingly— without his glasses. We walk out into bright sunshine wiping away stabbing tears.

The city's greatest fiddlers, litterateurs, gangsters, and wits were Jewish, of course. And so we devote our last hours to Migdal Shorashim, the tiny Jewish museum. Being within the czarist Pale of Settlement, the cosmopolitan port attracted Jews from all over the empire. "By the early 20th century," explains the museum's doleful curator, "Odessa had the world's third-largest Jewish population after New York and Warsaw." This is where native son Vladimir Jabotinsky developed his firebrand right-wing Jewish nationalism because cosmopolitan Odessa also suffered some of Europe's ugliest pogroms (my own great-grandparents' baby was murdered in front of them in 1905). Some 100,000 Odessa Jews perished in World War II; today, they number only around 35,000. "But we're still a vibrant community," declares the curator.

We peruse the cramped museum's ethnographic hodgepodge. A century-old cleaver has my mom flashing back to her grandmother Maria's gefilte fish.

"Next year in Jerusalem," the mournful man salutes as we leave. "No! Next year I want to rent an apartment *here* in Odessa!" my mother exclaims. "Can it be?" she wonders to me. "I've finally fallen in love with the city where I was born?" ✦

Adapted from "Odessa," by Anya von Bremzen.

Galata Bridge crosses the Golden Horn to Karaköy.

ISTANBUL

An ancient city shows its modern side

IF YOU WANT THE PERFECT SNAPSHOT of modern-day Istanbul, look no further than the Beyoğlu quarter, a collection of lively neighborhoods on the north bank of the Golden Horn, which is receiving a jolt of energy thanks to a slew of stylish hotel and boutique openings. Here, you're just as likely to find Converse-donning hipsters sipping raki—a cousin to absinthe—at a boisterous *meyhane* as Muslim women in head scarves shopping at trendy shops. In the Pera district, rising fashion star Serra Tucker has debuted the chic Misela, tapping into the city's vast network of tanneries and metalsmiths to produce bold statement handbags and clutches. At Old Sandal, in Galata, you'll get a taste of the city's flourishing reputation as a hothouse for the world's best cobblers. Peruse the shelves of leather boots and oxfords, or have a pair custom-made.

For years, Beyoğlu has had little in the way of alluring retreats. Enter the sexy Georges Hotel Galata, a refurbished 1800's-era apartment building on a cobblestoned back-alley with no signage or traditional check-in. A sleek glass elevator whisks you to 17 rooms and 3 spacious suites done up in exposed brick and luxe flourishes such as blue mosaic rain showers and L'Occitane amenities, with French doors that open onto balconies overlooking the Bosphorus. From there, it's a short walk down winding narrow streets to the Witt Istanbul Hotel. The 18 loftlike suites have full kitchenettes, slick leather sofas, and Turkish marble bathrooms—it's like the pied à terre you've always wanted.

GUIDE

STAY
Witt Istanbul Hotel
26 Defterdar Yokusu;
90-212/293-1500;
wittistanbul.com. **$**

Georges Hotel Galata
24 Serdar-i Ekrem Sk.;
90-212/244-2423;
georges.com. **$**

SHOP
Misela
28 Asmali Mescit Sk.;
90-212/292-2844;
miselaistanbul.com.

Old Sandal
10-A Serdar-i Ekrem Sk.;
90-212/292-8647;
oldsandal.com.tr.

Lounging by the
pool at the
Perivolas hotel.

SANTORINI, GREECE

A peaceful Greek idyll on the Aegean Sea

IF THERE WERE EVER A PLACE that could get by on its looks, it would be this mythic island. Whitewashed cave houses framed by bougainvillea and backed by blue-domed churches spill down the rim of an ancient volcanic crater; at sunset, the Sea of Crete is bathed in a rosy glow. Yet as compelling as the scenery may be, Santorini's true appeal lies in its wealth of diversions—extraordinary wines, black (or red or white) beaches, and archaeological sites from the prehistoric era, such as the Akrotiri settlement, often referred to as the "Minoan Pompeii." Make your base the white stone Perivolas hotel, in the village of Oia. Set within the alcoves of 300-year-old caves, the 20 suites have vaulted ceilings and private cliffside terraces that seem to hover at the crater's edge. For a romantic dinner, the open-air balcony at Assyrtico Wine Restaurant, in a renovated 1960's mansion in Firá, overlooks the volcanic islands of Nea Kameni and Palea. Order the flaky-pastry-wrapped *saganaki* (traditional fried cheese) with fig jam and local wine from Argyros Estate, then make your way back to Oia for a stroll along the nine-mile-long walkway.

GUIDE

STAY
Perivolas
*Oia; 30-22860/71308;
perivolas.gr.* **$$$$**

EAT
Assyrtico Wine Restaurant
*Firá; 30-22860/22463;
assyrtico-restaurant.com.* **$$$**

Elephants outside
a guest room
at Old Mondoro
Bush Camp,
in Lower Zambezi
National Park.

AFRICA +
THE MIDDLE EAST

MOZAMBIQUE

The ultimate castaway fantasy

A view of the bay from the terrace at Ibo Island Lodge.

Villa Sands, on Ilha de Moçambique. Right: An Ibo island local.

C AN AN ISLAND BE, in the best possible sense of the word, haunted?

On Ibo, in the Quirimbas Archipelago, off the coast of northern Mozambique—a place that is kinetic with the colors and textures of its past—I am compelled to consider the possibility. Ibo radiates with the memories of the Arab sultans and Portuguese explorers who came and went on the trade winds, enriching the surrounding coast with their cultural patrimony even as they plundered its resources. The echoes of their dominions merge along its tidal shores and in the near-deserted streets of its colonial Stone Town. Traces of vanquished prosperity and forsaken grandeur linger in mercantile arcades and crumbling Lusitanian villas in faded shades of yellow and pink. Trees grow up inside some of them, limbs reaching through windows; florid patches of black-green mold spread across their walls like great abstract watercolors.

That Ibo is so redolent of a rich history should come as no surprise: Mozambique is a country whose past has never quite relinquished its hold on the psychic landscape. Bordered by Tanzania, Malawi, Zambia, Zimbabwe, South Africa, and Swaziland, its coast stretches more than a thousand miles; in the north, it is a place of tidal flats and mangrove forests, coconut plantations, boundless blue skies.

Today, this coast is confronted with an electrified future. If you've read about northern Mozambique, it was likely in the context of the discovery of vast gas and oil fields in the Rovuma Basin and at various offshore sites, which has invited exploration of the 21st-century sort: planes and helicopters from major U.S., Russian, and Chinese energy conglomerates jostle for position on the runway of the one-hangar airport in Pemba, gateway to the Quirimbas.

Simultaneously, though, northern Mozambique's unique, frozen-in-amber heritage is attracting private investment, conservation organizations, and those in search of untrammeled beauty. A handful of the latter have turned their talents to hotel-keeping—here in the Quirimbas as well as on Ilha de Moçambique, some 200 miles to the south. Though their aesthetic visions vary, all marry respect for history, architecture, and nature with a passion for thoughtful design.

One of the first hotels to open was Ibo Island Lodge, on the edge of Stone Town on the northwestern coast of tiny Ibo (it measures only a couple of miles across). Bush planes ferry visitors back and forth to the island from Pemba on a 20-minute flight, though at low tide one could conceivably walk all the way from the mainland. Villagers, most from the Kimwani tribe, creak along Ibo's sand paths on rusty bicycles, banana bunches slung over the handlebars; young women wrapped in vibrant *capulanas* stroll hand in hand, their faces white with a hydrating paste made from the *musiro* tree. Silversmiths—part of a once-thriving tradition that in the past decade has been resuscitated by the Aga Khan Foundation—work in the shade of porticoes in Stone Town, shaping wire-thin segments of metal into intricate earrings and pendants. I take a walk around the island with Anli Madu, one of the lodge's easygoing guides, who was born and raised here; he translates as the village's healer explains shyly how she treats the patients whom the nurses from Ibo's lone infirmary have deemed beyond their care.

The lodge itself is housed in restored 19th-century Portuguese villas, set side by side at the sea rampart's edge. Earlier this year, a third villa at the south end of the property was added; it brings the number of rooms to 14 and can be booked as a fully staffed private villa. The mostly local waitstaff and housekeepers, young and quick to share a laugh, pad about with iced juices.

Ibo Island Lodge's owners, Zimbabwean Fiona Record and her husband, Kevin, have coaxed its interiors back to genteel, but not overly polished, life—good, because excessive polish would, here, be uncomfortably untrue. The décor mixes faded antiques from Goa with contemporary photography and carved teak and mahogany chests and sideboards. There are vintage clawfoot bathtubs in some suites, marble showers in others. Rooms open onto deep verandas running the length of each building; folding carved-wood Swahili screens between them afford privacy, while fans spin above—though in the early morning hours (when one of the staff comes with coffee) the breeze along the bay is still fresh.

Sailing a dhow off Ibo Island. Above: The Barracuda Villa at Azura at Quilálea.

That ocean, changeable but omnipresent, is a protagonist here. Ibo was key to the spice route plied by Arab sultanates as far back as the eighth century; it was they who purportedly built the fortification that later became the Fortim de São João, Ibo's oldest fort. Dramatic tidal fluctuations create massive flats around Ibo's rough coral coastline, so beach chairs and umbrellas don't factor into the setting. The lodge's solution for sunseekers is a dhow, which collects you from the nearby pier and heads north, toward Matemo Island, where you reach your own private paradise: a sandbar, newly emerged from the ocean. The crew sets up a tent and umbrellas; chairs and towels are laid in its shade; brunch (or lunch) is served. It's pure castaway joy, yours for hours without another soul in sight; until the tide turns, and the ocean starts to reclaim it.

If Ibo Island Lodge is the Quirimbas Archipelago at its most atmospheric, Azura at Quilálea, a private island resort that's a 40-minute powerboat ride to the south, is a Crusoe fantasy executed at the five-star level— the one that includes sundowners served by butler-hosts and Heidi Klein beachwear in the boutique. A tiny, half-mile-long coralline outcrop covered in marula trees and the odd baobab, Quilálea has been elegantly shaped without losing its essential wildness: the path that meanders from reception to the groovy sunken beach bar to the dive center is paved, but you might share it with the occasional (entirely harmless) monitor lizard. The nine thatched-roof villas are spare and cool, with polished concrete floors and floor-length linen curtains. Four are strung along the east coast; five face west, toward the Indian Ocean sunsets; Villa Quilálea blows out the template with significantly more space and a bathroom with a view. For all the guests, each of the exquisite meals is served in a different location on the island: one day my breakfast was in a tiny cove; that night I dined under a sea chestnut lit up by lanterns.

Stella Bettany, the Johannesburg-based British owner of Azura Retreats—which reopened Quilálea in late 2011— believes the island "has an immense soul. We wanted to keep that unique castaway quality," she says. Creature comforts and 2-to-1 staff-to-guest ratio notwithstanding, nothing about Quilálea is exclusive in the undemocratic and un-fun sense of that word. Millions went into the refurbishment, she notes, but most of it underground or back-of-house; so out front, despite a pronounced

chicness (aquamarine and turquoise prevail, with lots of grass matting underfoot), barefoot still feels like a perfectly acceptable dress code. Bettany champions Quirimbas culture as well; guests are encouraged to take the speedboat—or the resort's helicopter—to Ibo to visit the forts, Stone Town, and village (Azura collaborates with Ibo Island Lodge, whose guides are available for cultural tours). South African managers Paul and Kelly Ricklan are consummate hosts, moving fluidly from urbane chat to serious wilderness discourse to divespeak. "I lived in southern Mozambique for eight and a half years, and it's beautiful," Kelly Ricklan says. "But here the confluence of nature and culture is just unique. And it's far wilder." Azura guests can fish from the main beach and kayak the perimeter of the island. Or they can lie on their private decks and listen to the thump of

■ Northern Mozambique's unique, frozen-in-amber heritage is attracting conservation groups and travelers in search of untrammeled beauty.

waves against coral, appreciating how Azura's very cushy version of the Middle of Nowhere manages to impart an inimitably Mozambican sense of place.

There is no more definitively Mozambican place, however, than Ilha de Moçambique, off the coast of Nampula province—a bumpy but beautiful six-hour drive due south from Pemba. About two miles long and a couple of thousand feet wide, and reached by a long causeway, Ilha, as locals refer to it, is a 500-year-old fortified island city that is a microcosm of an empire and its demise. Vasco da Gama landed here in 1498 and the Portuguese colonized it in 1505, displacing the Arabs who had for centuries made this a principal port (its name is said to derive from that of Moussa Al-Bik, the sultan who controlled its trade). In 1507, it was made the capital of Portuguese East Africa, which it would remain for almost 400 years; in the mid 1600's, its population comprised Africans, Portuguese, Arab and Macanese traders, and Indians from the imperial provinces in Goa. Local children still scour the shallows

Ibo Island at low tide. Left: A stone terrace at Terraço das Quitandas.

for beads from Kerala and fragments of Jiajing Ming porcelain, remnants of 350-year-old shipwrecks, to sell.

The dissolution of Portuguese power was Ilha's saving grace: by 1898, when the capital moved to Lourenço Marques (now Maputo), slave trading had been outlawed for 20 years; by the 1950's, Nacala, to the north, had overtaken it as the primary port. Four centuries of commerce deserted Ilha in the space of 50 years, and much of the nonnative population followed (those who didn't made themselves scarce after 1975, with the arrival of independence). This near-desertion protected it from development, and in 1991, UNESCO sealed its status as a World Heritage site.

Ilha's Stone Town is a bigger, denser version of Ibo's—houses more tightly packed; streets more bustling, then and now—but equally magnificent in its half-disintegration. It harbors the oldest European church in the Southern Hemisphere: the Church of Our Lady of the Ramparts, constructed in 1522—white, austere, the searing African sunlight pouring through the cross-shaped embrasures cut into its thick walls.

These days, though, for almost every empty villa, or one bearing signs of habitation by locals, there is a

lime-render façade that has been conspicuously renovated. Ilha's promise isn't going unappreciated in Maputo, Johannesburg, or Cape Town—or farther afield. "French; Italian; French; German; Spanish; American." Eddie, the guide I've hired for the day, ticks off the proprietors' nationalities as we pass construction sites and restorations in the labyrinthine alleys. Private investment may have been encouraged by the establishment of a dedicated tourism authority last year, and is definitely encouraged by the easy

GUIDE

Poolside at Villa Sands. Left: Owner Nina Cássimo at her shop, Missanga.

affordability of a 2,000-square-foot villa here compared with, say, Morocco or Sicily (for those willing to abide Mozambique's convoluted property laws, dodgy infrastructure, and malaria hazards). One or two subtly stylish restaurants, serving improbably tasty thin pizzas or spicy prawn curries, dot the streets around the museum, a former seminary; a pretty new boutique, Missanga, sells smocks fashioned from *capulanas* and the odd brass relic pried from the bottom of the ocean.

Bright, whitewashed walls signal your arrival at Villa Sands, a luxurious 11-room inn in a former shipping warehouse at the water's edge. Its Stockholm-based owners purchased it in 2007, infused its interiors with a blend of contemporary minimalism and 19th-century Gustavian flourishes, and opened for business in 2011. The infinity-edged pool deck merges easily with the terrace restaurant, flush with the sea; the open lounge, with its Mies-inspired sitting areas and ornate European chandeliers, leaves the Afro-Lusitanian references to the rest. The slick result is unexpected, but totally appealing.

My own hotel's façade is similarly fresh, whitewashed. Three and a half centuries old, Terraço das Quitandas was restored by Isabel Osório and Sérgio Oliveira, its Maputo-based Mozambican owners. Beyond its doors is a ravishing time warp. *Quitanda* is the word for the local ornate carved-wood beds; one furnishes my two-room suite, which has saffron-yellow walls and a freestanding stone bathtub large enough for two. Makonde ebony carvings are showcased in alcoves; a delicate rocking horse, brought from India by Isabel's grandfather, gazes at me mildly from a corner. The living room is as long as the nave of a church, layered in antiques, along with Thai textiles and rugs and lamps from Morocco. The terrace is crowded with rattan furniture and plants in hand-thrown blue pots; hot-pink and tangerine bougainvillea wreathes an inviting fringed hammock. Fatima, the housekeeper's assistant, brings tea, with the wide smile she dispenses to compensate for her lack of English. "Besides the natural beauty and the amazing architecture, why here?" Isabel muses. "Because Ilha represents what we are: the mix of cultures, histories, people, food—left over centuries, by who passed and who stayed. It's made Ilha the place of everyone." +

Adapted from "Next Stop, Mozambique," by Maria Shollenbarger.

CAPE TOWN

No city captures the medley of global food traditions better than Cape Town—an urban center shaped as much by European colonialism as by its own indigenous culinary customs. At its colorful markets, haute gastronomic temples, and beachside shacks, you can sample the coastal port's ever-evolving "rainbow cuisine."

Carne Sa

*Braai*ing (grilling) is a national pastime in South Africa, and no one does it better than this locavore steak house (the meats are sourced largely from owner Giorgio Nava's ranch in Karoo). Try the free-range lamb, *braai*ed over coal, or the 24-month grass-fed sirloin, then top off the meal with a glass of Vin de Constance from the local Klein Constantia vineyard. *70 Keerom St.; 27-21/ 424-3460; carne-sa.com.* **$$**

Grand Café & Beach

It's hard to believe that the city's first beachside restaurant didn't open its doors until 2009—the outdoor cabanas and ocean-facing tables are perennially packed. Housed in a former helicopter hangar, the clubby interior is outfitted in Parisian wicker chairs, antique rugs, and candelabras. Capetonians gather for bistro classics such as smoked-trout salads and flatbread pizzas from the wood-burning brick oven. *Granger Bay Rd.; 27-21/425-0551; grandafrica.com.* **$$**

Hemelhuijs

The mood is playful at owner Jacques Erasmus's restaurant in trendy De Waterkant. Inside the black-and-white space, you'll find Scandi-modern blond-wood tables and whimsical objets d'art (deer busts spangled in plate shards; candlesticks sprouting tree branches). Come for brunch, when the place draws a stylish throng that feasts on cinnamon dumplings with house-made custard or poached eggs and artichokes. *71 Waterkant St.; 27-21/418-2042; hemelhuijs.co.za.* **$$**

Neighbourgoods Market

On Saturday mornings, the city's hipster bread makers and charcutiers gather at this collection of high-end artisanal food stalls in the suburb of Woodstock. Pick up pastries, coffee, and crêpes, then grab a seat at one of the communal wooden tables. Or bring a basket and stock up for a leisurely picnic on the beach. *Albert Rd.; neighbourgoods market.co.za.*

Pot Luck Club & Gallery

Chef-owner Luke Dale-Robert's low-key tapas spot is Cape Town's most buzzed-about new restaurant. An airy, loftlike dining room adorned with contemporary art curated by his fashion-designer wife Sandalene Olivier sets the perfect backdrop for the creative dishes prepared in an open kitchen: pork belly with red cabbage and apple slaw; blue-cheese mousse with salty-sweet walnuts. *375 Albert Rd., sixth floor; 27-21/447-0804; thepotluckclub.co.za.* **$$**

Roundhouse

When star designer Adam Tihany comes to town, he stops at this onetime Dutch East India Company guardhouse hidden in Table Mountain. The draw? An artful six-course tasting menu (beet carpaccio served with pickled eggplant and shimeji mushrooms; rib eye ornamented with onion petals). But the real gem here is the two-tiered lawn outside, dubbed the Rumbullion, where guests camp out on sunny afternoons for beer-battered fish and postcard-worthy views of Camps Bay. *Roundhouse Rd., The Glen, Camps Bay; 27-21/438-4347.* **$$$**

Test Kitchen

This sophisticated older sister to Pot Luck Club & Gallery made its debut on South Africa's culinary scene three years ago with an ambitiously innovative concept. Ingredients such as ginger and *yuzu* are poached and pickled to intensify their essence. Biltong (cured meat) and fresh catches like langoustines are presented in unexpected ways: the former alongside plum-cured foie gras, the latter with smoked quail and a corn-and-miso velouté. *Shop 104A, The Old Biscuit Mill, 375 Albert Rd., Woodstock; 27-21/447-2337; thetestkitchen.co.za.* **$$**

Tjing Tjing Bar

Ilze Koekemoer's love of all things Japanese is in grand display throughout her cocktail lounge in Cape Town's central business district: a wallpaper collage features photographs she took with her husband while in Tokyo, the red lacquer bar is lined with gold stools, and the dining room is decorated with pagoda-replica lamps. The small plates are mostly tasty pub fare (quesadillas; risotto balls) but the main crowd-pleaser is the handcrafted libations, whipped up with a precision you won't find in a traditional *izakaya*. Order a sweet-and-spicy Asian Persuasion (rum mixed with honey, chili, lime, and mint). *165 Longmarket St.; 27-21/ 442-4920; tjingtjing.co.za.* **$$**

Neighbourgoods Market. Left: A flatbread pizza at Grand Café & Beach.

Grand Café & Beach, overlooking Granger Bay. Right: A salad with orange, feta, walnuts, and dates at Hemelhuijs.

ZAMBIA

An under-the-radar safari destination

A tent at Chiawa Camp, on the Lower Zambezi. Opposite: Thornicroft's giraffes in South Luangwa National Park.

africa+the middle east

209

Safari essentials at Baines River Camp. Right: A crocodile on the Luangwa riverbank.

A Chiawa Camp canoe safari in Lower Zambezi National Park. Right: One of Chindeni Bushcamp's guest tents.

SUMMER AFTERNOONS ON THE Zambezi can reach 105 degrees, but with the sun at our backs and a breeze off the water, it felt oddly cool in our two-man canoe. We had paddled a quarter-mile upriver before slipping into one of the narrow channels that meander inland. Now we glided in calm water through pristine, bird-speckled wilderness. The grass glowed emerald green.

From our vantage the buffalo onshore loomed twice as large; elephants appeared as tall as baobab trees. But they posed us no threat on the water. The channel banks, on the other hand, were crowded with 15-foot-long crocodiles, their eyes like milky green marbles. At our approach they'd slither silently into the stream, then vanish in the murk beneath us. Meanwhile, hippos poked bulging eyes from the water to stare at us, unblinking—then they, too, would disappear below the surface. Our main concern was to avoid passing over these ornery beasts, since an angry hippo can easily topple a canoe. At which point the crocs become a problem.

I was up front, scanning the dark water for eyes. In back was my guide, Paul Grobler, a Zimbabwean expat with the droll affect of a Canadian comic. He also ends most sentences with "eh?"

"If we swamp, swim away from the boat, eh?"

Say what, Paul?

"Crocs attack the largest object first, and that's the canoe."

So I should just swim to shore and wait there?

"No, no, don't leave the water. Hippos and elephants see you as a bigger threat on land."

Oh. So I should just...discreetly tread water somewhere?

"Right," said Paul. "But keep away from the boat, eh?"

'd been hearing the word from Africa insiders: Zambia was the continent's great unsung safari destination, and unquestionably its best value. The game viewing is reliably excellent, the quality of local guides superb, and the parks offer a diversity of experiences seldom combined elsewhere: canoeing, fishing, boat rides, night drives, and, not least, walking safaris—a concept pioneered in Zambia's South Luangwa Valley by the late naturalist Norman Carr. "If you're serious about bush walking, Zambia is the place to do it," said safari outfitter Cherri Briggs of Explore Inc., who owns a house on the Lower Zambezi. In short, it's perfect for experienced Africa hands, but also makes a fine introduction for first-timers. (I was one myself.)

Zambia promised a more natural and authentic bush experience than its better-known counterparts—"like Kenya 30 years ago" was the refrain I kept hearing. Much of this derives from the lodgings themselves, which reflect a shifting ethos in safari travel. "Before, the priority was the lodge, and it was overdesigned for luxury," said Michael Lorentz, founder of Passage to Africa and Safarious.com. "These days, people simply want comfort—a lodge that's small, genuine, wild, and exclusive. The focus is more on the guide and on the safari experience itself." Zambia certainly fills that bill. While big-name safari companies have made inroads, the field is still defined by intimately scaled river lodges and bush camps, many of them founded and operated by Zambians— people like Andy Hogg, who started the Bushcamp Company, a collection of six camps in South Luangwa that find a tasteful balance between luxurious and rustic. Or Grant Cumings, whose family runs two long-standing properties, Chiawa and Old Mondoro, in the Lower Zambezi. With those camps as my bases—and with Briggs's expert counsel—I plotted out a 10-day trip.

PART 1: South Luangwa

South Luangwa National Park is among the most highly regarded game parks in Africa, yet it draws considerably fewer visitors than its equivalents elsewhere. The Luangwa River and its tributaries support a staggering concentration of wildlife, including 60 different mammals (among them 14 species of antelope) and 400 bird species. Given the mostly flat terrain—yellow-green grasslands and floodplains; groves of ebony and mahogany; countless oxbow lagoons—the park is ideally suited for walking safaris.

The Bushcamp Company's six properties are scattered in the remote southern end of the park, just a few hours' walking distance apart. Most visitors stay at several over a week or more, often hiking camp to camp (bags are delivered by vehicle). Tucked in unspoiled wilderness, sites are well removed from other lodgings. The quiet is remarkable. Even in peak season, you rarely pass another group; the valley seems to be yours alone.

The Bushcamps stand out for their chic design; their minimal footprint (they run on solar power, and most are dismantled at the end of each season); and, not least, their ace resident guides. (South Luangwa, in general, has a rigorous two-year training requirement for all walking guides, and park safety standards are extremely strict.) Each Bushcamp sleeps six to eight guests; meals and activities are usually communal.

■ Zambia promised a more natural and authentic bush experience than its better-known counterparts—'like Kenya 30 years ago' was the refrain I kept hearing.

All the camps are lovely, especially Chindeni, with its elegant teakwood decking and tents perched over a wildlife-rich lagoon, and Chamilandu, whose open-fronted tree houses face a stretch of the Luangwa River.

Mornings—especially those delicious hourlike minutes before dawn—quickly became my favorite time. How novel to be woken not by the marimba of an iPhone but by the thrum of bees around a flowering Natal mahogany tree. Its jasmine-y aroma sweetened the still-cool air. The buzzing found its counterpart in the basso grunts of hippos, yards from my bed, splashing back into the river after nocturnal forays inland.

As the sun rose over the pale misty hills, I'd join the other guests for a fireside breakfast: fresh melon, creamy porridge, and strong Zambian coffee. By 6:30, we were in the Land Rover, with guide Gilbert Njobvu at the wheel and our rifle-toting scout, Davey Banda, riding shotgun. (All walking groups are accompanied by an armed, park-appointed escort.) After a short drive we'd park, step out, and walk, single file, into the bush.

There was no trail to follow; Gilbert would improvise our course based on nearby signs of life.

In September—Zambia's early summer—the Luangwa River runs near-dry for long stretches, and the valley is anything but lush. This is peak safari season: animals congregate around the few remaining water sources, with less foliage to provide cover. Drained of color and liquid, much of the terrain is a dry and crackling brown. You think, *This could be autumn in Michigan*—but then you hear a rustle behind some shrubbery, and up pops the head of a giraffe. A Thornicroft's giraffe, to be precise, the rare subspecies unique to Luangwa. Gilbert motioned for us to follow, and we sneaked around behind him to emerge in a clearing. The rest of the tower—it's a "tower" of giraffes when stationary, a "journey" when on the move—stood beside a parched lagoon, attempting to quench their thirst.

Bush walks are not only about seeing wildlife firsthand, but also about the suggestion of wildlife: a tamped-down patch of grass, the sandy imprints of last night's hippo migration, and, of course, an infinite variety of animal droppings. Walking also brings you closer to things you scarcely notice from a vehicle—animal dens; medicinal plants; half-devoured bones. We came upon a buffalo skull, its nasal cavity shattered. "Lions did this," Gilbert murmured, *CSI*-style. "They'll attack the nose and mouth first, then hold it shut to suffocate the beast."

We became so attuned to rumors of wildlife that we once nearly missed the real thing. A leopard was lazing on a branch just above us as we passed beneath the acacia tree: a beautiful young male, paws dangling, tail curling like a cobra. It was Jason, a fellow guest from England, who spotted it first. Leopards tend to stay hidden by day, but this one was veritably posing. Prior to this, Jason told us, he'd visited eight African game parks and seen only a single leopard. After 26 hours in Luangwa, he'd already spotted five. (I wound up seeing 10 in as many days in Zambia.)

We continued on in the steadily increasing heat, past a dazzle of dozing zebra, past vast herds of impala with big soft anime eyes. From the river's edge we watched a dozen ecstatic crocodiles gorge on a hippo carcass. Their bellies were distended from the feast. When we passed the same spot two days later, the carcass was down to clean white ribs.

Dinner by lantern light at Chamilandu Bushcamp. Below: Spare ribs and salad at Chamilandu.

The senses sharpen considerably when your feet are on the ground. Without the rattle and fumes of an engine, the sounds and smells of the bush are heightened tenfold—like the sinister Jabba-the-Hutt chortle of unseen hippos, or the saccharine scent of the woolly caper bush, reminiscent of Necco wafers. Most of all, walking allowed us the luxury of sweet, slowly unspooling time—time for not merely spotting but for observing, time watch for a while. It's the difference between seeing a snapshot and watching a film: suddenly you have movement, context, character, plot.

"That infant is dying," Gilbert whispered. We were crouched under a sausage tree, watching a troop of baboons. He was right: a pink-eared newborn, his body limp, was being passed around by his mother and father and older siblings, who whimpered gently in distress. We watched this drama unfold for the better part of an hour, until the family quietly slouched away, perhaps preferring to grieve off-camera.

PART 2: Lower Zambezi

After a week in dusty South Luangwa, the shimmering sight of the wide, blue Zambezi came as a shock. Water, it turns out, changes everything.

Lower Zambezi National Park unfolds along 74 miles of Africa's fourth-longest river. (That's Zimbabwe on the opposite bank.) Wedged between the Zambezi to the south and a 4,000-foot-high escarpment to the north, the park is dominated by riverine woodlands and alluvial plains carpeted in mossy green grass. Though smaller and less biodiverse than South Luangwa, it is considerably lusher, even in the dry season.

A short drive and a 20-minute boat ride from Royal airstrip delivered me to Chiawa, set along a magnificent stretch of the Zambezi, from which vantage the camp seemed to disappear into the forest. Nine tents made of timber, reeds, and canvas are spread along the hillside. Chiawa is known for superb walking, fishing, and canoeing excursions, and the latter were surely the highlight of my trip. It helped that I was paddling with Paul Grobler, Chiawa's senior guide. Though our aforementioned croc and hippo dodgings made for some nerve-racking moments on the water, these were mitigated somewhat by Paul's deadpan wit.

There's a Zambian expression I love: "We'll make a plan." It means we'll deal with it. Paul uses it a lot.

"Huge croc just dove under the canoe, Paul."

"We'll make a plan."

There were lighter, lovelier moments: the sight of carmine bee-eaters nesting in the cliffside, their vermilion and teal plumage resplendent against crumbling sandstone. Or the sudden appearance of a Goliath heron—five feet tall, the largest heron on earth. Or the juvenile baboons playing king of the mountain atop a termite mound. And, later, the sun sinking over the Zambezi, turning the water to molten gold.

"This is so peaceful," I said to Paul as we drifted downstream, then abruptly swerved to avoid our umpteenth crocodile. "And also completely terrifying."

"Mmm," he replied. "We're relaxing at the edge of death."

My heart was still pounding when I stepped out of the canoe and onto the Chiawa dock. A porter handed me a gin and tonic, and I gulped it down with shaking hands. That night I lay awake with two vivid impressions: (1) I nearly got eaten today, and (2) I loved it.

By now I'd developed a serious guide-crush on Paul. (Did I mention he also dabbles in metalwork and astronomy?) The next morning, I was the first to sign up for his guided bush walk. It was like walking with Attenborough. We chanced upon a group of elephants clustered around a hole by the river. They were digging for the sand-filtered water below to give their young a safe, croc-free drinking source, Paul explained. Like a road crew at a manhole, some were working, others just standing around. One looked up and waved his trunk, as if flagging us past. Nothing to see here, people.

Elephants are the main draw at Old Mondoro, Chiawa's smaller and more primitive sister camp, which

sits in a glade of winterthorn trees, whose seedpods are pachyderm catnip. A local group hangs around camp all day, coming up to the bar, close enough to touch. (Don't.)

When my boat transfer from Chiawa pulled up just after lunch, a three-ton female elephant was standing beside the dock. For 20 minutes we could only idle in the river as she grazed, until she finally wandered off. There were six more bathing in the lagoon outside my hut. I was instructed to radio for a Land Cruiser to deliver me the 150 yards from my room to the dining pavilion, as the elephants made it too dangerous to walk.

Old Mondoro has four simple guest huts, with reed half-walls and canvas flaps that pull down at night. Out back, overlooking the river or lagoon, is a porch with a daybed and an outdoor shower and tub. I was enjoying a post-hike soak in the tub one morning—in the company of a chirping tree frog—when a bull elephant appeared in my backyard. His skin was wet from the river, and now he was gathering up sand and showering himself with dust. (This functions as both a sun guard and a parasite remover.) We performed our ablutions in tandem: I with bath gel, he with clouds of dirt. Soon he was completely

GUIDE

Sunrise at the Chamilandu Bushcamp, in South Luangwa National Park. Opposite: A young bull elephant in South Luangwa National Park.

beige. All that sand looked terribly itchy, I thought, and the elephant clearly agreed, for at this point he began scratching his belly with his penis, then scratching his penis by stepping on it. (A problem all men wish they could solve thusly.) I managed to film the final seconds of this odd ritual, until the elephant got embarrassed or annoyed—wouldn't you?—and marched off.

Back at Chiawa for my final day in Zambia, I met with owner Grant Cumings on the riverfront terrace. Grant was born in Lusaka, Zambia's capital, but spent much of his youth exploring the country's remote bush. After college in Florida, Grant returned home to open Chiawa, the first camp inside the park, in 1989.

After our chat, we watched a lone warthog skitter through the tallgrass by the river. Suddenly, three female lions sprang from the brush. Grant shot up, and a few other guests rushed beside us to watch. A kill looked certain, but the warthog pulled off a miraculous escape.

"Shall we pursue?" asked Grant, sporting a schoolboy's grin. Our impromptu group piled into the Land Cruiser and took off in the gathering dusk, the sky now streaked with rose. For 10 minutes we tracked the pride up the floodplain with no sign, until: "There!" Grant pointed left. My eyes fixed on a small mahogany tree, and at last I saw them: two, three, no, four lions hidden in the foliage, splayed on branches that barely held their weight. Grant inched the vehicle closer, and I caught one's eye. As she peered quizzically through the leaves, I snapped her portrait. (That photo now hangs over my desk.)

The evening was moonless and crystal clear as we continued northward. We wound up spotting a leopard on the prowl, two bush pigs, and seven civets in the space of 10 minutes. Then our host slowed to a stop at the crest of a rise, killed the engine, and switched off the lights.

Here we realized the advantage of an open-top Land Cruiser. A bowl of stars had emerged overhead. We leaned back, gazing at the strange constellations of the Southern Hemisphere. Orion laid on his side, resting. A breeze blew in from the escarpment, carrying the now-familiar scent of Natal mahogany. No one said a word. I remember thinking, I am already nostalgic for this. ✛

Adapted from "Zambia Up Close," by Peter Jon Lindberg.

KILIMANJARO, TANZANIA

Tackling Africa's greatest mountain

Nightfall at
Karanga Camp,
on the slopes
of Kilimanjaro.

GUIDE

"AS WIDE AS ALL THE WORLD, great, high, and unbelievably white in the sun, was the square top of Mount Kilimanjaro," wrote Ernest Hemingway in *The Snows of Kilimanjaro*. The peak—Africa's tallest, at 19,341 feet—is shrouded in wispy clouds, buttressed by a rain forest with thick moss, and crowned by an ice cap. It looms forbiddingly above a wildlife-rich savanna , yet is one of the most attainable climbs of the Seven Summits.

The easiest and most straightforward route to the top is along the Machame trail, a 14,000-foot ascent that wends its way past river gorges and the Shark's Tooth lava rock formation. Micato Safaris makes the eight-day challenge as comfortable as possible with such luxuries as a guide, a chef, and even porters to carry your gear. If you're inclined to make a more leisurely and scenic trek, opt for the 11-day hike up the Lemosho route with Alpine Ascents, which affords the least foot traffic. Added bonus: the journey includes visits to Tanzania's Tarangire National Park and Ngorongoro Crater. There's also a trip for extreme adventurers: Thomson Safaris takes athletic types up the Grand Traverse, a path that coils past caves and some of the mountain's last sections of untamed nature. The final leg ends when the group makes camp inside Kili's crater—a staggering 18,802 feet above sea level. As you gaze down at the vast grassland, you'll understand why Hemingway was so enchanted.

A room at Virunga Lodge, in Rwanda's Volcanoes National Park.

RWANDA

Searching for the elusive mountain gorilla

IN THE 1970'S AND 80'S, unregulated, rampant poaching in this central African state nearly swept the last mountain gorillas out of existence. But thanks to the late zoologist Dian Fossey, who fought fiercely for their protection, roughly 800 are now known to live in the wild. Northwestern Rwanda's Volcanoes National Park claims nearly a third of these families, and remains one of the last places on earth to observe the animals in their natural habitat.

Check in to Virunga Lodge, a slopeside safari camp just three hours by car from Kigali, the capital of Rwanda. The eight stone-and-tile bandas overlook the Euhondo and Bulera lakes. Through a partnership with Volcanoes Safaris, the lodge can secure park permits and arrange expertly guided treks up the gently graded foothills that lead into the dense evergreen and bamboo jungles. En route, keep a lookout for gorillas, golden monkeys, forest elephants, and a wide variety of bird species. Even if you're not lucky enough to spot the gorillas, the quest to find them is just as thrilling.

GUIDE

STAY
Virunga Lodge
Lake Bulera, Ruhengeri;
866/599-2737;
volcanoessafaris.com. **$$$$**

DO
Volcanoes Safaris
866/599-2737;
volcanoessafaris.com.

MARRAKESH

Once a bohemian outpost, the Red City lured free-spirited travelers to its dusty medina with the promise of dreamlike palaces, magical snake charmers, clairvoyant fortune-tellers, and romantic *riad*s. Now it's a stylish stop for the jet set, who come as much for the historic sites as for the world-class spas and galleries.

Bahia Palace
Colorful mosaic fountains, gardens redolent of orange and jasmine, and *zouak* (painted woodwork) ceilings—the Bahia Palace is considered one of the city's most treasured landmarks. In the medina on the edge of the Jewish Quarter, the grand viziers of Sultan Moulay el Hassan I constructed the Andalusian-style building over decades, housing their concubines in a network of rooms. It was ransacked in 1900. Now the palace receives visiting foreign dignitaries who explore the 20 acres of showstopping 19th-century design and vestiges of the kingdom's former opulence.
Derb Al Arsa, Riad Zitoun Jdid.

Dar Al-Ma'mûn
Marrakesh's most intriguing new project, the 2012-opened Art Center, lies eight miles outside the city center at the orchard-fringed Hotel Fellah. A rare nonprofit model is used to finance artist residencies and local education programs that promote regional talent and display their work. Stop by the impressive library, which houses more than 9,000 books.
Km 13, Route de l'Ourika; 212-525/065-000; dam-arts.org.

Galerie 127
With its exposed-brick walls, sleek granite floors, and austere gray palette, it would be easy to mistake Nathalie Locatelli's industrial-chic space—the first of its kind in North Africa—for a gallery in New York's Chelsea neighborhood. Enclosed in an Art Deco building in New Guéliz, her collection is equally modern: contemporary travel images and regular exhibits by big-name local and international photographers (Carole Bellaiche; Alejandra Figueroa) attract an eclectic crowd of global art aficionados and trendy Moroccan denizens.
127 Ave. Mohammed V; 212-524/432-667; galerienathalielocatelli.com.

Jardin Majorelle
This botanical garden, designed in the early 20th century by the Orientalist painter Jacques Majorelle, was acquired in 1980 by Pierre Bergé and Yves Saint Laurent. Surrounded by walls painted the cobalt universally known as bleu majorelle, the 12 acres have colorful local flora, an excellent Moroccan-focused bookshop, and the Musée Berbère, with Berber art from Saint Laurent's own collection. Escape the summer heat in Café Bousafsaf's leafy courtyard, where chicken *tagine* and couscous lunches end with house-made vanilla ice cream.
Rue Yves Saint Laurent; 212-524/313-047; jardinmajorelle.com.

Maison de la Photographie
A three-story *riad* museum, the Maison de la Photographie hosts rotating exhibits of its 8,000-plus-piece private photography collection; most pictures are quotidian scenes of the city taken between 1870 and the 1950's. A highlight: black-and-white shots of native tribesmen cloaked in traditional woolen *haik*s (blankets). Swing by the rooftop salon, which serves steaming cups of sweet mint tea with almond *briouat*s (stuffed pastries).
46 Rue Souk Ahal Fes; 212-524/385-721; maisondelaphotographie.ma.

Medersa Ben Youssef
Once the largest Koranic school in Morocco, the 15th-century Ben Youssef (attached to the mosque of the same name) is a confluence of carved cedar, colorful *zellij* tile work, and ornate stucco. Classic Saadian design touches are manifested in rose-hued walls marked with Islamic calligraphy—especially intricate in the prayer hall—and Moorish archways that open up to a sun-splashed courtyard where sheikhs used to preach. Book a private tour, which includes a visit to the former living chambers of many of the 900-odd students.
Place Ben Youssef; 212-524/292-515.

Spa at the Royal Mansour Marrakech
At King Mohammed VI's hotel—a showcase of Moroccan artisanship—the palatial, 27,000-square-foot, white-filigree-and-glass spa is virtually a city in itself. A wrought-iron atrium leads to a wellness lounge stocked with lemon and ginger juices, while a seemingly endless menu of treatments (black-soap scrubs; argan-oil massages) are administered in suites that have private terraces and plunge pools. Opt for a hammam using the sumptuous Marocmaroc skin-care line, then complete the royal pampering at the beauty salon, a gleaming temple of white marble.
Rue Abou Abbas al Sebti; 212-529/808-080; royalmansour.com.

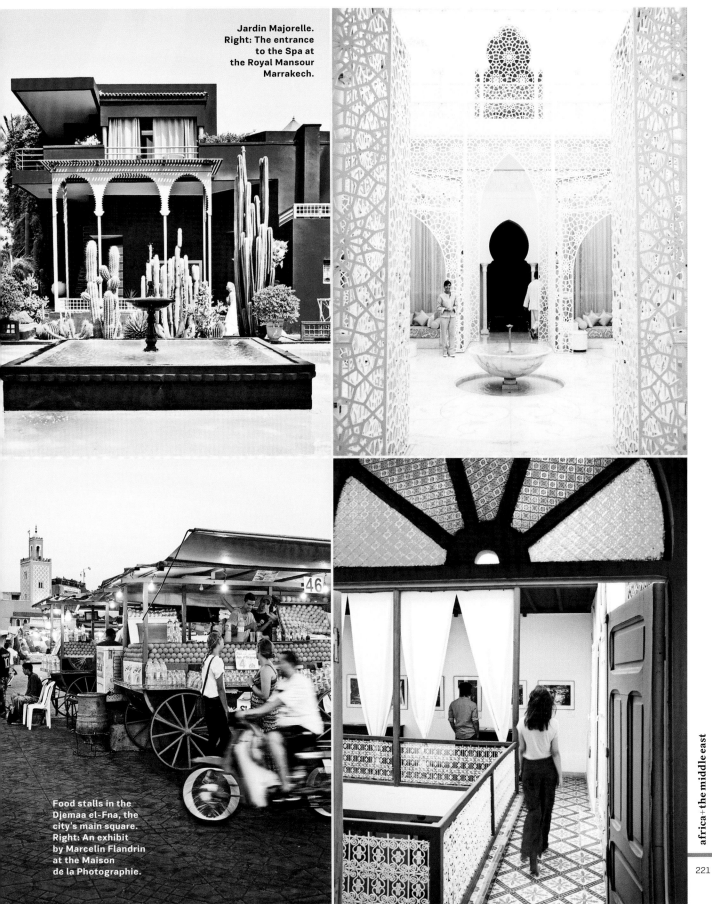

Jardin Majorelle. Right: The entrance to the Spa at the Royal Mansour Marrakech.

Food stalls in the Djemaa el-Fna, the city's main square. Right: An exhibit by Marcelin Flandrin at the Maison de la Photographie.

Tel Aviv's
Design Museum
Holon.

TEL AVIV

High design along the Mediterranean

ISRAEL'S YOUNGEST CITY has often been defined by its inexhaustible
nightlife and thriving beach culture; it fronts some 10 miles
of sky-blue shoreline. But a burst of entrepreneurial creativity is
quickly transforming Tel Aviv into a center for architecture and
design. First came architect Ron Arad's surrealist Design Museum
Holon, whose swirling concrete façade became an instant icon
when it opened in late 2010. Now the movement is turning toward
hospitality. Case in point: the Alma Hotel & Lounge, a mint-
hued retreat in the White City neighborhood's Bauhaus district.
Set in a landmark 1925 building, the property is the area's latest
fashionable arrival—its 15 boho-chic rooms are large and airy,
with Chinese antiques, stained-glass windows, and a riot of vibrant
colors. Rising-star chef Yonatan Roshfeld is the mastermind
behind the hotel's three culinary experiences, which range from
casual (Tapas Ahad Ha'am) and experimental (the Lounge) to
fine dining (Herbert Samuel). In-the-know gourmands are also
heading south to Delicatessen, a haute take-out spot from
restaurateurs Mati and Ruti Broudo, who kick-started Tel Aviv's
upscale-foodie trend two decades ago with the opening of the
city's first high-end espresso shop, Coffee Bar. Here, they've done
it again, with three floors that house a kosher deli, a café, and
a French-bistro-inspired restaurant. When the beach is busy or
the sun too hot, come to feast on roasted shrimp skewers, lentil
salads, or even the irresistible chicken schnitzel.

GUIDE

STAY
Alma Hotel & Lounge
23 Yavne St.; 972-3/630-8777; almahotel.co.il. **$$$**

EAT
Coffee Bar
13 Yad Harutsima; 972-3/688-9696; coffeebar.co.il. **$**

Delicatessen
79/81 Yehudah HaLevi; 972-3/968-1010; delitlv.co.il. **$$**

DO
Design Museum Holon
8 Pinhas Eilon St.; 972-7/3215-1515; dmh.org.il.

Shanghai's
Yu Garden, with
a view of the
Pudong skyline.

ASIA

RAJASTHAN, INDIA

A regal land of over-the-top palaces and temples

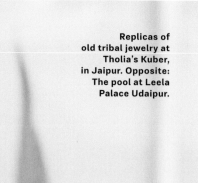

Replicas of
old tribal jewelry at
Tholia's Kuber,
in Jaipur. Opposite:
The pool at Leela
Palace Udaipur.

Overlooking
Jodhpur. Right:
The private
salon at Hot
Pink, a boutique
in Jaipur.

A spa tent at
Leela Palace Udaipur.
Left: Traditional
clothing for sale at
Ganesh Handicraft
Emporium, in Udaipur.

NEVER EXPECTED TO FIND MYSELF in a jewelry store in Jaipur, cupping a plum-size sapphire in my palm. Cool to the touch and the color of a swimming pool, the gem was unadorned, the better to show off its clarity. This was just one of many trinkets I got to play with that afternoon. There were enameled turban-pieces studded with diamonds, curved scabbards adorned with vibrantly colored precious stones, and a gold chess set. "Go ahead, pick it up!" I was urged toward whatever was in front of me. No gloves, no problem. Welcome to Rajasthan.

India's largest state, in the arid northwest, is the locus of the country's most glamorous past, and today it's a major draw for anyone seeking an immersion in courtly history (as well as in textiles, jewelry, antiques, and spices). The center of Rajput power since the sixth century A.D., Rajasthan is thick with imposing forts and carved marble temples that look like towering pinecones. The most concentrated way to get to know the region is through its three main cities—Jaipur, Jodhpur, and Udaipur, each with its own flavor—but between and among them, the scrubby Thar Desert and Aravalli Range are rich with pilgrimage sites and glimpses of village and rural life almost unchanged since the feudal era.

The bug first bit me thanks to Waris Ahluwalia, the designer of House of Waris, which produces handmade scarves and gold-and-gem jewelry with heraldic motifs and a dash of punk. I was previewing one of his collections at Colette in Paris, and he started to explain how the artisans in his Jaipur network would undertake his enamel work using centuries-old techniques. Waris was born in India but grew up in New York; his connection to Rajasthan came while visiting there with his parents as a kid and deepened as an adult in search of craftspeople to execute his designs. "The skill there is extraordinary," he said, his eyes getting wider. He hunched his shoulders, imitating the way they sit over small charcoal fires in their tiny workrooms to melt the gold and then hammer and channel-cut it to hold rivers of powdered glass.

Rajasthan may find itself at a crossroads, with a growing number of visitors, ambitious infrastructure initiatives, and a brand-new hotel boom creating pockets of real slickness. But as I learned when I visited, Waris was right: it's not just a monument to the past. There may now be supermarkets and good highways and IT jobs, with a Jaipur metro under way, but the area is in no danger of losing what makes it most special.

JAIPUR

As the capital of the state, Jaipur is usually the first stop on a Rajasthan itinerary. It's a strong shot of color and noise and activity, especially impactful after the relative order of Delhi, where most overseas travelers first touch down. Founded, as the Mughal Empire was falling in the early 18th century, by a Hindu soldier-king obsessed with architecture and astronomy, the city is one of India's first examples of urban planning, built along a grid system with the massive City Palace and an extraordinary 18th-century observatory at its heart. To celebrate a visit in 1876 by Queen Victoria's son Prince Albert, the city's storefronts and houses were painted salmon pink, and they've remained so ever since. Shopkeepers' wares extend out into the streets. Egg-size *pani puri* (chile-and-potato-stuffed fried bread) bob in boiling oil. Traffic surpasses the usual cacophonous mix of scooters and cars, to include camel-drawn carts, painted elephants, pigs, and, of course, cows. Businesspeople rush to their next appointments, passing long lines at stands for *lassi* (a yogurt drink), hurrying past women in the brightest possible saris and men in dhotis and loosely knotted turbans whose brilliant colors change according to the message of the moment: mourning, betrothal, celebration, welcome.

This street-level mix of country and city can seem deceptively humble compared with what's behind the doors of all those pink-washed shops. Because let's not be too noble: people may come to Jaipur to see the 16th-century Amber Fort or the lacy Palace of the Winds, but the most dedicated activity for most, undertaken with Formula One levels of intensity, is shopping. (Perhaps it's only natural to get to it while your wallet is still heavy and the selection is the best; Jodhpur and Udaipur are not light on goods, but there is less variety.) Among the better-known jewelers—the famous Gem Palace, on M.I. Road; Tholia's Kuber, just down the block; the stunning Royal Gems & Arts, inside a mansion covered in 17th-century frescoes—historically significant bling is there to be fondled, along with less aristocratic pieces at prices that make springing for your first emerald worth it.

Jaipur is a hub of contemporary creativity, too. You see it in the mix of Indian fashion designers such as Manish Arora and Abraham & Thakore on sale at Hot Pink, the chic shop owned by Munnu Kasliwal in the Narain Niwas Hotel where French jeweler Marie-Hélène de Taillac is artistic director. And in the same way that she and House of Waris use age-old methods to push beyond traditional aesthetics, Alexander Gorlizki is

■ India's largest state is the locus of the country's most glamorous past and a major draw for anyone seeking an immersion in textiles, jewelry, antiques, and spices.

revamping Rajasthan's other most famous craft, miniature painting. His works are surreal and graphic, though the brushstrokes and motifs remain as they were during the art's 16th- and 17th-century golden age. They're executed by his partner Riyaz Uddin, a master painter, and his staff of seven, based in an apartment-style atelier in Jaipur's ancient Muslim quarter.

Looking out from Uddin's second floor onto the neighborhood around us revealed a *Rear Window* of cottage industries: a vat for tie-dyeing sat on one roof. Across the street inside a shady room, stonecutting and polishing went on at full tilt. As we walked around, I heard a faint plonk-plonk sound coming out of a building. Uddin explained that the men inside were hammering away at books on the ground in front of them, making pages of silver leaf. Each would have started out with about 150 pieces of silver the size of

a piece of spearmint gum, separated by thin sheets of paper. I understood what Waris meant back in Paris when he said, "Anything I can dream up, they can make."

JODHPUR

If Jaipur is about ground-level immersion in craft and industry, Jodhpur, set on the eastern edge of the Thar Desert, is more of a vertical: the squat buildings inside the 15th-century city are dwarfed by the Mehrangarh Fort, its sandstone walls set on fire by the sun.

The largest of its kind in India, Mehrangarh Fort is still under the control of the Rathore family, who laid the foundation in 1459. They continue to use it today: in 2010, a massive processional mural at Jaipol Gate was restored for the wedding of the crown prince, who will one day be the 37th Marwar king.

King? In the largest democracy in the world? Well, kind of. Even after India achieved independence in 1947, the maharajah families retained most of their local authority and wealth, and received sizable allowances from the state. It was only in 1970 that Indira Gandhi took all that away, compelling many royals to repurpose or give up their estates. As so often happens when aristocracies fade, power rests among those canny enough to adapt their fortunes. Kings became businessmen, and palaces became hotels and museums, with tax breaks if the family remained in residence. Jodhpur's Oxford-educated Gaj Singh II, the current maharajah, became a diplomat and an MP, and transitioned his holdings into the highly successful Mehrangarh Museum Trust. But he celebrated his golden jubilee in 2002. So: no more investiture, officially, but a whole lot of power and ceremony. In village homes today it's still common to see portraits of and even shrines to the (former) local king.

Many people visiting Rajasthan come during wedding season, traditionally from September to January. "The wedding business has completely changed the way people see monuments and land here," said Raghavendra Rathore, a fashion and product designer, member of the royal family of Jodhpur, and the proprietor of two Jodhpur-area heritage hotels. "As India opens up, there's a fear that we're losing our indigenous identity," he continued. So the drive to play maharani for the week (Indian weddings are traditionally six-day affairs) is a welcome celebration of cultural history. When I was

On the terrace
at Udaipur's
Taj Lake Palace,
overlooking
Lake Pichola.

Thaal at House of Bedla, in Udaipur. Right: Royal Gems & Arts, in Jaipur.

in Rajasthan, every evening I heard the fireworks and saw the searchlights shooting out from palaces and mega-hotels rented out by wealthy families. Traffic would come to a halt as men in their finest Nehru-style tailoring and women in explosively glittering saris would emerge from Lexuses. But it was in Jodhpur that I saw a real cross section, from elephant-glutted mega-bashes in the hills outside of town to a simple procession through the old city. The groom, in a red silk jacket and a gold sash and turban, rode atop a donkey while his bride, ablaze in a crimson sari, followed along, serenaded by friends and family with trumpets and kazoos.

UDAIPUR

A whitewashed city of palaces, parks, and temples, draped with bougainvillea and nestled inside the green Aravalli Range, central Udaipur is hilly but small enough to take on by foot. The city is built around four man-made lakes, but its moniker "the Venice of the East" is a bit overblown. (For one thing, there are no canals.) But Udaipur doesn't need the comparison. It's evocative in its own way, especially in the bustling market that winds around the City Palace Museum and

encircles the elaborate Jagdish Temple. Three stories of heavily carved, lingam-shaped pillars dedicated in the 17th century to the preserver god Vishnu, the temple is very much in use among the local community today. It's a pilgrimage site, too, but don't be fooled: the most elaborately outfitted sadhus hanging around are less ascetic holy men, more models of a sort, ready to pose for pictures in exchange for tips.

Udaipur is a major draw for Indian tourists, too, especially prosperous neighboring Gujaratis eager to escape their state's strict ban on alcohol. Rajasthani saris, like the ones at the sari shop inside the City Palace Museum, are dyed exceptionally bright, and the antique textiles at Ganesha Handicrafts Emporium, just outside the palace gate, often wind up on sale in New York galleries. Udaipur's maharajahs are among India's longest-ruling, in an unbroken line since the eighth century A.D., and the family jumped into professional hospitality ahead of the national curve, transforming its 18th-century summer palace on an island in Lake Pichola into the Jag Niwas hotel in the 1960's. In the hands of Taj Hotels, Resorts, & Palaces, which has managed it since 1971, the Taj Lake Palace has more recently inspired a game of waterside one-upsmanship that has the townspeople shaking their heads in amazement. First came the behemoth Oberoi Udaivilas in 2002, which takes up more than 30 acres on the northwestern shore of Lake Pichola. Four years later the Lake Palace underwent a stem-to-stern restoration. Then, in 2009, up came the Leela Palace Udaipur on an eastern bank. Everything from the foot massage at check-in and the hammered silver thrones to the armies of butlers and bellhops is fabulously over-the-top.

But one doesn't always have to play the "big, better, best" game that Rajasthan so often puts on. The most delicious food I ate on my trip came from family cooking demonstrations, not in formal banquet halls on Versace china. As culinary immersion becomes a bigger part of tourism worldwide, cooking classes are now common in smaller heritage hotels and homestays. Drawing on family recipes guarded by palace kitchens for generations, this cuisine is becoming a proper subgenre, dubbed "maharajah cooking" by the local press. In 2006, after a decade leading culinary seminars across India, Udaipur's Vijay Singh Bedla and his wife, Sugan Kumari Bedla, turned their family residence into a B&B, House of Bedla, with an extremely active kitchen manned by Sugan and their 24-year-old son,

Karan. "Thankfully, everyone in my house is a foodie," Bedla said on the afternoon of my visit.

After a dip into a family history rich in tales of palaces and feasts, we headed upstairs to the B&B's patio to eat. Since Udaipur is one of the few parts of Rajasthan with local seafood, the menu focused on freshwater whitefish, one marinated in coriander chutney, as a starter, the other served with tangy pickled gravy. Rajasthani food tends to be hearty and spicy, with rich meat curries for those whose caste status (or modern practices) allows for meat. But our fish, smoked chicken, sweet potatoes with fresh fenugreek, and slow-cooked eggplant were complex and subtle. "Each noble family here has fought so many battles, and each keeps their own history books," Bedla explained, as he told stories of his ancestor's gallantry in protecting Europeans during the Sepoy Mutiny in 1857. "We've maintained that tradition," he said, referring simultaneously to the food set before us and his family's past. This reverence for what came before is one of the most striking facets of life in Rajasthan, but it's on afternoons like this one that it comes most deliciously alive. ✦

Adapted from "Jewels of Rajasthan," by Alexandra Marshall.

GUIDE

Riverside dining
at Deck1.

CHIANG MAI, THAILAND

A riverfront neighborhood reborn

WANDERERS HAVE LONG BEEN DRAWN to the Rose of the North for its otherworldly landscapes of cascading rice paddies, dawdling roadside water buffalo, and gilded Buddhist temples. In the past decade, Thailand's third largest city has also become a hotbed of Asian style and design, and a foodie haven for those in search of local Thai cuisine. These elements converge in the hip Wat Gate quarter, a leafy neighborhood with a slew of revamped hotels and family-run restaurants. At the 137 Pillars House Chiang Mai, former headquarters of the 19th-century teak exporter East Borneo Company, the 30 suites mix historic Thai architecture with mod flourishes (ruby-red pillows and chairs; white leather sofas); rooms open up to well-shaded verandas with daybeds that look out onto a palm-studded tropical garden. For dinner, Hinlay Curry House is known for its spicy pumpkin curry and flaky roti—leave room for the house-made creamy coconut ice cream. A lively after-dark scene unfolds at nearby Deck1, where well-to-do Bangkok weekenders let loose. Tangy mai tais and regional dishes (order the giant prawns in tamarind sauce) are served alfresco, with a backdrop of unbeatable views of the Ping River.

GUIDE

STAY
137 Pillars House Chiang Mai
2 Na Wat Gate Soi 1;
66-53/247-788;
137pillarshouse.com. **$$$**

EAT
Deck1
14 Charoenraj;
66-53/302-788;
deck1.raringinda.com. **$$**

Hinlay Curry House
8/1 Na Wat Gate;
66-53/324-621. **$**

BANGKOK

Culinary treasures in Bangkok come from many sources—ramshackle family-run restaurants; bustling night markets; elegant dining rooms; high-design hotels. Whether grabbing a meal means rubbing elbows with the city's monied elite or trying to land a table at a boisterous cafeteria-style hall, these places all have one thing in common: authentic flavors that dazzle the senses.

Bo.lan

Husband-and-wife team Dylan Jones and Bo Duangporn Songvisava pioneered Bangkok's Slow Food movement with the opening of Bo.lan. Devotees swear by the grilled beef curry, an intricate layering of hand-pounded red paste, freshly extracted coconut milk, double-cooked meat, and notes of Kaffir lime and cassia leaves. *42 Soi Pichai Ronnarong, Songkram Sukhumvit 26; 66-2/260-2962; bolan.co.th.* **$$$**

Issaya Siamese Club

A green-trimmed 1920's villa on the edge of the Sathorn district is the flagship of native son Ian Kittichai's rapidly expanding culinary empire. Try his updated Thai classics, such as the red-chili-glazed sea bass and the spicy lamb *massaman*—the finest you'll find anywhere.

4 Soi Sri Aksorn, Chua Ploeng Rd.; 66-2/672-9040; issaya.com. **$$**

Jidori-Ya Kenzou

Hidden in a side alley lined with Japanese *izakayas* near the Emporium shopping mall, this pint-size slice of Tokyo specializes in yakitori made with free-range chicken. Order the simple skewers, the work of grill masters who stoke embers with *washi* (paper) fans to give them a pungent smokiness. *10/12 Soi 26, Sukhumvit Rd.; 66-2/661-3457.* **$$**

Or To Kor Market

When locals are in the mood for spicy sausages and curries, they head to this upscale food market in the Chatuchak district. A legion of purveyors hawk organic produce, spices, and fruit; street vendors in the back draw throngs for braised duck noodles, jasmine rice, and *saba* fish curry. Make sure to order dessert: the *kanom krok* (cupped rice cakes filled with coconut pudding) is a standout. *Kamphaeng Phet Rd.*

Park Society Restaurant & Bar

Partially cantilevered off the 29th floor of the Sofitel So Bangkok hotel, Park Society is the ideal roost for taking in panoramic views of Lumpini Park. But the city's movers and shakers come for more than the vistas; a French-inspired menu (duck foie gras; Hokkaido scallops with niçoise dressing and *pomme purée*) is served by a young waitstaff dressed in chic uniforms from fashion designer Christian Lacroix. Join the après-dinner crowd on the terrace lounge for Bellinis spiced with pink peppercorn—the ultimate nightcap. *2 N. Sathorn Rd.; 66-2/624-0000; sofitel.com.* **$$$$**

Raan Jay Fai

It's hard to believe that this casual, open-air café peddles some of the city's most expensive seafood. But chef-owner Jay Fai has made her one-woman show *the* place for crab omelette and basil-and-red-chile drunken shrimp noodles cooked in a wok over a coal-fired stove. The dish packs a lot of heat, so you'll need an ice-cold Singha beer to counteract the spice. *327 Mahachai Rd.; 66-2/223-9384.* **$$**

Ruea Thong

Don't be put off by the no-frills storefront—behind the door you'll find a cozy neighborhood spot in Thonglor that specializes in Thai comfort food. You can't go wrong with the staples: *yum khai dao* (fried-egg salad) and *gaeng som cha-om tod* (sour curry with acacia-leaf omelette). *351/2 Soi 55, Sukhumvit Rd.; 66-2/185-2610.* **$**

Thanying

Chef M. R. Sorut Visuddhi—son of the former head cook for Queen Rama VII at Sukhothai Palace—turns out the city's best royal cuisine inside a charming white house decorated with antiques. Get a window table overlooking the tropical garden and feast on small plates such as *puu phat phong karii* (crab stir-fried with eggs and curry powder) and *tom khaa kai,* a traditional chicken coconut soup, culled from age-old family recipes. *10 Pramuan St.; 66-2/236-4361; thanying.com.* **$$**

Water Library

Restaurants in Thonglor tend to favor flash over substance, but Singapore-born chef Haikal Johari executes a seriously ambitious tasting menu at Water Library, with just a 10-seat chef's table. Expect fusion plates such as *sous vide* Dover sole with a miso sabayon and white chocolate paired with *matcha* green tea and wasabi. *12 Soi Thonglor, Sukhumvit Rd.; 66-2/714-9292; mywaterlibrary.com.* **$$$$**

Preparing a meal at Raan Jay Fai. Right: The view from Sofitel So's Park Society Restaurant & Bar.

Kanom koh (ice cream wrapped in *mochi*) at Issaya Siamese Club. Left: The restaurant's garden.

KOH SAMUI, THAILAND

A far-flung holistic retreat

The entrance to one of the wellness sanctuary pavilions at Kamalaya, in Koh Samui.

Beachside at Kamalaya. Above: Ingredients for an herbal compress, one of the resort's many sleep aids.

M Y INSOMNIA—I'M UP for an hour or so a couple of nights a week—is mild but destructive. It makes my afternoons mountainous. I become the dead-eyed cyborg whose chilling dispassion is revealed in the final reel; my laser setting is Chocolate Pudding.

My troubles started about 15 years ago, and—as is the case for millions of people around the world—they've made me on various occasions a less curious, patient, or extroverted person. My inability to sleep well has robbed me of hours of my life. I want these hours back. So when I learned that Kamalaya, in Koh Samui, the posh "wellness sanctuary" on the Thai island, offers a sleep-enhancement program, I heard a proverbial bell ring.

I will admit to a certain amount of unease regarding the phrase "wellness sanctuary"—as was corroborated by my first hour or two at Kamalaya. I encountered a plethora of scented candles, pensive-looking guests, spirit houses, marigold garlands, and allusions to non-socket-related "energy." After my greeter handed me an appointment card and told me to show up at the Wellness Center the next morning, I toured both my room and Kamalaya's common areas and devised the following definition: wellness sanctuary (n.): *A place where they hide all the clocks and coffee, then give you an appointment for 9:35 a.m.*

Lulled by Kamalaya's lush surroundings, I gradually became more charitable. Centered around a cave temple formerly used by Buddhist monks, the 59-room resort is located in a jungle ravine that spills precipitously down to a private beach. The setting is at the same time sybaritic and rugged; more than once I daydreamed about showing up for breakfast wearing only a Speedo and crampons.

The five-night Sleep Enhancement program includes four massages, two rounds of acupuncture, two sessions with a naturopath, and two sessions with a life coach, all of which take place in the Wellness Center. Though having 90-minute foot massages two days in a row is

probably as close to heaven as I'll ever get, it was the latter two components of the regimen that were the most helpful to me. In a cozy office overlooking the sun-dappled Gulf of Thailand, I told my thirtysomething Australian naturopath, Emma, about my insomnia. "Sometimes at midnight I'll stand at my kitchen sink in my underpants eating breakfast cereal in heavy cream," I admitted. "Or sometimes at three a.m. I'll sauté Krispy Kreme doughnuts in butter." Emma's eyes widened and she exclaimed, "How are you not as big as a house?" I explained that I swim three times a week and walk about an hour a day. I also said that my insomnia often occurs on nights when I've been drinking.

A good part of Emma's counsel was suggestions I've heard many times before: no TV or computer before bedtime; slow down on caffeine and alcohol and spicy or sugary foods, especially at night; establish a regular bedtime, etc. However, in discussing my diet and sleeping patterns, we made two big discoveries. First, I don't eat enough protein during the day, which may be why I need afternoon naps, which later interfere with my night sleep. Second, I drink too much grapefruit juice—and the vodka can't be helping matters.

My two sessions with Emma's colleague Smitha, a life coach from southern India, were equally helpful. Smitha taught me a breathing exercise (after taking a full breath, you inhale slightly more, first into your rib cage and then into your chest). After this, I became so relaxed that I was able to meditate effectively for the first time in my life. Then Smitha had me close my eyes and narrate to her my thoughts as I imagined walking at night from my bed to my refrigerator. By asking me a lot of questions, she helped me pinpoint my motivation for night eating. I realized that I'm a self-generating vortex of low self-esteem and approval seeking and that, to my sleep-deprived brain, heavy cream and butter are a kind of gastronomic applause. *Thunderclap!*

Fairly heavy, no? Admittedly, I don't go to a shrink, so I'm a somewhat wide target. Fortunately, though, not

all of my Kamalaya experience was like looking at myself naked in a mirror. I interlarded the soul searching with physical activity. I swam in the resort's infinity pool and the ocean; I walked 20 minutes one day to a nearby zoo. Once I rang a huge gong in the lobby: not a terribly strenuous form of exercise, but it made a big impression. I also took advantage of the many free wellness-related classes that Kamalaya offers. The bodily challenges posed by yoga and tai chi sessions in the hilltop open-air yoga pavilion were greatly aided by the sun's magisterially lifting up over a scattering of nearby islands off in the gulf: nature was doing her damnedest, so I'd better, too. Meanwhile, I tried to keep on top of the 19 pills a day that Emma had given me, including magnesium for daytime and Somnium for night. But by day three I'd tapered off significantly: too much to swallow.

The Kamalaya staff are mostly Thai; they wear what look like pastel-colored judo outfits, and they steeple their fingers in a *wei* whenever you come across them. One night at dinner, one of them handed out small

GUIDE

STAY
Kamalaya
102/9 Moo 3, Laem Set Rd., Na-Muang; 66-77/429-800; kamalaya.com.

paper tags to the eight of us at the Community Table. Most were there to work on other issues: weight loss, smoking. We were told to write down a wish. I asked Teresa, an elegant Swiss guest in her fifties, about hers: "Are you going big picture, or are you going specific? World peace or new vacuum cleaner?" Teresa smiled and said, "Somewhere in between." My brain flashed on the phrase *Roomba Without Borders*.

Half an hour later, down at the beach, Teresa and I and about 15 other guests took part in the Thai custom known as floating lanterns. We tied each of our wish-bearing tags to a four-inch-tall rectangular paper balloon with a ball of flammable wax at its base. After the wax was ignited, the balloons lifted up, up, up into the sky until, about 30 minutes later, all these twinkly, ectoplasmic airships had slipped away into the void. While watching this majestic sight, I fell into conversation with Mohammed, a young guest from Bahrain, who asked how I'd slept so far at Kamalaya. "Beautifully," I reported. "But the test is when I get back to New York."

When I returned home, I did feel wonderfully rested. I was tan. I had lost six pounds—which I chalked up to alcohol deprivation, Thailand's heat, still mighty in October, and all the times I'd walked up and down Kamalaya's steep hill. Since my return two months ago, I'm eating more protein during the day and I've whacked all the nighttime grapefruit juice. I'm laboring to get my glug-glug-glug down to glug-glug, or perhaps just glug. I'm still waking up as often as I was before, but now, thanks to deep breathing, I'm able to shorten how long I stay awake about 50 percent of the time. And I've weaned myself off the sleep aids Emma gave me.

Breaking a pattern of sleeplessness will, I'm sure, take years and years, so the fact that I've already experienced a reduction is deeply heartening. I will soldier on. Perhaps it's those Kamalaya-induced dreams that now keep me asleep: often have I dreamed of those papery spaceships, floating my nighttime imaginings up, up into infinity. ✦

Adapted from "Chasing Sleep," by Henry Alford.

BORACAY, PHILIPPINES

An island on the verge

ONCE A BACKPACKING HAVEN with only the most basic accommodations, this five-mile-long island now rivals better-known Asian destinations such as Phuket and Koh Samui, Thailand, as a sybaritic hideout. A 45-minute flight from Manila brings you to either Kalibo or Caticlan, where boats connect directly to White Beach, with powdery sand that might just be the softest in the world. The thatched-roof Mandala Spa & Villas, Boracay's newest hotel, has a renowned wellness program led by health guru David Ross: early-morning yoga, mind-body lectures, and detox diets (mangoes only) are all on the menu. For those less spiritually inclined, there are plenty of other diversions, from Moroccan-inspired dinners at the waterfront Kasbah restaurant up the road and the hotel's Hilot Trilogy spa treatment, to simply napping on your private terrace hammock overlooking the Sulu Sea.

GUIDE

STAY
Mandala Spa & Villas
*Station Three,
Barangay Manoc-Manoc;
63-36/288-5858;
mandalaspa.com.* **$$**

EAT
Kasbah
*Station One, White Beach;
63-36/288-4790;
kasbahboracay.com.* **$$**

A craggy spot
on Boracay's
western shore.

ASIA

From the highest reaches of the Himalayas to the lush rain forests of Sri Lanka, Asia's natural beauty is unparalleled—a vast terrain of verdant mountains; arid, sprawling deserts; and ice-capped, windy crags. Often, the best way to experience the continent's diverse topography is on a guided journey with an expert outfitter.

Bhutan
With its nomadic inhabitants and well-preserved monasteries, eastern Bhutan is steeped in Buddhist culture. Pack your camera for the Merak-Sakteng trip from Asia Transpacific Journeys (*asiatranspacific.com; six days from $3,000),* where you'll pass hillsides filled with wild rhododendrons, wander through remote monasteries, and meet the indigenous Brokpa people. Once the journey ends, spend a couple of days at the stylish Uma by Como, Bhutan (*comohotels. com;* **$$$**), in the untouched Punakha Valley. A breakfast of ginger-and-lime muffins with house-made watermelon jam, followed by a traditional Bhutanese hot-stone massage, will help you unwind.

Burma
Explore the sacred pagodas and primeval hinterlands of this get-there-now destination with Backroads (*backroads. com; eight days from $4,398).* Guided hikes stop at the Pindaya Caves, Green Hill Valley elephant camp (where visitors can give the residents a bath), and Inle Lake, with its floating gardens and stilted villages.

India
India's northern region of Ladakh draws both intrepid travelers and culture buffs. In the villages of Stok, Taru, and Nimoo, among others, Shakti Himalaya (*shakti himalaya.com; eight days from $4,397)* runs a network of seven homestays (think three-room houses with cedarwood furniture and en suite bathrooms). Guests can take guided tours of nearby communities and historic sites, including the village of Chilling, known for its metalsmithing. The Wild Walk with Wild Frontiers (*wildfrontierstravel.com; 10 days from $2,904)* includes a four-day backpacking trek in the Kashmir Himalayas through spruce forests and open mountainsides across the Sonomus Pass. Camp by glacial rivers and picnic in the Sind Valley before reaching the ancient capital of Srinagar, where *shikaris* (guides) ferry travelers to traditional houseboats on Dal Lake— floating mini-hotels complete with sundecks and elegantly appointed rooms.

Mongolia
Few places feel more far-flung than Mongolia—after all, this central Asian country borders Siberia, which is pretty much synonymous with "edge of the world." On a group tour with Nomadic Expeditions (*nomadicexpeditions.com; 13 days from $5,795),* adventurers can see petroglyphs in the Gobi desert; visit the Flaming Cliffs, where a nest of dinosaur egg fossils was first discovered; and interact with Kazakh hunters. The excursion starts in the capital of Ulaanbaatar and ends in the Gobi at the Three Camel Lodge, with endless views of the Gobi-Altai mountains. For a more physically rigorous exploit, REI Adventures (*rei.com; 11 days from $5,099)* leads hikes into Hustai Nuruu National Reserve and the Moilt Valley on the Mongolia Multisport trip. Travelers will spot herds of wild *takhi* horses and marmots, spend nights in traditional Mongolian *ger,* ride two-humped Bactrian camels, and hike the Khongoryn Els sand dunes.

Nepal
The snowy, often-treacherous peaks of the Himalayas attract high-altitude hikers, but if you don't want to summit Mount Everest, G Adventures (*gadventures.com; 15 days from $1,399)* will take you through Sherpa villages and glacial moraines to the mountain's South Base Camp. Less challenging tours of Everest are also available, including a trek on the Annapurna Circuit with Epic Tomato (*epictomato.com; 15 days from $7,880),* which cuts through traditional yak-herding communities before crossing into Tibet.

Sri Lanka
Since the country's civil war ended in 2009, this island in the Indian Ocean has been on the cusp of a tourism boom. Red Savannah (*redsavannah. com; 14 days from $5,352)* organizes custom itineraries, which might include a trip to a tea plantation, a climb up the 7,559-foot-high Adam's Peak, and excursions to Wilpattu and Yala national parks— home to one of the densest concentrations of leopards in the world. You'll check in to Heritance Kandalama (*heritancehotels.com;* **$$**), on the forested banks of the Kandalama Reservoir outside the town of Dambulla, where the 152 rooms look out on the Sigiriya rock fortress. Don't miss the three-hour journey from the hotel through the jungle to the ancient Aligala Caves.

A camel ride in Mongolia's Gobi desert. Left: A village in Nar Phu Valley, Nepal.

Crossing a bridge in Bhutan. Right: Children entering Trongsa Dzong temple, also in Bhutan.

HONG KONG

The art world turns its eye east

WHEN ART BASEL ARRIVED in Hong Kong for the first time, in 2013, the city's role as a major player on the global art scene was cemented. But a few savvy international tastemakers had already planted their flags in the center of the emerging Asian market. New York transplant Lehmann-Maupin opened in a Rem Koolhaas–designed space in the historic Pedder building, one of the last remaining examples of Neoclassical architecture in the city. Hard-core contemporary art collectors come to the gallery for the well-curated mix of Eastern and Western talent, from Korean multimedia artist Lee Bul to American sculptor Teresita Fernández.

On the southern side of Hong Kong Island, the industrial Wong Chuk Hang neighborhood is lined with small galleries and design ateliers. Among the best is Spring Workshop, a multifaceted space that showcases a range of experimental installations by local artists.

Art, it seems, is everywhere in Hong Kong these days—even in restaurants. At the new hot spot Duddell's, chef Siu Hin Chi serves Cantonese classics in an Art Deco–style mansion decorated by London-based designer Ilse Crawford. Throughout, you'll find an eclectic array of artwork: black-and-white brush paintings, contemporary sculpture, and rotating exhibitions in the upper-floor galleries.

GUIDE

EAT
Duddell's
1 Duddell St., third floor,
Central; 852/2525-9191;
duddells.co. **$$$**

DO
Lehmann-Maupin
407 Pedder Bldg.,
12 Pedder St., Central;
852/2530-0025;
lehmannmaupin.com.

Spring Workshop
Remex Centre, third floor,
42 Wong Chuk Hang Rd.,
Aberdeen; 852/2110-4370;
springworkshop.org.

Falling into the
Mundane World,
an Art Basel
installation by
Tam Wai Ping
in West Kowloon.

asia

247

CHINA

Avant-garde architecture changing the skyline

The view from Shanghai's World Financial Tower. Right: The Rocco Yim–designed Guangdong Museum. Opposite: Guangzhou Opera House.

CHINA IS IN THE MIDST of what may be the biggest building boom in human history, surpassing the creation of the Pyramids and the Great Wall, outstripping the celebrated buildup to the 2008 Beijing Olympics. Tens of millions of the country's 1.3 billion population are flooding into its cities, where progress is the theme and the future is the goal, and ever-taller buildings are pumping up skylines into steroidal versions of Manhattan. Posters promoting the image of the new China as a First World country proudly display fast sports cars, bullet trains, and iconic buildings poised to lift off.

Consider the view of Shanghai's central business district, Pudong, from the Bund, the gracious esplanade of old buildings fronting the Huangpu River, built during the city's colonial period of foreign concessions. On the bank opposite, the spectacular jumble of new Chinese architecture—globes, pagodas, pyramids, dish stacks, and glassy tubes, along with a wafting stingray—may cause you to blink, but it is real, and the hallucinatory combination of disparate shapes and materials is dazzlingly illuminated at night.

China has become the world's experimental architecture lab, for both international and Chinese architects. Zaha Hadid, Norman Foster, Steven Holl, Rem Koolhaas, Frank Gehry, Kohn Pedersen Fox Associates, Pei Partnership Architects, and Gensler are just a few of the high-profile architects and firms hired to design the country's new buildings, their names representing labels of quality in China, much like Armani and Prada among fashion houses, and Ferrari and BMW among cars. And now Chinese architects are themselves catching on and breaking out, the first of a new generation that will earn its place on the ubiquitous architecture posters advertising China's cities. In May 2012, Hangzhou architect Wang Shu became the first Chinese national to be awarded the Pritzker Architecture Prize, that discipline's Nobel.

asia

At a dinner after the 2012 Pritzker Architecture Prize ceremony in Beijing, Hadid—a juror for the awards—commandeered a colleague's iPhone to inspect the latest innovation spawned in China's architectural petri dish. Even she, a Pritzker laureate, seemed surprised and impressed by the hypnotically curvilinear, first-of-its-kind Phoenix International Media Center, by Shao Weiping of the Beijing Institute of Architectural Design's Un-Forbidden office (known as BIAD UFo). The firm has applied new parametric software to create a building that looks like a spherical pouf turning in on itself, with its diagonal steel structure swelling, and then falling into a hole, the lines bending out of sight.

Capital cities normally benefit from all the government buildings—embassies; palaces; bureaucratic headquarters—that confer on them the stately quality of being a capital. But Beijing is not content to reign, like Washington, simply as a capital. It has thrown its hat into the ring as a commercial hub of the country, erecting high-rise structures mile after mile, many of them with iconic shapes that draw on every available inspiration—from imperial hats to Euclidian geometry.

Still, with a long history of imported design influences, it is Shanghai that continues to be China's main architectural stage. The Shanghai Oriental Sports Center, by the German firm Von Gerkan, Marg & Partners Architects, is an acropolis of colonnaded buildings set in picturesque lagoons and sheathed in a membrane of panels whose grid lines stretch like rubber. Almost too pretty, the crowd-pleasing buildings are nonetheless impressive, vaulting acrobatically over huge interior spaces. Farther outside town is Shanghai's second recent architectural masterpiece, the campus of Giant Interactive Group's headquarters, by Los Angeles– and New York–based architect Thom Mayne, of Morphosis. Mayne has riffed on the open landscape to create a twisting, swooping, two-and-three-story sod-covered building whose backbone heaves like the spine of a dragon on the hunt, leading to a head that cantilevers over a lake. The zigzagging forms of the building dig into the landscape, hunkering into the ground.

Not to be outdone in the architectural sweepstakes of China's competing city-states, Guangzhou (the former Canton) has welcomed several elegant towers in its new central business district that confirm the

Guangzhou's International Finance Center. Below: The Tea House, in Shanghai, designed by Archi-Union.

world-class sophistication of the country's building culture. On the north shore of the Pearl River, British firm Wilkinson Eyre Architects designed a super-tall structure, the Guangzhou International Finance Center, with a twin or at least a partner planned nearby. The two will bracket a huge plaza fronting the city's new opera house and museum, themselves a study in contrast and a postcard of cultural ambition.

The very cubic new Guangdong Museum, with an irregular, Mondrianesque pattern of punched windows deeply set in the façade, was designed by Hong Kong architect Rocco Yim and faces, on the opposite side of the plaza, the very organic Guangzhou Opera House (by Zaha Hadid Architects), another masterpiece in China's new and growing collection. Hadid won the competition for the opera house when she presented paired structures, the main stage and a smaller black-box hall, as rocks smoothed over by a stream.

On the opposite bank of the Pearl River, the structurally ambitious Canton Tower offers a rooftop observation deck with a drop-dead panorama. Designed by Dutch architects Mark Hemel and Barbara Kuit of Information Based Architecture (IBA), together with Arup, the international engineers, the building's LED lights create rainbows of shifting color.

Under construction nearby is another exercise in acrobatics, a vast commercial and office block of daringly cantilevered floors, all set askew, by Andrew Bromberg of Aedas Architects in Hong Kong.

China's huge population has required huge buildings, but there are Lilliputian efforts in the country's architectural Brobdingnag. Japanese architect Kengo Kuma led a group of architects in the recently completed Sanlitun Village, in Beijing, inspired by the city's courtyard houses and low-rise *hutong* neighborhoods. The shops, a collection of minimalist cubes, encircle sunken courtyards—one cube has a façade of oversize polka dots.

Beijing's up-and-coming MAD Architects added the stainless-steel Hutong Bubble 32 to the corner of a traditional Beijing building, breathing fresh architectural air into the courtyard complex and the otherwise drab neighborhood. In a trendy, though out-of-the-way, arts complex in the Yangpu district of Shanghai, Philip F. Yuan of Archi-Union Architects built a back office for the firm that he calls the Tea House, with curves of concrete and spaces that reimagine the ancient tradition of a teahouse.

Wang Shu, the 2012 Pritzker winner, also started small, establishing a boutique practice, Amateur Architecture Studio, and operating outside the expectations of most architects hired to construct China's large-scale trophies. Working with craftsmen and with materials recycled from buildings lost to China's tsunami of modernization, Wang has cultivated an architecture inspired by the country's ancient traditions of calligraphy. He designed the classroom and dormitory buildings at the Xiangshan Campus of the China Academy of Art, outside Hangzhou, as Modernist garden pavilions, notable for their use of raw concrete and natural woods, all conceived poetically as microcosms of the larger landscape. At his powerful, moving, and even mysterious Ningbo History Museum, Wang used rubble throughout his design, with full confidence in his unorthodox and contrarian methods.

Wang represents the shifting of the tide. China, which has been an importer of architecture, may be on the verge of releasing its first architectural exports: an emerging group of Chinese talents inspired by their own unique roots. ✦

GUIDE

DO

Canton Tower
222 Yuejiang West Rd., Guangzhou; 86-20/8933-8222; cantontower.com.

Guangdong Museum
2 Zhujiang East Rd., Guangzhou; 86-20/3804-6886; gdmuseum.com.

Guangzhou International Finance Center
5 Zhujiang West Rd., Guangzhou; 86-20/8888-8808; gzifc.com.

Guangzhou Opera House
1 Zhujiang West Rd., Guangzhou; 86-20/3839-2888; gzdjy.org.

Ningbo History Museum
1000 Shounan Middle St., Ningbo; 86-574/8281-5555; nbmuseum.cn.

Sanlitun Village
19 Sanlitun St., Beijing; 86-10/6417-7110; taikoolisanlitun.com.

Shanghai Oriental Sports Center
300 Yongyao Rd., Shanghai; 86-21/2023-2008; orientalsportscenter.cn.

Tea House
1436 Jungong Rd., Shanghai; 86-21/5596-7071; archi-union.com; by appointment.

Adapted from "All the Architecture in China," by Joseph Giovannini.

TOKYO

Delicate silk fans. Hand-painted wooden chopsticks. Rock T-shirts and punk shoes. Whether you're looking for traditional Japanese treasures or edgy local fashions, Tokyo's sheer range of offerings makes the city one of the best places in Asia to shop.

Dog Harajuku
With studded geisha sandals and rhinestoned biker jackets by owner Kai Satake, Dog Harajuku is a treasure trove of boundary-pushing clothes and accessories. The hodgepodge collection has caught one celebrity's eye: pop princess Lady Gaga stops in during her Asia tours. *3-23-3 Jingumae, B1, Shibuya-ku; 81-3/3746-8110; dog-hjk.com.*

Ginza Natsuno
On a backstreet off the Ginza's main drag lies Ginza Natsuno, a tiny, cluttered temple to the chopstick. The walls are lined with many rare examples made of wood, lacquer, and gold leaf by Kyoto's best traditional and avant-garde artisans. *6-7-4 Ginza, Chuo-ku; 81-3/3479-6116; e-ohashi.com.*

GR8 Boutique
Cutting-edge fashion draws the city's trendy set to this stall inside the Laforet gallery mall. Best bets: the Ambush x Reebok collaboration, a special-edition line of metallic blue and red sneakers, and printed T-shirts by cult brand Kokon to Zai. *1-11-6 Jingumae, 2.5F, Shibuya-ku; 81-3/3408-6908; gr8.jp.*

Haibara
You'll be tempted to frame the postcards and patterned *washi* paper from this stationery firm founded in 1806 in the Marunouchi/Ginza area. The shop also carries a well-curated selection of hand fans, wallets, and mobile-phone cases. *2-7-6 Nihonbashi, Chuo-ku; 81-3/3569-0952; haibara.co.jp.*

Hokuroku Sousui
The Japanese have always been purists—and they're going green, too. Enter Hokuroku Sousui, which specializes in plant-based hand soaps, herbal teas, and pillows with decorative paper cases. *2-7-2 Marunouchi, 4F, Chiyoda-ku; 81-3/6447-2881; hokurokusousui.com.*

Kitte
The revitalized Marunouchi district has been transformed into a luxury super-site where mixed-use skyscrapers such as Oazo, Brick Square, and Tokia make shopping a high-rise adventure. The latest addition? Kitte, an airy, multilevel complex of small retailers in the former Central Post Office opposite Tokyo Station (*kitte* means postage stamp). Don't miss H-Tokyo, a charming handkerchief boutique that will custom-embroider pocket squares on the spot. *2-7-2 Marunouchi, Chiyoda-ku; jptower-kitte.jp.*

Lisn
A coveted line of the 300-year-old Shoyeido, a legendary fragrance house, the sleek Lisn sells more than 150 blends, including aromatic combinations that reflect each season. *5-47-13 Jingumae, Shibuya-ku; 81-3/5469-5006; 2.lisn.co.jp.*

Mandarake Henya
Fine workmanship elevates ordinary objects to art, and in this city artistry can be found in many forms—even the humble toy. Browse the reverent displays of early Japanese-made tin robots, atomic Kaiju monsters, and action figures in a mod gallery straight out of *2001: A Space Odyssey*. *Nakano Broadway Mall, 5-52-15 Nakano, Nakano-ku; 81-3/3388-7004; mandarake.co.jp.*

Sacai
Minimalism meets industrial chic at this urban sanctuary, where the sensory overload of neon-pop Tokyo fades away. Here, Comme des Garçons protégée Chitose Abe continues to evolve Sacai, her moody, experimental clothing brand, made with handcrafted fabrics and subtle flourishes (lace; crocheted trim). *5-4-44 Minami-Aoyama, Minato-ku; 81-3/6418-5977; sacai.jp.*

6% DokiDoki
Influenced by everything from Kabuki theater to gangsta rap, Tokyo's ever-evolving street scene is never dull—and the Harajuku district is where to get the look. Channel your inner Lolita at this pink-and-yellow-hued boutique, stocked with ruffled miniskirts, Day-Glo charms, and oversize bow-tie barrettes. *4-28-16 Jingumae, 2F, Shibuya-ku; 81-3/3479-6116; dokidoki6.com.*

Tanaka
Most tourists come to Kappabashi (Tokyo's "Kitchen Town") to pick up plastic sushi key chains and refrigerator magnets, but the real find is the wooden black-and-red lacquerware at Tanaka. Peruse the shelves lined with small decorative objets d'art, chopsticks, bento boxes, bowls, and other serving pieces. *3-5-5 Kojimachi Sandenbiru, 4F, Chiyoda-ku; 81-3/5215-2156; kappaseli.com.*

Hokuroku Sousui's pared-down accessories. Right: Employees at 6% DokiDoki.

The entrance to Mandarake Henya. Left: Shoes on display at GR8 Boutique.

The minimalist Zen garden at Ryoan-ji.

KYOTO, JAPAN

A spiritual land of pristine nature

THE GARDENS OF KYOTO have for centuries defined a unique and subtle aesthetic—an otherworldly fusion of landscape and design. The city served as the country's capital for more than 1,000 years, from 794 to 1868. Emperors and shoguns built palaces there; Shinto and Buddhist priests erected temples; all of them raised gardens that today showcase the Japanese people's deep love of the natural world.

For an inside look at these wondrous green spaces, start your journey at Sento Gosho, a typical stroll garden that dates back to 1630 and invites visitors to wander; it's filled with charming arched bridges; dark, limpid pools; and delicate stepping-stones. In contrast, the city's many minimalist Zen gardens were created for meditation. At the five-century-old Ryoan-ji, 15 boulders are arranged among a bed of gravel raked into distinctive patterns—the point is to open your mind to reflection. There are no flowers or birds here, only locals sitting silently on a wooden terrace. Perhaps one of the most beautiful gardens in the world is Saiho-ji, the Moss Temple, designed in 1339 by the Buddhist monk Muso Kokushi as a means of attaining enlightenment. Explore the eight acres of woodland, with its series of small linked ponds that form the Japanese characters for words like *heart* and *courage*. The park creates a tapestry of textures and shades—and the sense of calm is absolute.

GUIDE

DO
Ryoan-ji
*Goryono-Shita-cho, Ukyo-ku;
81-75/463-2216; ryoanji.jp.*

Saiho-ji
*56 Matsuo Jingatani-cho,
Nishikyo-ku;*

*81-75/391-3631;
reservation required.*

**Sento Gosho
(Sento Imperial Palace)**
*Kyoto-Gyoen, Kamigyo-ku;
81-75/211-1215;
reservation required.*

A look out over Mount Rotui on the French Polynesian island of Moorea, with Cook's Bay in the distance.

AUSTRALIA +
NEW ZEALAND
+ THE SOUTH
PACIFIC

FRENCH POLYNESIA

In search of the get-away-from-it-all fantasy

Guest bungalows
at Hotel Kia Ora
Resort & Spa,
on Rangiroa atoll.
Opposite: Playing
a ukulele on the
island of Fakarava.

Black pearls
from Moorea.
Right: The dining
area at Raimiti,
on Fakarava.

The restaurant at
Tetamanu Village,
a guesthouse
on Fakarava.
Left: Biking on
the grounds
of Hotel Kia Ora.

'M NAKED—AND ALONE—walking over an exposed bed of coral under scorching sun. The open Pacific slams into the reef a few feet to my right. The wind rips past my ears. I turn inland and (gingerly) thrash barefoot through dense underbrush, beneath palm and *tiare* trees. A hundred yards later I break out and the turquoise lagoon is waiting. I step into the placid water up to my knees. There is no wind on this side of the atoll. When I take another step, a blacktip reef shark, about four feet long, darts from behind a coral outcrop to my left; it's close enough that I feel the water displace on my legs as it swims off. That I don't jump out of my skin—or do anything except laugh and say "Cool"—coupled with the fact that I'm naked and tromping around like nature boy, lets me know that my time in French Polynesia is having the desired effect.

I had come to the South Pacific to escape. For most of my life I'd harbored this fantasy—disappearing to a remote island, vanishing without a trace. When I saw the movie *Cast Away* (filmed in Fiji), the only thing I couldn't understand was why Tom Hanks wanted to get off the island. And I'm not the only one: in this age of the "black-hole resort," where high prices are paid for the privilege of no Internet or phone, there's a growing awareness that the more hyper-connected we are, the more we have to fight for any true connection. Personally, I find it increasingly difficult to hear myself think, or even to slow down enough to try—and the more I consult my iPhone, the more difficult that becomes. So I decided to check out.

Strung out nearly halfway between South America and Australia, covering an area roughly the size of Western Europe, the 118 islands and atolls of French Polynesia have been the stuff of dreams since explorer Louis-Antoine de Bougainville wrote in 1771 that the local women possessed the "celestial form of that goddess Venus." When Paul Gauguin arrived almost a century and a quarter later to paint the scantily clad natives, the deal was sealed.

But when I arrived in Papeete, the capital of French Polynesia, on the island of Tahiti, it was anything but the paradise I had imagined. Moldering buildings and exhaust-choked streets greet the visitor. Seedy shops selling black pearls—French Polynesia's number one export—cluster beside tattoo parlors. Clothes hang from drooping lines. Of French Polynesia's 270,000 residents, nearly two-thirds live on Tahiti, most of them crowded into and around Papeete.

There's a decrepit charm to the city, and I find myself lingering longer than expected. But perhaps the best thing that can be said about Papeete is that it's where you catch the ferry to Moorea,

11 miles across the Sea of the Moon. The remnant of volcanic mayhem, where jagged peaks plunge into foliated and impenetrable valleys, heart-shaped Moorea is where Polynesian dreams begin to come true.

"The idea of time, it is very foreign here," Philippe Guéry tells me under passion-fruit and mango trees on the edge of Opunohu Bay, one of the two deep and shockingly lush inlets that dominate the island's northern coast. The age-old lament of "island time" holds true in French Polynesia, but with a distinctly French existential shrug of the shoulder. "The concept of tomorrow, in a way, it does not exist," Guéry says. He and his wife, Corinne, came to Moorea from the Basque region of France seven years ago and have no intention of going back. "Why?" he spreads his arms wide by way of explanation.

Farther round Cook's Bay, I find Ron Hall, a native of southern California who came to French Polynesia back in the 1970's to crew on actor Peter Fonda's yacht. Fonda went back; Hall didn't. "No wonder there was a mutiny," he says, referring to the famous uprising that occurred on the *HMS Bounty* in 1789 (two film versions of the mutiny were shot on these islands). "Would you have gone back to Manchester?"

There's an easy welcome on Moorea, and riotous beauty, but there are fences and locked gates as well as several large resorts with the obligatory overwater bungalows. "The modern world has arrived. They've gotten to us," Hall tells me. "You need to head out to the Tuamotus. You're at nature's mercy out there, on the edge of the world."

Sounds perfect.

Rising barely 10 feet above sea level at their highest point, the 78 atolls that make up Tuamotu Archipelago are palm trees, sand,

and that's about it. Small coral islets string themselves out like beads on a necklace and encircle vast lagoons, while the open Pacific pounds the outer reefs. It's in the lagoons of these tentative claims at land that most of the world's black pearls are farmed, and it's in their ocean passes that some of the best scuba diving is done.

The singular oasis of sophistication on scruffy Rangiroa sits on the bank of the Tiputa Pass, one of two deepwater channels that funnel life in and out of the massive lagoon. Denise Caroggio, an elegant grande dame, arrived in Papeete from Paris in 1979 and found her way here nearly 15 years ago. "When I first arrived," Caroggio leans close, her blue eye shadow perfectly applied, "there was one plane a week. After two days I called Air Tahiti and said there was an emergency and that I needed to get off." She laughs and looks out across the churning pass from the deck of her chic, seven-suite pensione, Les Relais de Joséphine. "Then I fell in love with this pass. All life has to go right past my backyard."

The majority of Rangiroa's 3,000 residents live in the village of Avatoru—the main metropolis of the Tuamotus, with its two banks, post office, and handful of stores. There is one paved road, and in the evenings I ride my bicycle under the few dim streetlamps, past simple houses, while blue light flickers out from otherwise unlit windows. The air is pungent with the smell of *tiare*, the white, star-shaped flower that keeps French Polynesia smelling like perfume. Inside one of the island's five churches, a choir practices; the voices carry across the open water of the lagoon.

Back at Les Relais de Joséphine, my simple, elegant, thatched-roof bungalow furnished with reproductions of French-colonial antiques is steps from the pass. I lie in my four-poster bed, the sliding doors open wide, and watch dolphins leap from the water.

Aside from the charms of Caroggio's salon, and the overwater bungalows at the glamorous Hotel Kia Ora Resort & Spa, Rangiroa's appeal is a raw one. "It's what Bora-Bora was twenty years ago," Kia Ora manager Gerard Garcia tells me. "It's still pristine here, still remote." But when I see a cruise ship sailing through Tiputa Pass, I know Rangiroa is not isolated enough. One hundred and fifty miles to the southeast, I find the spot that is: Fakarava, population 700. Dogs sleep in the shade of ironwood trees; snails twice the size of my fist inch across the crushed-coral road; the sun burns

down. "There's a lot of quiet here," Margareth Burns assures me from behind the register of the island's bakery, Boulangerie Havaiki. The island's sleepy Tetamanu Village guesthouse also runs a dive center.

A small boy, just leaving the island's lone school on his bicycle, overtakes me on the road and the race is on. Laughing, we pedal hard until he leaves me in the dust next to a lagoon-side outdoor restaurant with hanging shells. Cecile Casserville, a former ski instructor from the Alps, opened Teanaunua 11 years ago with her Moorean partner, a sarong-clad Adonis named Enoha Pater. "We have been all over the Tuamotus, and there is something special here. You feel it right away, no?"

I nod, savoring freshly grilled tuna Casserville has just prepared for me. "We don't like cities, cars, noise. This is what we want." A few feet away in the clear water a five-foot nurse shark circles, waiting for scraps—Pater saunters over and obliges. "But if you want real peace, go south. It is very remote. You will be happy there."

And then I'm in an open-hulled boat, racing over still water toward an isolated motu in the southern part of the lagoon. Already a wild and insubstantial spot, Fakarava begins to break apart. The motus become more spread out, more inhospitable. Signs of life are few, then nonexistent. After nearly two hours, a small dock juts out into the water from a lush motu. As the boat ties up, a few simple buildings are seen hiding among the palms, just back from the coral-bound coast. A weathered man with white hair walks out to greet me.

Eric Lussiez, from the Republic of the Congo, is a man of artistic temperament with a survivor's demeanor, and he's created a South Seas paradise of

GUIDE

STAY
Hotel Kia Ora Resort & Spa
Rangiroa; 011-689/931-111; hotelkiaora.com. **$$$$**

Les Relais de Joséphine
Rangiroa; 011-689/ 960-200; relais-josephine- rangiroa.com. **$**

Raimiti
Fakarava; 011-689/710-763; raimiti.com. **$$$$**

Tetamanu Village
Fakarava; 011-689/713-834; tetamanuvillage.pf. **$**

EAT
Teanaunua
Rotoava, Fakarava; 011-689/934-065. **$$$**

DO
Tetamanu Diving Center
Fakarava; 011-689/713-834; tetamanuvillage.pf.

Transporting a kayak on Moorea. Above: A palm-frond cottage at Raimiti.

simplicity called Raimiti. On a small and narrow motu he has built nine cottages, four on the lagoon and five—a hundred yards away—on the ocean. The first thing Lussiez shows me is how to operate my kerosene lamp. My small cottage, made of palm fronds, has hot running water, a wide bed, and no electricity.

"You are the only guest. You will have quiet," Lussiez tells me, and walks away.

I stand in front of my cottage and look out over the lagoon. The air is still. Then the longer I don't move, the more my surroundings come to life. The aroma of the *tiare* flower is strong. Frigate birds dive into the water. Hundreds of silver, nearly translucent fish leap out of the lagoon in unison. A snail inches along beside my toe. This is where I've wanted to be—even before I knew of its existence. This place is deeply familiar, in the way only somewhere you've never been to before can be.

At dawn, I'm on the ocean side of the atoll, atop a wide bed of coral. There are nearly a hundred primitive towers of stacked coral—cairns—lining the coast. The silhouetted statues are an eerie sight before the sun comes up over the Pacific.

"I built the first one," Lussiez says when I see him later, "and then guests continued. I hope you will add to the garden." Lussiez settled in French Polynesia 35 years ago. "I had a restaurant on Moorea for thirty years, and would come here, just for myself. But then...." He shrugs. And in his shrug, I understand. Perhaps it's a result of being so close to the edge of the world, but the paradoxical sensation of so much peace, and feeling so alive, is impossible to ignore.

Late in the day I'm back in the coral garden, stacking a tower high, laying small claim on this moment in this place. Sweat rolls down my back as I lift and place large chunks of coral and add to my creation. Without really noticing, I slip out of my bathing suit. It's when my work is done that I turn inland, thrash through the undergrowth and emerge beside the lagoon, where I step into the water and the blacktip reef shark zips past me. I laugh. For an instant I wish I had my camera, and it occurs to me I have no idea where my iPhone is—and then I realize, I don't care where it is. It's going to be very difficult to put my clothes back on. ✦

Adapted from "Escape to the South Seas," by Andrew McCarthy.

The St. Regis
resort on
the shores of
Bora-Bora.

BORA-BORA

A postcard-perfect beach escape

WHAT COULD BE MORE SEDUCTIVE than a bungalow perched over a turquoise lagoon? That's the essence of Bora-Bora, a geographically blessed sliver of French Polynesia. At its heart lies the 2,385-foot-high jagged peak of Mount Otemanu; on its fringes are tiny motus and a coral reef that swirls with colorful marine life. The 100 thatched-roof villas at the St. Regis Bora Bora Resort jut into the sea in a rolling Y-formation; languorous afternoons are spent on the private decks (which come with whirlpools and outdoor showers) gazing out at the powdery white sands of the bay. But you didn't come all the way to the South Pacific simply to lounge. Follow dive master Laurent Graziana—an island mainstay for more than 15 years—on an underwater journey with Diveasy to meet moray eels, blacktip reef sharks, and giant manta rays. Then join other travelers for sundowners back at the sand-floored Bloody Mary's, where the chef serves fresh-off-the-boat *poisson cru* (a local take on ceviche).

GUIDE

STAY
St. Regis Bora Bora Resort
Motu Ome'e BP 506;
011-689/607-888;
stregis.com. **$$$$$**

EAT
Bloody Mary's
Povai Bay; 011-689/677-286;
bloodymarys.com. **$$**

DO
Diveasy Bora Bora
011-689/792-255;
diveasyborabora.com.

AUCKLAND, NEW ZEALAND

The North Island's largest and most urban city is earning some major culinary cred with a multicultural mix of new and timeless restaurants—and the odd craft-beer bar. For the ultimate epicurean tour, look no further than these seven spots.

Coco's Cantina

On nondescript K Road in central Auckland, you'll find this no-frills restaurant, packed with young hipsters. The ultracasual atmosphere is a mash-up of mismatched furniture and menus scribbled on clipboards. Try one of the Italian-inspired small plates—risotto balls; bruschetta; polenta fries— and a craft brew. If you have to wait for a table, belly up to the bar or make your way to the leafy courtyard out back for great people-watching. *376 Karangahape Rd., Newton; 64-9/300-7582; cocoscantina.co.nz.* **$$$**

Depot Eatery & Oyster Bar

It may sit in the shadow of a huge casino, but don't let the offbeat location deter you— chef Al Brown's seafood canteen is the buzziest spot in town. The place pays homage to its home country, with black-and-white photographs of Maori children on the walls and locally sourced ingredients: freshly shucked shellfish; kahawai fish cakes; hapuku belly seasoned with herbs and fresh lime. Snag a table outside and order a *quartino* of Sauvignon Blanc to complement your meal. *86 Federal St., Central Business District; 64-9/363-7048; eatatdepot.co.nz.* **$$$**

Ebisu

A sophisticated crowd fills this dimly lit converted warehouse, where exposed brick, dark leather booths, and hewn-timber columns provide the backdrop for chef Yukio Ozeki's *izakaya*-inspired dishes. To start, the soft-shell crab with orange *ponzu* and wasabi mayo, followed by the seared duck breast or rib-eye (known here as scotch) fillet. There's also a formidable drinks list, with more than a dozen traditional sakes. *116-118 Quay St., Britomart; 64-9/300-5571; ebisu.co.nz.* **$$$**

Engine Room Eatery

The interior of Natalia Schamroth and Carl Koppenhagen's bistro looks like a large family kitchen: bowls of fresh fruit and house-made tarts line black countertops, while shelves are stocked with cookbooks (including *The Engine Room Eatery,* the restaurant's own award-winning volume). Order the signature twice-baked goat cheese soufflé from an ever-changing seasonal menu of comfort classics, scrawled on a blackboard hung over an open kitchen. *115 Queen St., Northcote Point; 64-9/480-9502; engineroom.net.nz;* **$$$**

French Café

Owner and chef Simon Wright's temple to gastronomy is outfitted with crisp white tablecloths, oversize glass windows, and large abstract murals—the perfect setting for his eight-course degustation menu that puts an elevated twist on classic French roasts (quail with bacon, chestnuts, and croissant sauce; caramelized pork belly with seared scallops). *210 Symonds St., Central Business District; 64-9/377-1911; thefrenchcafe.co.nz.* **$$$$**

SPQR

Housed in a former motorcycle shop, SPQR is the social epicenter of the chic Ponsonby neighborhood. On any given night of the week the place is jammed with fashionistas and aspiring movie stars— and the wine just flows. The kitchen turns out tapas-style dishes (fresh Stewart Island oysters; char-grilled calamari; salmon gravlax cured in Hendrick's gin). But the thin-crust pizza is the highlight, made with unconventional toppings like smoked salmon and watercress. *150 Ponsonby Rd., Ponsonby; 64-9/360-1710; spqrnz.co.nz.* **$$$**

Zus & Zo

Not far from the beach at Herne Bay, this shabby-chic brunch favorite is an ode to Holland, with white wooden stools, rustic flower boxes filled with tulips, and a bicycle parked by the bench out front. The menu follows suit, specializing in organic Dutch standouts: *dikkertjes* (pancakes) topped with apple, banana, and berry compote; mushrooms with blue cheese and Black Forest ham on sourdough. Don't miss the fresh pastries (apple tarts; date scones), made daily, and the city's best cup of coffee. *228 Jervois Rd., Ponsonby; 64-9/361-5060; zusandzo.co.nz.*

Mango-and-crab *maki* with *tobiko* and baby coriander at Ebisu. Right: Ebisu's dining room.

Bruschetta with *burrata,* romesco, arugula, and toasted almonds at Coco's Cantina. Left: A server at the restaurant.

Kayakers explore a sheltered lagoon in Abel Tasman National Park.

SOUTH ISLAND, NEW ZEALAND

Adventure in a nature lover's utopia

NEW ZEALAND'S SOUTH ISLAND is home to the nation's tallest mountains as well as the lowest plains—it is bigger, wilder, and far less trammeled than the northern part of the country. This stunning expanse of topographic extremes is one of earth's last frontiers; nearly one-third of the island is either protected park or reserve. On the pristine northern coast, the 55,672-acre Abel Tasman National Park is perhaps the island's most picturesque parcel of land, with golden beaches, granite cliffs, and quiet estuaries populated by tui and pukeko birds. The 32-mile Abel Tasman Coastal Track traces the Tasman Sea; off its shores, you can kayak alongside orca pods and colonies of fur seals. Or sign up for an 11-day trek through nearby Nelson Lakes with Black Sheep Touring Co. that ends with a rafting adventure inside a cave illuminated by the country's famous glowworms.

Heading down the western coastline, the climate begins to cool. The 3 million-acre Fiordland National Park, carved by glaciers 20,000 years ago, dominates the area's farthest reaches, with snowy summits and primeval rain forest. On a journey with REI Adventures, you'll hike for three hours on the park's Kepler Track and take a boat to Milford Sound, a fjord whose jaw-dropping backdrop—clear icy waters; cascading narrow waterfalls; mist-shrouded peaks—was dubbed the Eighth Wonder of the World by Rudyard Kipling a century ago.

GUIDE

DO

Black Sheep Touring Co.
800/206-8322; blacksheep touring.co.nz; 11 days from $4,005 per person.

REI Adventures
800/622-2236; rei.com; 11 days from $5,170 per person.

WELLINGTON, NEW ZEALAND

A creative capital in an otherworldly terrain

A guest room at Ohtel.

Flying over Mount Ngauruhoe. Below: Blue moki sashimi at Ortega Fish Shack & Bar.

OUNT NGAURUHOE, 10 A.M. Half a morning's hike across a treeless, lunar landscape of black lava boulders—covered with colonies of white-green lichen and ferns as tiny as babies' toes—gets me to the foot of the volcano. Each rock along the trail looks like its own world, and every few minutes I've bent down for a close look, imagining myself shrinking to microscopic size, these flecks of plant life rising up like otherworldly forests.

A few yards on, a crossroads: the spot where the intrepid quit the trail for the tough climb to the summit, from whence the views—down into this mountain's red-streaked, sulfurous crater and out across a spiny trail of sister volcanoes—are said to be spectacular.

Looking up, scanning the mountainside, I count scores of hikers' improvised tracks, braided in the loose gray scree. For a few fearful moments, I hesitate—the grade is steep, about 45 degrees. I scrunch my hat down to my ears so the cold mountain wind won't snatch it, and with each step, add my own trail of sliding, shaky footprints to the plaits.

Until the 2001 premiere of *The Fellowship of the Ring*, the first part of Peter Jackson's film trilogy based on J.R.R. Tolkien's *Lord of the Rings* novels, this peak, standing 7,500 feet high on the Central Plateau of New Zealand's North Island, was known only as Mount Ngauruhoe, in honor of an ancient mythological hero of New Zealand's indigenous Maori people. Yet the mountain is so classically, conically volcanic that Jackson used it as the model for the key landmark of Tolkien's epic story, Mount Doom—a name that, for some, is now interchangeable with its actual one.

No part of New Zealand has been more changed by Jackson's movies, and by the growing film-production industry they sparked here, than the city of Wellington, at the North Island's southern tip. Despite being the country's capital, Wellington has long lived in Auckland's shadow, known to the wider world primarily as the place to catch the ferry to the South

Island's geographic wonderland. But Wellington's show-business success has brought status to the city and helped nurture a vibrant scene of restaurants, cafés, boutiques, and galleries now commonly referred to as Wellywood.

Peter Jackson's is the name above the titles, but the city's rising visibility owes at least as much to Richard Taylor and his partner Tania Rodger. The soft-spoken couple's main business, Weta Workshop, and its sister company, Weta Digital, based in the northern suburb of Miramar, have produced special effects and props for *The Lord of the Rings* as well as *District Nine, Avatar,* and the Narnia films. Weta has also helped refurbish a 1920's theater in Miramar called the Roxy, which opened the week I arrived in Wellington. The theater is

■ On warm days the whole city rushes to the waterfront: running, strolling, and biking along a boardwalk that winds from the Oriental Bay neighborhood past Te Papa.

a throwback to the classic Art Deco movie palaces, with custom brass and bronze details and even a gourmet restaurant, Coco, in the lobby.

Over a lunch of lamb burger with *halloumi* cheese and pea compote, Tania Rodger explains that Wellington's evolution into a film capital is attributed to its denizens' can-do style. "It's our attitude that it's possible to make things happen here that makes things happen here," she tells me. There is an ongoing chicken/egg debate, she says, about whether Wellington's success was born of this town's culture or the best of Wellington culture was born of the box-office jackpot. The question is probably irresolvable, but there's no doubt that the business and the culture are enjoying a fine romance.

Take Logan Brown Restaurant & Bar, Wellington's most coveted dining spot. It's packed to the rafters with an after-work Wellywood crowd supping on locally sourced ingredients like Cook Strait butterfish with fennel soubise under the vaulted ceiling of what used to be a bank. Or Ortega Fish Shack & Bar, where a perfect piece of salmon or blue moki, fresh as the afternoon, is presented in an atmosphere thick with gossip of the day's filming. The cafés—such as Caffe L'affare and the Castro-kitsch-crammed Havana Coffee Works—could be at home in Seattle or San Francisco; many have their own coffee roasters and all are served by seriously dedicated baristas. The best bar in Wellington, Motel Bar, which opened just as the *Lord of the Rings* odyssey began, became legendary when the actors playing hobbits—and the special-effects guys who made the actors into hobbits—made it their post-production hangout. On a Friday night at Motel, I ask Tommy the bartender to suggest a cocktail. After peppering me with questions—"What time did you eat? What did you eat? Did you have wine? White or red?"—he pulls down a bottle with a hand-lettered masking-tape label: "Duck Fat Rye." It was rendered, he explains, on the stove in his apartment. He mixes his take on a Sazerac, which is quite possibly the softest, most graceful drink ever to slide across my tongue—a response I am sure is evident by my expression. "Tommy turned me from a boozer," says the owl-eyed stranger sitting next to me, "into a drinker."

For all its charms, Wellington is still a bit of a diamond in the rough. Its main drags, Lambton Quay and Courtenay Place, are clogged with lowbrow retail shops, and its bohemian Cuba Street feels like an unreconstructed Lincoln Road, in Miami's South Beach. Richard Taylor believes the lack of upkeep is owed to a sort of collective inferiority complex. "We're a tiny small town in a country that nobody knows," he says. "We're still sort of realizing that we can be a player." New Zealand has a population of only 4.4 million, about half of whom live in rural areas, and most residents of the North Island don't spend much time worrying about the country's role on the global stage. With almost no poisonous spiders or snakes, and no native mammalian predators, New Zealanders have only cataclysm to fear—which Wellingtonians especially do, since their town is built directly on a fault line that is due for a major correction. Many here were chastened by the February 2011 Christchurch earthquake, which killed 185 people and damaged more than $20 billion worth of property. Yet they are resigned to living at the earth's mercy, beholden to its

Weta Workshop co-owner Tania Rodger *(left)* and film editor Jamie Selkirk at the Roxy Cinema. Left: Te Papa museum.

Paua ravioli at Logan Brown Restaurant & Bar. Left: Diners at Caffe L'affare.

The Wellington waterfront. Right: A bartender at Motel Bar.

highs and lows, fearful of its uncertainty and relishing its virtuousness.

Which is why, on warm days when the sun comes out, the whole city rushes to the waterfront: running, strolling, skateboarding, and biking along a boardwalk that winds from the swank Oriental Bay neighborhood past Te Papa, the immense national museum (whose treasures include the largest colossal squid ever caught), toward the old downtown and government center. When I told one man I met, the English sculptor Max Patté, whose half-ton, eight-foot sculpture of a naked man almost falls off the edge of the boardwalk, about my plans to summit Mount Ngauruhoe, he supplied me with a typical Wellingtonian anecdote. "My first year in New Zealand, I drove up five times in hopes of making the trek," he said, "and five times the weather drove me home. But when I made it—it was amazing." People here take nothing for granted; they'll keep at it until they get the thing done.

Patté wished me good luck with the weather.

MOUNT NGAURUHOE, 11 a.m.

I am (I think) almost halfway up Mount Ngauruhoe. But one knee—a knee I've hurt every few years since I was a teenager—starts feeling shaky, so I stop for a rest.

I wish I could get to the top. I've never looked into a volcano. And part of me says to go for it, even if I think I might fall in. But I cannot separate the part of me that wants this experience purely for the sake of it, from the part of me that's embarrassed for not thinking I can do it, the part of me that's made of the worst kind of pride.

I think about my good luck with the weather. And I remember that statue, the man giving himself over to gravity, and try to let that symbol lead me on.

Since I was little, I've imagined New Zealand as an ideal of pristine, remote exoticism: a chiaroscuro landscape of peaks and valleys inhabited by funny-looking flightless birds. Though real life rarely fulfills those kinds of fantasies, New Zealand does.

A few evenings before, I'd taken a guided night hike through Zealandia, a nature preserve in the hills above

Wellington. We saw a tuatara lizard—crouching, munching on something, staring at us with zero interest—and not one, not two, but three kiwis—implausible-looking creatures, like little feathered footballs on legs. "A three-kiwi night!" exclaimed my guide, Jane. "I've never had one of those before!"

During that hike, just above the horizon, I caught a glimpse of the first constellation I remember learning about as a child: Orion, the hunter. In the Southern Hemisphere, he's turned counterclockwise, lying on his back, and is known, I'm told, as "the Pot." The northern heavens' grand hero is, in the southern skies, a piece of kitchenware. To me, that contrast of concepts dramatizes the understated humility of this place. I later asked a bus driver how New Zealanders see themselves in the grand scheme of things. "We don't," he replied, but with some encouragement, continued. "We look after New Zealand. And for four million people, we've done quite well."

MOUNT NGAURUHOE, 12:15 p.m.

If I could keep climbing, I would. But I can't, is the truth. My legs won't hold me. Or, I don't think they will hold me. I sit. Eat a couple of energy bars. Take a good look at the view from here. Take some pictures. I love what

I see. Yet still, it's not the top. I won't make it to the top. My disappointment in that shortcoming swells until, bizarrely, it feels bigger than any of the mountains in my view.

When I pick my way back down Ngauruhoe and cross past Mount Tongariro, though, the land stops me thinking, shrinks me and carries me—through a massive crater's bowl, up a mountain and down, down to twin pools, crème-de-menthe green, and as I keep descending, trees rise up around the path's subtropical, loamy-smelling end. That night I fill one whole page of my journal describing the different shapes of fern fronds I saw—E.T.'s-finger-shaped ferns, sine-wave ferns, backslash ferns, starburst ferns, opera-glove ferns—before collapsing on the hard mattress of a roadside motel and sleeping, in the deep rest that follows a day when you've done all you can.

Coming back to New York, the jet lag is wrecking, the worst I've ever had. In my apartment, I lie on the sofa re-watching *The Return of the King*, and the ending brings tears to my eyes—for Frodo's journey makes it impossible for him to return home the same.

This time, though, I also see how the *Lord of the Rings* movies rhyme with the place and the people that made them. These are movies about little people drawn into a grand story, people compelled by circumstances to carry, for a time, burdens of power. They are not consumed by those burdens, but changed by them and made more fully themselves.

That's more or less how Wellington has handled its period in the spotlight, which won't be over for some time to come. The film director James Cameron bought a reported $16 million property in New Zealand, where he will film two sequels to *Avatar*. Though Cameron is not known for humility—accepting the 1998 Oscar for directing *Titanic*, he hollered, "I'm the king of the world!"—who knows what effect Wellington's magic may have on him? After all, it's the kind of place that can give a creature of the rat race some strange and freeing thoughts.

In other words, there's more to climbing a mountain than making it to the top—a lesson I could only have learned in a place like Wellywood. ✦

Adapted from "Journey to Middle-Earth," by Michael Joseph Gross.

GUIDE

STAY
Ohtel
66 Oriental Parade, Oriental Bay; 64-4/803-0600; ohtel.com. $$

EAT AND DRINK
Caffe L'affare
27 College St.; 64-4/385-9748; laffare.co.nz.

Coco at the Roxy
5 Park Rd., Miramar; 64-4/388-5555; roxycinema.co.nz. $$$

Havana Coffee Works
163 Tory St.; 64-4/384-7041; havana.co.nz.

Logan Brown Restaurant & Bar
192 Cuba St.; 64-4/801-5114; loganbrown.co.nz. $$$

Motel Bar
2 Forresters Lane, second floor; 64-4/384-9084; motelbar.co.nz.

Ortega Fish Shack & Bar
16 Majoribanks St.; 64-4/382-9559; ortega.co.nz. $$$

DO
Roxy Cinema
5 Park Rd., Miramar; 64-4/388-5555; roxycinema.co.nz.

Te Papa
55 Cable St.; 64-4/381-7000; tepapa.govt.nz.

Zealandia: The Karori Sanctuary Experience
End of Waiapu Rd., Karori; 64-4/920-9200; visitzealandia.com.

MELBOURNE

If you want to surf, go to Sydney. If you want to shop, the answer is Melbourne, a city with the charm of a small town and the hedonism of a modern metropolis. Whether you're on a quest for an out-of-print cookbook, colorful handmade vases, or a Hentsch Man overcoat, Australia's style center has it all.

Books for Cooks

At this old-school bookstore, you'll find an encyclopedic collection of 40,000-plus new and vintage culinary titles: celebrity toque bibles, Parisian pastry compendiums, and classics like the delightful *Mr. Wilkinson's Favourite Vegetables* line the shelves. Should your tastes run to the more esoteric, there's a free worldwide search service for rare tomes that will help you hunt down that needle in the haystack. *233 Gertrude St.; 61-3/8415-1415; booksforcooks.com.au.*

Captains of Industry

Up a rickety staircase in the Central Business District, sartorial partners Thom Grogan and James Roberts have transformed an urban loft into a men's club for the city's dapper set. They may come for finely made bespoke suits, but this isn't a pop-in, pop-out kind of tailor. An organic café serves pork-and-cauliflower sandwiches and rich espresso, while a barber sends customers off with *Mad Men*–era coifs. *2 Somerset Place; 61-3/9670-4405; captainsofindustry.com.au.*

Incu

This contemporary, wood-paneled boutique sells trendsetting men's-wear brands discovered by the owners, brothers Vincent and Brian Wu, on their travels around the globe. Look for labels such as Saturdays Surf NYC, Hentsch Man, and Weathered—Incu's in-house line. Don't miss the regular showroom sales, where the previous season's gear can go for less than $100. *83 Kerr St.; 61-3/9662-3730; incu.com.*

Metal Couture

Goth meets glam at this moody atelier of cult jeweler William Llewellyn Griffiths, who has collaborated with the likes of Dolce & Gabbana and Vivienne Westwood. His "heavy metal couture" rings, brooches, and bangles are inspired by tattoo art and Baroque architecture. Hollywood A-listers, including Billy Bob Thornton and Russell Brand, are among Griffiths's admirers. *122A Gertrude St.; 61-3/9419-2547; metalcouture.com.*

Mud

An eye-popping trove of refined, Australian-made ceramics—in shades like minty green, watermelon red, and duck-egg blue—fill this light-splashed housewares shop. Also on display: playful Chilewich teaspoons and placemats and iconic modern tables and chairs from the 1970's by legendary German designer Dieter Rams. *181 Gertrude St.; 61-3/9419-5161; mudaustralia.com.*

Nevenka

Tucked away on an upscale retail lane in the CBD, Rosemary Masic's petite boutique is known for its hippie-chic designs inspired by her Eastern European heritage: brightly patterned dresses; form-fitting Italian cotton jackets; paisley silk pants. *12 Howey Place; 61-3/9663-5873; nevenka.com.au.*

Pieces of Eight

Behind a dramatic glass-and-steel façade, gallery owner Melanie Katsalidis sells objets d'art and handcrafted jewelry—multicolored block necklaces; emerald rings— by such Melbourne artisans as Nina Oikawa and Lucy Folk. The space also includes an open artist-in-residence studio for patrons interested in getting an inside look at how custom pieces are made. *28 Russell Place; 61-3/9663-3641; piecesofeight.com.au.*

Polyester Records

In this digital age, a timeless record store for fans of vinyl is a rarity. Here, musical foragers can uncover old albums, buy concert tickets, or simply strike up a conversation with an in-the-know staff member who has the scoop on everything from Norwegian black-metal bands to the latest Aussie indie-rock groups. *387 Brunswick St.; 61-3/9419-5137; polyesterrecords.com.*

Rose St. Artists' Market

Taking cues from similar collectives in London and Brooklyn, this community of craftspeople sets up shop in a warehouse-like space every weekend to sell their treasures: letterpress cards; cotton linens; embroidered scarves. When your mettle (and pocketbook) has been exhausted, head to the rooftop of the market's Young Bloods Diner, where chef Sascha Randle serves up an all-day brunch (rhubarb and the market's sour-cherry buckwheat porridge; coddled eggs with duck confit) accompanied by craft brews. *60 Rose St.; 61-3/9419-5529; rosestmarket.com.au.*

Women's wear at Nevenka. Left: Pieces of Eight jewelry store.

Eighteenth-century-inspired jewelry on display at Metal Couture. Right: Perusing the pottery at Mud.

TASMANIA, AUSTRALIA

The next great food destination

OFF THE SOUTHERN COAST OF AUSTRALIA, the rugged island of Tasmania has recently been transformed from a culinary backwater into a legitimate farm-to-fork dining destination. The capital of Hobart first emerged as a stomping ground for young, inspired chefs from Sydney and Melbourne, but now the movement is headed farther afield. Just outside the city, the cultural center MONA Pavilions has been making waves with its sleek metallic cubical villas, edgy art museum, and buzzy restaurant, the Source, run by French chef Philippe Leban. Local dishes such as venison with red-cabbage kimchi and pan-fried scallop gnocchi with chard draw sophisticated urbanites, who come as much for the food as for the rich reds and pale ales from the on-site winery and Moo Brew microbrewery. An hour's drive northeast lies another gastronomic retreat: the glass-and-wood hotel Saffire Freycinet, overlooking the granite peaks of Freycinet National Park. Here, Aussie chef Hugh Whitehouse pushes the envelope with adventurous food-foraging programs to nearby Marine Farm—you'll suit up in waders, pull Pacific oysters straight from Coles Bay, then eat them with just a squeeze of lemon and a glass of sparkling Tasmanian wine on a white-clothed table in the water. What better way to get a taste of Tassie?

GUIDE

STAY
MONA Pavilions
655 Main Rd., Berriedale; 61-3/6277-9900; mona.net.au. **$$$**

Saffire Freycinet
2352 Coles Bay Rd., Coles Bay; 61-3/6256-7888; saffire-freycinet.com.au. **$$$$$**

EAT
The Source
655 Main Rd., Berriedale; 61-3/6277-9904; mona.net.au. **$$$**

Saffire Freycinet guests tasting oysters straight from the water in Moulting Lagoon.

TRIPS DIRECTORY

A thatched-roof villa at Azura at Quilalea, in Mozambique.

INDEX

Beach clothes hang from a rock face in Tulum, Mexico.

CONTRIBUTORS

Henry Alford

Gini Alhadeff

Luke Barr

Colin Barraclough

Andrea Bennett

Kate Betts

Anya von Bremzen

Jennifer Chen

Andrea Cooper

Laurel Delp

Stephen Drucker

Jonathan Durbin

Mark Ellwood

Emily Fiffer

Jennifer Flowers

Peter J. Frank

Eleni N. Gage

Joseph Giovannini

Ron Gluckman

Michael Joseph Gross

Elizabeth Gunnison Dunn

Frances Hibbard

Eriko Horiki

William Hide

Misha Janette

David Kaufman

David A. Keeps

Stirling Kelso

Peter Jon Lindberg

Heather Smith MacIsaac

Kim Foley MacKinnon

Alexandra Marshall

Keita Maruyama

Connie McCabe

Andrew McCarthy

Kevin McGarry

Daphne Merkin

Heidi Mitchell

Shane Mitchell

Bob Morris

Mark Morrison

Kathryn O'Shea-Evans

Samuel Polcer

Roxana Robinson

Julian Rubinstein

Adam Sachs

Kashiwa Sato

Andrew Sessa

Dani Shapiro

Maria Shollenbarger

Gary Shteyngart

Emma Sloley

Scott Spencer

Bree Sposato

Jessica Su

Mario Testino

Henry Urbach

Verbal

Shivani Vora

Jeff Wise

Alexandra Wolfe

Jane Wooldridge

Joe Yogerst

Yoon

A view of Marrakesh's Djemaa el-Fna square.

PHOTOGRAPHERS

Hotel guests on
folding chairs outside
the Panorama Alm,
in Kitzbühel, Austria.